LIFE IN LA LIGA

THE STORY OF SPANISH CLUB FOOTBALL

RAB MACWILLIAM

This edition first published in Great Britain in 2019 by

ARENA SPORT
An imprint of Birlinn Limited
West Newington House
10 Newington Road
Edinburgh
EH9 1QS

www.arenasportbooks.co.uk

ISBN: 9781909715745
eBook ISBN: 9781788851701

British Library Cataloguing-in-Publication Data
A catalogue record for this book is available on request from the British Library.

Designed and typeset by Polaris Publishing, Edinburgh
www.polarispublishing.com

Printed in Great Britain by MBM Print SCS Limited, East Kilbride

CONTENTS

ACKNOWLEDGEMENTS   v

INTRODUCTION   vii

SPAIN: A BRIEF HISTORY TO 1900   1

SPAIN'S AUTONOMOUS COMMUNITIES   6

PART ONE: THE EARLY YEARS   9

PART TWO: FROM LA LIGA TO EUROPE   97

PART THREE: LA LIGA AND EUROPE   141

PART FOUR: 'TIME FOR CHANGE'   175

PART FIVE: WALKING SPANISH   231

FURTHER READING   312

INDEX   314

ACKNOWLEDGEMENTS

I'd like to thank Dan MacWilliam, my late father, for taking me to watch my first football match at Inverness's Clach Park in the Highland League when I was around five or six. He also drove me down to Glasgow on a few occasions for big games at Hampden and Ibrox when I was still a kid. He initiated and encouraged my love for the game, and for this, and much else, I will always be grateful.

More specifically, I greatly appreciate the feedback I received on earlier drafts of this book from my son Nick MacWilliam and Simon Liebesny – Gooners both – and from my Stoke Newington neighbours, Pat Newman (who spends several months of the year in his villa in Murcia) and José Fernández (a Gijón man and a proud supporter of Sporting de Gijón). I much appreciate their opinions and comments.

At Arena Sport, freelance copy editor Ian Greensill carried out a meticulous job, and saved me a good deal of embarrassment by pointing out several basic errors in my text. Any errors which remain are down to me, not Ian nor anyone else. My publisher and editor, Pete Burns, had the courage to contract me to write this book, and Pete has been immensely supportive and helpful throughout the project.

Last, but by no means least, my wife Anne Beech listened to my arcane Spanish football stories, ignored my cursing and raving at my computer, and permitted me sole access to the downstairs study with the same combination of compassion, understanding and disbelief which she has brought to our thirty-five year partnership. Many thanks, my dear.

INTRODUCTION

As a young lad growing up in the Highlands of Scotland, I spent every spare moment kicking a ball around – in my primary school playground, local park, back yard of my house, anywhere I could find – pretending to myself that I was Denis Law strutting imperiously around Hampden Park or Jim Baxter lording it over Ibrox.

I preferred playing the game to watching it but, when my father took me to Ibrox and Hampden or when I saw games on TV, the Rangers side of the early 1960s, which included Baxter, John Greig, Willie Henderson et al., became my boyhood heroes. I was also enthralled by the Real Madrid team which, in the 1960 European Cup final at Hampden Park, ruthlessly and sublimely destroyed Eintracht Frankfurt.

I watched grainy, black-and-white television replays of that game, often described as the greatest game of football ever played, and marvelled at the passing skills, dribbling talent, goalscoring ability and footballing artistry of, in particular, Di Stéfano,

Puskás and Gento. This was in a different class altogether to the football I knew, and that game initiated my enduring interest in Spanish club football.

When my playing days were over, I became a spectator and student of football, and I continued my attachment to the game as a book publisher in London by publishing a number of football titles, in particular British club histories. More recently, as an author I have written several books on the game without having incurred the burden of becoming a specialist on any of its aspects, as I am a generalist at heart when it comes to football.

However, although a few of my published titles, normally historical in their focus, have covered the European game, this is the first book which I have written exclusively about the game in Spain, the country whose club football had so fascinated me when I was a boy.

I have followed the fortunes of such clubs as Sevilla, Barcelona, Atlético Madrid, Real Betis, Real Madrid and Athletic Bilbao, as well as the many other clubs which have constituted, in differing eras and with varying degrees of success, the 'Primera División' ('La Liga') and the 'Segunda División', or second tier, of Spanish club football.

Over the years, I have watched Spanish clubs in both domestic and European competitions, and have gained an insight into, and an admiration for, the game as it is played at the highest levels in Spain. More importantly, and as nothing beats being a spectator in the stadium while a match is being fiercely contested, I relished the European evenings I spent standing on the North Bank at Arsenal's old Highbury Stadium.

At Highbury, I watched my local club Arsenal play – in the European Cup, UEFA Cup and Cup Winners' Cup – such sides as Valencia, Real Zaragoza, Deportivo de La Coruña, Real Mallorca, Celta de Vigo, Villarreal and Real Madrid. There always seemed to be a heightened air of expectation and excitement in the stadium when a Spanish club was our opponent, more so than with any other European club. As was proudly proclaimed in the 1960s by Spain's Tourism Ministry, and as was obvious on the pitch: 'Spain is different'.

This being the case, I decided to write this book for the reader who is interested in Spanish football and football generally but who has a far from expert knowledge of the game's origins and development in the country, and also of its contemporary influence within Spain and, more recently, in European competition. In the book I do not presume a facility in the Spanish language (or languages) as, when using Spanish Castilian (or Basque or Catalan) words and phrases, I provide English translations. Also, for those readers who may be unfamiliar with certain Spanish cities and regions, I try to convey, as concisely as I can, 'the spirit of place'.

As I was researching and writing this book, I discovered that Spain is indeed different. The story of club football in Spain is significantly more complex and diverse than I had previously supposed, and much more so than that of most other footballing nations. This complex diversity, albeit in a modified form, remains in the Spanish game to the present day.

Alongside the history, I have included short biographies of personalities and outstanding players, famous and infamous incidents and matches, humorous and occasionally tragic events, club and regional rivalries, instances of chicanery and double-dealing, the role of the media and the fans, Spanish football terminology and other reflections on aspects of the Spanish game.

Finally, and importantly in my view, it is impossible fully to comprehend Spanish club and regional football without the inclusion of a brief historical and political background. So, from time to time in the book I provide this information. The development of the club game in Spain has been so intimately involved with wider domestic political events that, without such an explanatory context, some of what I say would be either misleading or meaningless. However, as this is very much a book about football, I keep to a minimum these necessary contextual guides.

The book is organised chronologically into five parts which, coincidentally or not, is a structure which mirrors changes in the country's wider social and political development. This chronological perspective is an approximate guide rather than a rigid framework as, from time to time, I feel it may be more helpful and interesting for the reader if I veer across various time periods to illustrate certain points, such as a player's career trajectory or aspects of some clubs' eccentricities, the latter abounding in Spanish football.

This book, though, remains essentially a history from the late nineteenth century to the present day, and is organised in as linear and as progressive a manner as I can manage and as is possible when one considers the idiosyncrasies inherent in its subject matter.

Part One describes the origins of club football in Spain, from the late nineteenth century in Andalucia, the Basque Country and Catalonia to the other administrative regions, and the speedy development of football clubs across Spain from the initiation of the Copa del Rey in 1903 to the introduction of La Liga in 1929.

Part Two considers football's growing professionalism, organisation, popular appeal and socio-political importance, from the formation of La Liga, through the impact on the game of the Spanish Civil War, to post-Civil War club and league reconstruction and the emergence of European-wide club competitions in the late 1950s.

Part Three covers the dramatic twists and turns in domestic club football in the 1960s and 1970s. It also explores the story of Real Madrid in the European Cup from 1955 to 1960 and its growing rivalry with Barcelona, as well as the arrival on the European stage of other intra-continental tournaments and the involvement in these of Atlético Madrid, Real Zaragoza, Valencia, Athletic Bilbao and other Liga clubs.

Part Four concerns itself with the domestic dominance of Real Madrid in the 1960s and 1970s and the re-emergence of Athletic Bilbao, Barcelona, Valencia and Real Sociedad in the early 1980s. It also discusses the fluctuating fortunes of such clubs as Real Betis, Deportivo de La Coruña, Espanyol, Real Mallorca, Málaga, Villarreal, Alavés and Celta de Vigo up to the present day.

Part Five discusses Real Madrid and Barcelona in La Liga and the 'new' Champions League, from Real's 'vulture squad' and Barcelona's Cruyff-inspired 'dream team' to the close of the 2017/18 season. I also consider the twenty-first century re-emergence of Atlético Madrid, Sevilla and Valencia in La Liga and the UEFA Cup/Europa League, and look at current trends and domestic developments in La Liga. The book concludes with a reflection on season 2018/19, and a brief Further Reading list.

The above description and structure may give the impression that the book is a solemn, scholarly tome, of interest mainly to historians, sociologists and the like: far from it (although I don't wish to discourage such learned academics from reading it). Nor is the book an attempt to explain Spain's unique, confusing and, on occasion, brutal political history.

Rather, *Life in La Liga* is aimed firmly at the general reader who is intrigued by Spanish club football and who is interested in discovering more about its origins, development and the players, competitions and external events which have shaped the game and which, particularly in recent years, have made Spanish clubs the most successful footballing sides in Europe.

I have attempted to keep the book as informative, entertaining and readable as is possible when dealing with such a frequently chaotic subject. I have also tried to follow the wise dictum of the US crime novelist Elmore Leonard who, when asked why his books are so entertaining and engaging, replied: 'Simple. I just leave out the boring bits.'

So bear with me, and follow this remarkable footballing story as it unwinds, modernises and reaches the multi-million pound industry of the present day.

Rab MacWilliam, London, June 2019

SPAIN: A BRIEF HISTORY TO 1900

When the English traveller Richard Ford wrote in 1845 that Spain was 'a bundle of local units tied together by a rope of sand', he neatly captured the essence of this country, whose historical and cultural experience was very different to that of most other countries in Western Europe.

While the country is today a modern, unitary, liberal-democratic state, and is regarded by its fellow nations as an equal and valued member of Europe and the international community, there remains an undercurrent of truth in Ford's observation. In the words of the Spanish government's 1960s promotional slogan which was designed to attract tourists to the country: 'Spain is different'.

Spain has long been a land of disputation, conflict and extremes, concisely expressed in the Spanish proverb 'three Spaniards, four opinions'. From the rugged Atlantic regions of Galicia and Asturias and the mountain ranges and deep valleys of the Basque Country, through the central dusty highlands of Castile and the sun-drenched Mediterranean shores of Andalucia, to the Balearic and remote Canary Islands and the more temperate hills and plains of Catalonia and Valencia, its often stunning landscapes and micro-climates reflect, and in some instances have defined, Spain's political, linguistic and social diversity.

Spain's history has also been varied and distinctive, embracing innovation and conservatism, and harmony and turmoil. For over 1,500 years, the country was occupied by Romans, Visigoths and Islamic 'Moors', the last being the most enduring and significant influence on today's Spanish state.

After the late-fifteenth-century Christian 'Reconquista' had ended the final semblance of Moorish rule, the country's imperial colonisation of Latin America resulted in Spain becoming one of the major military and trading powers in the world throughout the sixteenth and early seventeenth centuries: its 'Golden Age' of global supremacy.

Thereafter, Spain gradually entered into a period of decline and political introversion, fuelled by domestic arguments and strife as well as by the rise of competitive European colonial states. The internal economic factors grew in their severity and they were numerous, including the vast disparity in living standards between the peasantry and the land-owning aristocratic elites under the oppressive 'latifundio' system. There was also a growing economic imbalance and contrast between the large expanding cities, with their access to mineral and trading wealth, and the ever-increasing poverty of the majority of the population based in the countryside.

The political situation was equally troubling. The overarching power of the monarchy, and the constant squabbling between the Habsburg and Bourbon dynasties, did little to alleviate the immiseration of the Spanish people. The ubiquitous Catholic Church maintained a firm hold on all aspects of Spanish life, preaching a rigid conservative obedience and promoting a widespread religious intolerance of all other faiths. And the escalating demands for cultural and linguistic autonomy from the central state which were made by a number of areas within Spain, in particular the Basque Country and Catalonia, were continual obstacles hindering the creation of a viable unitary Spanish state.

Any one of these largely self-inflicted problems was, by itself, sufficient to concern and destabilise a country insistent on the centralisation of power but which remained neo-feudal and reactionary, with its elite's eyes still fixated on Spain's past triumphs while it ignored the probability of impending economic collapse. But taking all these factors together, it was clear that urgent measures had to be taken to alleviate these seemingly intractable problems, or Spain was heading towards disaster.

By the late eighteenth century, the ideas generated by the Enlightenment, which had begun in Scotland and had found its full expression in France earlier that century, were slowly filtering into Spain. These promoted the primacy of reason, along with its accompanying emphasis on liberalism, democracy and modernity, as the principles which should govern the minds and actions of individuals and states.

Despite desperate attempts by Spain's Church, monarchy, moneyed elites and military to keep at bay these threatening notions, these fresh and relatively egalitarian ideas found receptive homes in the minds of Spain's expanding bourgeoisie, who were becoming concerned and affected by the worsening economic and political condition of the country. Aside from the ethical and moral issues involved, the current situation was bad for business.

Even by Spain's historically divisive standards, the nineteenth century represented one of the most politically chaotic periods which the country had until then experienced. As the century began, the country had forged a temporary internal truce and, with British assistance, had sent Napoleon's troops homeward to think again. However, Spain remained riven by internal disputes and bitter rivalries, the main obstacles to the creation of a nascent modern state being, again, the Church, the overbearing and over-indulged military, the monarchy and the rural land-owning classes.

Nevertheless, despite the ferocity of these constraints, in 1812 Spain proclaimed its first Constitution, which proposed such much-needed reforms as universal male suffrage, freedom of the press, ultimate power to reside in the democratically elected 'Cortes' (national government) and, crucially, the declaration of Spain as a unitary state.

These reforms were suppressed by the monarchy and the groups in the country who were engaged in the bloody Carlist Wars, dynastic struggles and aristocratic feuding, in their attempts to maintain Spain, in the interests of all traditionalists, as their own fiefdom, free from foreign interference. Ranged against these formidable barriers were the growing numbers of progressive, enlightened thinkers and activists, usually found in the larger cities.

In 1873 Spain's First Republic was declared, but within less than two years and the election of four consecutive presidents, the Republic was quashed by the military, who restored the monarchy and 'invited' King Alfonso XII, of Bourbon lineage, to save Spain from 'chaos'. It was to be almost sixty years before a Second Republic was instituted.

Despite this military coup, Spain established universal male suffrage, and entered a brief period of relative stability. Government alternated between Liberal and Conservative parties, but rigged elections and electoral fraud were common, these usually being arranged by local 'caciques' (powerful land-owning figures in the countryside). So, in effect, there was little real progress made towards modernisation and reform.

Then, in 1898, Spain's self-image was shattered. The USA had declared war on Spain and had humiliated the country by acquiring Puerto Rico and then Cuba, the final remnant of Spain's once-mighty Latin American colony. Known to this day as 'El Desastre' ('The Disaster'), the shock to Spain of the loss of Cuba was profound, and the country again mourned the loss of its empire.

However, even at this low point in Spain's history, growing numbers of people in different parts of the country were becoming excited by the introduction of a new sport. Football had arrived in Spain, football clubs were being formed across the country and, as the game quickly spread across Spain, national depression was giving way to enthusiasm for the game and political differences were being slowly absorbed into football rivalries.

But, this being Spain, the game was soon to become inextricably enmeshed in much wider, more complicated issues than simple football matches.

SPAIN'S AUTONOMOUS COMMUNITIES

In his book *The Spanish Labyrinth*, Gerald Brenan wrote that a Spaniard's loyalty 'was first of all to his native place, or to his family and social group within it, and only secondly to his country and government'. This pervasive sentiment has been a constant theme in Spanish history, and the regional pride, and often the accompanying sense of 'difference' which this has generated, has been the main obstacle to the creation of a unified Spanish nation.

The Spanish Constitution of 1978, drawn up and agreed by representatives of all the main political parties, secured the country's transition to democracy in the immediate post-Franco years. One of its principal achievements, in an attempt to defuse the historical antagonisms between the centre and the peripheral regions (in particular Catalonia and the Basque Country), was the Constitution's political and geographical configuration of Spain into a quasi-federal state consisting of seventeen 'communidades autónomas' ('autonomous communities').

The Constitution did not offer 'federalism', as the term is generally understood. Rather, it was a form of decentralised devolution. The Communities were granted 'the right to autonomy or self-government' but within 'the indissoluble unity of the Spanish nation', with the state retaining full sovereignty. Where possible, the constitutional boundaries between the Communities roughly followed the borders of the medieval kingdoms and the Iberian regions prior to the initial unification of the country. By 1983, the Communities had been established. They are as follows:

Andalucia. Provinces: Almería, Granada, Jaén, Córdoba, Málaga, Seville, Cádiz, Huelva. Capital: Seville.
Basque Country. Provinces: Álava, Biscay, Gipuzkoa. Capital: Vitoria-Gasteiz.
Galicia. Provinces: A Coruña, Lugo, Ourense, Pontevedra. Capital: Santiago de Compostela.
Principality of Asturias. Capital: Oviedo.
Cantabria. Capital: Santander.
La Rioja. Capital: Logroño.
Navarre. Capital: Pamplona (Iruña).
Aragon. Provinces: Huesca, Zaragoza, Teruel. Capital: Zaragoza.
Balearic Islands. Largest islands: Mallorca, Menorca, Ibiza, Formentera. Capital: Palma de Mallorca.
Catalonia. Provinces: Lleida, Barcelona, Girona, Tarragona. Capital: Barcelona.
Valencian Community. Provinces: Alicante, Castellón, Valencia. Capital: Valencia.
Murcia. Capital: Murcia.
Canary Islands. Largest islands: Tenerife, Fuerteventura, Gran Canaria, Lanzarote, La Palma, La Gomera, El Hierro. Capitals: Santa Cruz (Tenerife), Puerto del Rosario (Fuerteventura), Las Palmas (Gran Canaria), Arrecife (Lanzarote).

Extremadura. Provinces: Cáceres, Badajoz. Capital: Mérida.

Castilla-La Mancha. Provinces: Albacete, Ciudad Real, Cuenca, Guadalajara, Toledo. Capital: Toledo.

Castile and León. Provinces: Ávila, Burgos, León, Palencia, Salamanca, Segovia, Soria, Valladolid, Zamora. Capital: Valladolid.

Community of Madrid. Capital: Madrid.

PART ONE

THE EARLY YEARS

The clouds of steam and the screeching of rusty brakes announced the train's arrival in Antwerp's Central Station on that afternoon in August 1920.

The train and its carriages had travelled from Spain, and its passengers included a diverse collection of athletes, trainers and officials. The Olympic Games were being held in Belgium, and among the runners, swimmers, high-jumpers and polo players was the football squad, the first time in the country's history that Spain's top footballers had united as a national team to represent their country abroad.

The squad consisted of twenty-one footballers, of whom fourteen were from the Basque Country, four from Barcelona and three from Galicia. Under the Olympic rules they all had to be amateurs, but this basis for selection was not a problem as Spain would not recognise professional football until 1925. They were, however, all from the north of the country, as these regions contained the leading clubs and the most skilful exponents of this relatively new sport.

The official Spanish reason for this northern bias – an explanation offered by somewhat piqued representatives from the country's central heartland and its southern regions – was that these players were used to grass turf pitches, unlike players in much of the rest of the country, and the Olympic matches were all to be played on turf. Perhaps so, but nevertheless these northerners were undeniably Spain's most talented and experienced footballers.

The first modern Olympic Games had been held in 1896 in Athens, an appropriate location given that the Olympics were last contested in Greece over 1,500 years previously. In this new era for the quadrennial tournament, football had been considered an 'exhibition sport' in the 1900 Paris Olympics, but in 1908 the authorities at the London Games had deemed the game worthy of 'competitive' status. In London it had also become the first Olympic team sport.

The proposed Berlin Olympics of 1916 had, unsurprisingly, been cancelled, and Antwerp had been chosen for the first competition since the Stockholm Games in 1912, largely due to the destruction and suffering which Belgium had witnessed during the First World War. Also, because of the War, such previously hostile countries as Germany, Austria, Hungary, Bulgaria and Turkey had not been invited to Antwerp, thereby to a degree diluting the 'international' element of the Olympics.

Spain, as a 'neutral' country during the War, had been invited, and saw its invitation to participate as a recognition that the country was no longer perceived as an isolated addendum to the rest of the world, although its own Olympic expectations, at least in football, were not particularly high.

In the event, and through no fault of the Spanish players – who included such national luminaries as Athletic Bilbao's Belauste and 'Pichichi' and Barcelona's Samitier and Zamora – the football tournament developed into something of a lottery. Spain began brightly enough, beating Denmark 1–0, but they lost 3–1 to Belgium in the quarter-finals. Belgium went on to defeat Czechoslovakia in the final, but its gold medal was gained by default as Czechoslovakia, angered by the decisions of the British referee, walked off the pitch in protest before the match had ended.

The Czechoslovaks were then banned, and the French, as the defeated semi-finalists, had already packed up and gone home. So, the destinations of the bronze and silver medals were to be decided by the remaining countries, which comprised Sweden, Italy, Spain and the Netherlands. Spain's first match was against Sweden. At the end of the game, after Spain had won 2–1, there were only seven Swedes and eight Spaniards remaining on the pitch, and the tie was described in a local newspaper as 'the most barbaric and brutal game ever seen on a football field'.

This match gave birth to a phrase which, over the years and particularly during the fiercely nationalist Francoist authoritarian regime, the Spanish would embrace with pride: 'La Furia Española'. Heartened by their Swedish survival, the 'Furia' disposed of Italy and the Netherlands, and emerged from the tournament clutching their prized silver medal.

In its first appearance on the footballing world stage, Spain had gained the international respect it had craved and which the country felt it deserved. This silver medal was a critical motivating factor over the coming years in generating widespread public interest and enthusiasm in football, the legitimation of professionalism in the game, the establishment of new football clubs and the inauguration of a national league.

***

Within twenty years or so of football's arrival in Spain, the game was already beginning to contribute significantly to the consolidation of a wary sense of unity in a country in which several areas actively encouraged the continuation of a socially fractured and culturally divided nation.

While Spain's internal conflicts gradually diminished as the country tentatively embraced a sense of nationhood, these potent rival legacies became expressed through football loyalties and were vigorously contested on football pitches, as clubs from all regions of the country met each other in regular national league and cup competitions.

Although the fortunes of the national team have fluctuated, Spain today is home to some of the world's most admired club sides, and Spanish club football is widely regarded as representing the contemporary game at its finest.

As the following pages will demonstrate, in the majority of cases and at least initially, it was through the influence and guidance of the British – the innovators of modern football – who first planted the seeds from which grew what is now the Spanish national game.

At the end of the nineteenth century, Britain's commercial concerns, interests and influence still pervaded much of the world. So it's no surprise that the new game of 'association football', which accompanied the travels of British businessmen, sailors, workers and students, was soon revealed to its many overseas trading partners as well as to the local inhabitants.

Football in European countries typically began at the larger ports, as the local workers, who observed British sailors and workers kicking around a ball and who were intrigued by the game, decided to copy their visitors and then formed football clubs. For example, the oldest organised football clubs in Italy, France, Germany and Belgium were established, respectively, in the busy ports of Genoa, Le Havre, Hamburg and Antwerp. The popular appeal of the game was such that, within just a few years of its introduction, football clubs proliferated across the continent, and Spain was no exception.

In order to discover the origins and spread of Spanish club football, it seems sensible to begin by looking at the game's development in each of the main Spanish regions. I begin with Andalucia, a sprawling land mass in the south of the country, where the whole thing kicked off almost 130 years ago.

***

ANDALUCIA

As was the case in many other European countries, the major coastal cities in Spain, in particular Bilbao and Barcelona, discovered football mainly through trading contacts with their British connections. Enthusiasts in these cities readily embraced the game, and they wasted little time in setting up football clubs. However, unlike most of Europe, the game of football had its origins in a predominantly underdeveloped region of the country: Andalucia.

Located to the south-west of Seville, the Andalucian capital, and close to the Portuguese border, the Atlantic port of Huelva had been established by the Phoenicians around 1,000 BC, was later occupied by the Romans and Moors, and became in the late nineteenth century the home of the first football club to be founded in Spain.

The reason for Huelva's undisputed status as 'El Decano' – the 'dean' or 'oldest member' – of Spanish football lies in its proximity to the Rio Tinto ('Red River'), which rises in the Sierra Morena mountains to the north of the town and which enters the Gulf of Cádiz near Huelva. Upstream and close to the river were the world's oldest copper mines, first excavated over 5,000 years ago and reputed to have been the fabled King Solomon's Mines.

During one of Spain's frequent internal power struggles, in 1873 a British-led consortium seized the opportunity to acquire from the Spanish government, for somewhat less than its market value, the mines and the surrounding land, and established the Rio Tinto Mining Company. During the 1870s British and Spanish workers developed the necessary infrastructure, including the forty-mile rail link with Huelva so that the extracted copper could be exported across the world. These workers spent their spare time, if they had any, playing 'foot-ball', as the game was then known in the area.

Today, the land is under Spanish ownership but, when under British control, the Rio Tinto mines had become the world's leading copper supplier. As well as bringing over experienced mining workers from Britain, the company employed local people from Andalucia, one of the poorest regions in Spain, as well as unemployed workers from across the country, mainly from the northern regions of Galicia and Asturias.

The majority of the engineers, technicians, drilling managers, doctors, accountants, middle managers and directors, however, were British, and they established in Huelva a bi-cultural, quasi-apartheid social system. Living in relative luxury and isolating themselves from the Spanish workers, and enjoying an expatriate, sybaritic lifestyle in what became known as Huelva's 'barrio ingles' ('English quarter'), these people also played occasional games of football, which were observed by the local Spaniards who quickly developed an admiration and a facility for the game.

After the arrival of the British, football kick-abouts had become common in the area but there had been no attempt to form or register an official football club. The appointment of Doctor William Alexander Mackay as head physician at the Rio Tinto Company was to change all this. Mackay had been a keen football player when a medical student at Edinburgh University, and he had enthusiastically joined in the casual games around Huelva.

He soon assumed responsibility for all Rio Tinto Company ball games, when he was approached by a group of young Spaniards who wanted to learn more about football. He decided, along with these Spaniards and one of his British co-workers, Charles Adam, to form a football club in the port. On 23 December 1889, Huelva Recreation Club was founded. Later known as **Recreativo de Huelva**, it is the oldest football club in Spain.

The club's first game – and the first football match under FA rules to be played in Spain – took place the following year, on 8 March 1890, at Seville's Tablada Hippodrome against Sevilla FC, a team of British expatriates drawn mainly from the Seville Water Works. With only two Spanish names on each team sheet, Huelva lost 2–0.

Huelva and Caithness

Lybster is a small village on the coast of Caithness, the northernmost county in the United Kingdom. I mention Lybster in the context of a book on Spanish football because Dr William Mackay, the man who brought football to Spain, was born here in 1860 and brought up in the village, then a busy herring port.

I was intrigued to discover this, as my mother was also born and spent her youth in Lybster. I enjoyed some of the happiest weeks of my childhood in this small harbour village, which nestles on the east coast of the austerely beautiful county of Caithness, located over 600 miles north of London.

In 2014, Lybster Council received a request from Huelva for the village to send its local amateur football team, Lybster FC, to visit the Andalucian city to play Recreativo de Huelva, in honour

---

of Dr Mackay. The Council discovered that Mackay had indeed been born in the village, and agreed with alacrity.

The doctor, known in Huelva as 'Don Alejandro', was not only instrumental in establishing Spain's oldest club, he was also behind the building in 1892 of the club's Velodromo Stadium, he was club president from 1903 until 1906, on behalf of the club he was awarded in 1909 the 'Great White Cross' by King Alfonso XIII, he has a street named after him in Huelva, and he was awarded the title of Freeman of the City. He eventually moved back to Scotland, and he died in the Highland town of Tain in 1927.

A thirty-strong contingent from Lybster FC flew out on a four-day trip to Huelva in the summer of 2018, and the Caithness team were beaten 5–0 by a Recre side who fielded members of their 2006 team, their last appearance in La Liga. Lybster retaliated by playing Jamesie Mackay, a sixty-five-year-old veteran. In 2019 – the 130th anniversary of the Don founding Huelva – the Spanish club will visit Lybster for the return match. Football is a sentimental game, is it not?

By the early years of the twentieth century, Recreativo de Huelva was competing in regional Andalucian competitions, and the club was also a founder member of the Real Federación Española de Fútbol (Royal Spanish Football Federation) which, after four years of protracted regional disagreements, was finally established in 1913.

Although in 1906, 'Recre' had reached the final group stage – effectively the semi-final – of the Copa del Rey, a 3–0 defeat by Madrid FC ended its hopes, and Huelva had to wait almost 100 years before it surpassed this stage in the competition: in

2003, Recre reached the Copa del Rey final but were beaten 3–0 by Real Mallorca. Almost all the players in the 1906 game were British, but by 1913 Recre's regular first team was composed entirely of Spaniards and the club had adopted the blue-and-white striped shirts which it wears today.

Like so many of the pioneering clubs in Spanish football's history, Recre has since achieved little in the way of major success but, one way or another, it survives. Throughout its existence, the club has moved from regional leagues to journeying between the second, third and fourth levels of Spanish league football.

Recre has played five seasons in the top division, La Liga, the highlight of which was its 3–0 victory (revenge is sweet, if a long time coming) over the superstars of Real Madrid (Madrid FC, as was) at the Bernabéu Stadium in December 2006, a result which was one of the biggest shocks in the history of La Liga. By 2009/10 the club was back in the second tier, and today it plays its football in Segunda B. Over the last few years Recre has survived financial crises with the help of their loyal supporters – one being Dr Mackay's grandson, who is president of the Huelva Supporters' Trust – and sympathetic external assistance.

In 2016 news emerged that Recreativo de Huelva was in serious financial trouble, a far from uncommon problem in Spanish football. The club owed millions of euros to the tax authorities, and it could not pay staff and player wages. El Decano faced the real threat of extinction. The club's owner, Huelva City Council, had to sell. In the summer of 2018, the club was acquired by Eurosamop for the sum of one euro. It is too early to predict what the future may hold for Spain's oldest football club but, given its historical importance, one hopes that El Decano will not disappear from the Spanish footballing map.

League structure précis

In Part Two of this book, I will be describing in some detail the structure and format of the Spanish league system. However, as I mention the league in these opening pages, I here give a brief synopsis. The Primera División, or La Liga, is the highest level, and sits above the Segunda, the second level. The third level was the Tercera until 1977, which was when Segunda B was introduced in its place, relegating the Tercera to the fourth and bottom level of the Spanish national football league. Here is where the regional and local leagues begin. The league's rules are rather complicated, as you will discover.

Elsewhere in Andalucia – and outwith many of the larger cities, particularly Seville, Granada, Cádiz, Córdoba, Málaga and Jaén – football was relatively slow to engage the interests of the predominantly rural inhabitants of the region. Indeed, **UD Almería** did not open its doors for business until 2001 but, coached by manager Unai Emery, it became in 2007/08 the youngest established club to reach La Liga since the Spanish league's formation in 1929.

The arid soil and hot climate, the dusty and mountainous terrain, the communication and travel problems, the cultural barriers, the 'pueblo' (village-centred) attitude, and the prevailing widespread poverty did little to encourage the development of the game in much of rural Andalucia. However, in the south-west of the region, trading contacts with the British, as in the case of Huelva and Seville, were frequent, and football became established here in the early years of the twentieth century.

Seville

I recall, a good few years ago, wandering around Seville's Jewish Quarter and discovering a small bar hidden away in a maze of winding lanes close to the city's imposing cathedral, which was once a mosque.

I went into the shabby old bar and I was delighted to find that the walls were covered with old, black-and-white photos of football games. Such bars are rare. One's entry is frequently accompanied by suspicious glances from the regular drinkers, as these bars are normally to be found in 'enemy' territory.

Closer inspection revealed that the bar was devoted to Real Betis, and it was probably the only such place of homage in that relatively affluent, touristic part of Seville, an area commonly regarded as the natural home of Betis's city rival, **Sevilla FC**. In fact, the rivalry, and mutual disdain, is intense, and has been so for over a hundred years.

Sevilla FC lays claim to being 'Spain's oldest football club devoted entirely to football', having been formed by a gathering of young Scots and Spaniards in January 1890 as Sevilla Foot-Ball Club. The title of 'Spain's oldest football club' is contested by several clubs, notably Athletic Bilbao (who formed in 1898 but did not achieve official status until 1901), Tarragona (established in Catalonia in 1896 as a sports club but who did not form a football team, today's Segunda División Gimnástica de Tarragona, until 1914) and, of course, Recreativo de Huelva who, by common consent, lead the pack.

The first president of Sevilla was the Elgin-born British vice-consul to Seville, Edward Farquharson Johnston, and the nationality of the early players was overwhelmingly British. In 1905 Sevilla Fútbol Club was formally registered. Two years later, competition arrived in the city when some local polytechnic students formed Sevilla Balompié, 'balompié' being the literal

Spanish translation of 'football'. The pervasive national usage of 'fútbol' is another indication in Spain of the sport's British origins.

The year 1909 marked the beginning of the rivalry between what became the city's two major clubs. The mutual enmity began as a result of neighbourhood and class realities. Sevilla was a club largely composed of middle- and upper-class players and directors from the affluent side of the River Guadalquivir, based mainly in and around the Nervión area of the city.

In 1909, a talented young player from Triana – then the working-class, gypsy-dwelling heart of Seville – became available for acquisition by Sevilla, but the club's board, wishing to retain their and the club's 'burguesa' ('bourgeois') status, decided not to sign him, on the basis of his unacceptably uncouth class background: after all, he was 'just a simple worker' from a poor family.

This decision was fiercely contested at board level and led to the resignation of at least two directors, who promptly linked up with Balompié to form a new club, Betis Balompié, which was based on the less affluent Triana bank of the River Guadalquivir. In 1914 King Alfonso XIII granted Betis the name 'Real', and it became **Real Betis Balompié.**

This split in the Sevilla board resulted in one of the club's enduring nicknames, one with a more pejorative and barbed edge than the standard 'rojiblancos' ('red-and-whites') and 'Nerviónenes' ('the ones from Nervión').

The directors who resigned in indignation at the club's overt class bias, and who helped to form Betis, presented Sevilla FC with a gift of a white handbasin with a red stripe (Sevilla's colours), accompanied by a note offering 'a farewell which, for life, you will use to collect shed tears, not for your failures but for our successes'. The Spanish word for a handbasin is 'palangana', and many still refer to Sevilla as 'los palanganas'.

In 1915 the first game between the two clubs narrowly went Sevilla's way, by a 4–3 scoreline, but such was the crowd violence and general mayhem, on and off the pitch, that the referee had no choice but to abandon the match. In 1918 – the second game in what became the 'Seville Derby' – most of the Betis players were on 'mili' (National Service) while many of the wealthier and better-connected Sevilla team managed to avoid 'mili'. So Betis deliberately and provocatively fielded a team composed of inexperienced youngsters, and they were beaten 22–0. This 'moral victory' by Betis made the club's point and, one hopes, more than compensated for the footballing humiliation. To date, there have been 114 'Derbies', with Sevilla well ahead on points.

Today, both Seville clubs are influential members of the Spanish football establishment, but this perceived class antagonism lingers on. Sevilla has become by some distance the more successful club in the city, but a working-class, underdog, left-wing sentiment still clings to Betis (a prominent supporter in recent years was the Socialist Party's leader Felipe González), whose motto is the indefatigable 'Viva el Betis manque pierda': 'Long live Betis even when they lose'.

'Alcohol, Alcohol . . .'

If one were to encounter an inhabitant of what is one of the oldest and historically most important ports in Europe, one might expect to encounter at least a degree of haughty reserve. If so, no one appears to have informed the Cádiz CF fan base of what is expected from them. More likely, though, is that they have paid no attention, given that, according to Sid Lowe in the *Guardian*, they are '. . . the best in Spain . . . a special breed with impenetrable thick accents, missing teeth, and who sing about booze'.

Cádiz sits on the Atlantic coast, around fifty miles south-east of Huelva. The city was established by the Phoenicians in 1100 BC, and is today home to the Spanish Navy. Despite being one of Spain's more venerable football institutions (Cádiz CF was formed in 1910) and aside from two solitary seasons, the club's only continuous spell in La Liga was the eight seasons between 1985 and 1993, when its highest placing was twelfth. The club can currently be found in Segunda.

But the fans of the old club don't appear particularly distressed by its relative lack of success. In fact, they don't appear to be particularly bothered about winning, so long as they are enjoying themselves. This cheerful acceptance of their status is conveyed in one of their 'songs':

'Alcohol, Alcohol, Alcohol.
We come here to get drunk, the result doesn't matter at all.'

They have also been spotted at matches waving flags, emblazoned with the message 'Arbitro, guapetón' ('Referee, you're gorgeous'), a refreshing change from 'Who's the wanker in the black?'

In 1492, King Ferdinand II of Aragon and Queen Isabella of Castile received the surrender of the 'Moors' from the Alhambra Palace in Granada and, with this grand gesture, these devout Catholics signalled an end to the Christian 'Reconquista' of Spain, almost 500 years after it had begun in the north of the country.

The departure of the Islamic people who had ruled Spain for

over 700 years, as well as most of the 'moriscos' (Islamic followers who had converted to Christianity, at least nominally), came in 1606 when, with the Christian brutality which was typical of those times, they were forcibly expelled from the country.

The Alhambra – a magnificent, brooding fortress and a tribute to Islamic architecture – looms imperiously over the city of Granada, which lies to the east of Seville and is located on the other side of the Sierra Nevada from Málaga. Formed in 1931, **Granada CF** became, in 1941/42, the third club from Andalucia to enter the top tier of Spanish league football, La Liga. The club remained in La Liga for twenty years, but then went into sharp decline as financial problems mounted, and it collapsed at one stage as low as the fourth tier.

However, by 2002 the club was back in Segunda and, in 2010/11, Granada again reached La Liga, thirty-five years after the club had last been in the top tier. It remained in Primera for six seasons, dropping into Segunda for 2017/18. The fact that Tony Adams (a name Arsenal fans may recall) was manager during that particular Liga season obviously had nothing to do with Granada's temporary fall from grace.

The Mezquita, or Great Mosque, is at the heart of the splendidly enigmatic city of Córdoba, once the vibrant, multiracial and religiously tolerant capital of Islamic Al-Andalus, which occupies the fertile Guadalquivir river plain to the north of Seville. Its football club underwent various incarnations in its earlier years, re-emerged in 1954 as **Córdoba CF** and spent several years in La Liga in the 1960s.

Its highest Liga position is fifth in 1964/65, but during the following four decades, the club groped its way around the relative obscurity of the Segunda and Tercera. They did reach Primera again in 2014/15, but a 0–8 home thrashing by Barcelona, Luis Suárez claiming a hat-trick, ensured Córdoba's relegation that season, and the club was back in Segunda.

The city of Jaén, in the northern foothills of the Sierra Nevada, is admired for the quality of its olive oil production. Perhaps a bottle or two of this revitalising liquid will help to smooth the upward path of the city's football club, **Real Jaén**, whose current league status could benefit from a bit of assistance. An early arrival, of 1922 vintage, whose history includes three seasons in the 1950s in La Liga, 'los lagartos' ('the lizards', due to the all-white strip) seem to prefer the Tercera, which is where the club is normally to be discovered, sheltering under a rock.

The Mediterranean port of Málaga, birthplace of Picasso, was one of the pioneers of Andalucian football when Málaga Foot-Ball Club was set up in 1904, as the game was played on the dockside quays by British sailors in the declining years of the nineteenth century. As appears to be the norm in Spain, the club adopted various guises as the years passed and, as CD Málaga, spent a couple of seasons in La Liga in the 1950s and began to settle into La Liga in the 1970s.

In 1993, another club, **Málaga CF**, was born, and very quickly advanced up the ladder to La Liga where, with the occasional slip from grace, the club remained from 2000 to 2018, when it was relegated. It is, however, too determined a club to remain there overlong, and will probably soon be back in La Liga, where it belongs. Málaga's European adventures will feature later in this book.

Having languidly drifted across the romantic, humid lands of Andalucia, I now turn my attention to an entirely different region in terms of climate, geography, culture and language. I refer to the north of Spain and, in particular, to the harsh, mysterious world of the Basque Country.

***

BASQUE COUNTRY

Bilbao

Around 500 miles north of Seville, gazing out at the stormy Bay of Biscay, stands the bustling seaport of Bilbao, the largest city in the Basque Country.

By the late nineteenth century, Bilbao's population was approaching 100,000. It was a fast-expanding city, with its shipbuilding, railway yards and steel mills, in particular, being significant contributors to its local economy and its trading links with other European countries, including Britain. It also possessed the nucleus of a business-oriented middle class, geared towards innovation and profitable commercial expansion.

This industrialising mini-economy with a receptive commercial culture was, aside from a few exceptions such as Barcelona, in marked contrast to much of the rest of Spain which was economically backward, agrarian and in thrall to the 'latifundios', the large, privately owned estates.

Since 'El Desastre' of 1898, and the consequent collapse of the important colonial market, much of rural Spain – in particular, the central, inland regions – was again experiencing isolationism, internal political strife and recurring power struggles, against a background of economic decline and increasing poverty. In the early years of the twentieth century, internal emigration to the larger towns and cities was increasing, but the rural peasantry who remained on the land were penurious and close to starvation.

However, this was far from the case in the areas surrounding the major ports, in particular Bilbao. British miners had been arriving in the Basque Country from north-east England cities, such as Sunderland and Newcastle. Shipyard workers also headed to Bilbao from the southern English coastal cities of Southampton and Portsmouth to take advantage of the economic benefits of industrialisation in the city. These immigrants brought with them the British game of football.

In 1898, these British workers formed Bilbao Football Club. In the same year, Spanish students back home from English universities, where they had discovered and enjoyed football, established Athletic Club in the city. Prior to this, in 1894, the two groups had played each other in casual games at Lamiako on the east bank of the River Nervión, the workers winning 6–0 in the first fixture.

In 1901, the students met at the city's Café Garcia, and there they drew up the rules and regulations for **Athletic Club**. Despite the club's claim for an 1898 founding date, 1901 is the general consensus (outside the Basque Country). By this early stage in its history Athletic Club had already adopted a cause: Basque nationalism, a philosophy underlying what many Basques perceived as their and their region's unique character.

The Basque Country consists of four Spanish (and three French) regions, these being Álava, Gipuzkoa, Navarre and Vizcaya, which was home to Bilbao. The first three regions were relatively underdeveloped and, importantly, lacked an industrial middle class. Vizcaya was different, Bilbao was without question the Basques' most important city, and so Athletic Club was to become, at least in the eyes of the club, the standard-bearer for the Basque cause.

The Basques were and are an anomaly in Spain and, indeed, in Europe. Their origins remain obscure, and their settlement of the lands around the south-east Bay of Biscay predates the arrival of the Celts. Their language is entirely different to Spanish Castilian, and is unique in Western Europe. Their culture, although heavily Catholic-influenced, is also very much their own and has little in common with Castilian. Although in these regions there are many who consider themselves Spanish, there is a sizeable number which does not and which considers itself Basque, and Basque only.

In 1894, Sabino de Arana had founded the Partido Nacionalista Vasco (PNV), a radically conservative Basque nationalist political party, and he coined the term 'Euskadi', loosely meaning 'the Basque community'. Another Basque word – 'Erdaldunak' – means 'people who speak a different language', and could then, and now, be applied to many people within this region whose preferred tongue is Castilian. In any event, shortly after its establishment, Athletic Club and the PNV became close allies, with the former embracing the policies of the latter.

The word 'Euskadi' continued to resonate throughout Spain until relatively recently, when the Basque armed separatist group ETA ('Euskadi Ta Askatasuna': 'Basque Homeland and Freedom') laid down its arms after four decades of bloody struggle against the Spanish state.

Meanwhile, after the legal foundation of the club in 1901, Bilbao and Athletic briefly merged, under the name Vizcaya, to contest the Copa de la Coronación, the forerunner of the Copa del Rey. Five clubs – Vizcaya, FC Barcelona, Madrid FC, New Football de Madrid and Español – competed in this celebratory tournament, and Vizcaya beat Barcelona 2–1 in the final to claim the Cup. The Copa, held in Madrid, was the venue of the first match between Barcelona and Real Madrid (as Madrid FC were later titled), and the Catalan club won 2–1.

In 1903 the alliance between the two Bilbao clubs became a permanent merger, under the name Athletic Club. (Also in 1903, a group of Basque students formed Athletic Club Madrid, known today as Atlético Madrid, and forged strong, if temporary, links with Athletic Club.)

Athletic Club claimed the inaugural Copa title in 1903, and again in 1904 and 1911. In 1913, the club inaugurated their new stadium – San Mamés – known as 'La Catedral' by the faithful (in both senses). This stadium was to be Athletic's home for the next 100 years.

The Spanish football federation decided in 1914 that, as the Copa was becoming so popular with national football clubs, it would end the existing practice of free entry into the competition and replace this with a series of regional play-offs, with each regional winner allowed into the Copa.

However, this decision did not deter Athletic Club. With the invaluable presence of striker Pichichi, it was unstoppable between 1914 and 1916, winning the trophy three times in succession.

Pichichi

England has the Golden Boot, Italy has the Capocannoniere ('head gunner'), Turkey has the Gol Kralligi ('goal king'), Germany has the Torjägerkanone ('top scorer cannon'), and most other footballing countries have a similar annual award for the leading goalscorer in their top football league. Spain has the Trofeo Pichichi, a prize named after a Basque player who, 100 years ago, was a supremely talented forward and prodigious goalscorer for his club, Athletic Club of Bilbao.

Rafael Moreno Aranzadi was born in Bilbao in 1892 into a wealthy middle-class family. His father had been a mayor of the city and his uncle was Miguel de Unamuno, a Basque poet, essayist, philosopher and prominent academic. Educated at a private Catholic school, and under family pressure to follow an academic career, Aranzadi briefly studied law but, since his youthful experiences of the game on the playing fields by the River Nervión, he had known that football would be the overriding priority in his life.

A precociously skilful footballer, he ditched his legal studies and, in 1911, he joined Athletic, established only ten years previously. He was, at just over five feet in height, on the small side, and he became known as 'Pichichi', an affectionate nickname meaning 'little pigeon' or 'little duck'. He was a confident and self-assured youngster and, despite (or perhaps because of) his lack of inches, he was a master at the art of dribbling, heading (perhaps surprisingly) but, above all, goalscoring.

In 1913 Pichichi claimed the first goal ever scored at Athletic's magnificent new San Mamés Stadium, against fellow Basques Real Unión, and he scored a hat-trick in the 1915 Copa del Rey final against Español. Immediately recognisable on the pitch by his white bandana (to protect his head from the thick laces then in use on footballs), this little footballing genius, christened by newspapers 'El Rey de Shoot' ('The Strike King'), scored 200 goals in 170 games for Athletic Club, his only club, between 1911 and 1921.

He played five games for Spain's first national team in the 1920 Olympics, scoring one goal, and he retired from football in 1921. Although he was once their hero, an increasing number of Athletic fans considered that his individualistic attitude and 'celebrity lifestyle' were affecting his play, that he was becoming arrogant and selfish on the pitch, and made their feelings known vocally during Athletic games. Pichichi's pride and self-esteem were under attack, so he gave up playing. He then briefly tried his hand at refereeing, but quickly found that to be tedious. In March 1922, he contracted typhoid from dining on contaminated oysters, and he died at the age of twenty-nine.

His death was mourned in Bilbao, and he became a footballing legend, a status ensured by his unparalleled goal tally, his loyalty to the club and his early death. In 1926 Athletic installed a bust of Pichichi at San Mamés, and it is customary for all visiting teams to leave a bouquet of flowers beside the bust. A painting of Pichichi and his wife, against an idyllic rural Basque landscape, hangs in the club president's office.

Pichichi was Spanish football's first sporting superstar. In his honour, *Marca*, the Madrid-based daily Spanish sports newspaper, initiated the 'Trofeo Pichichi' at the beginning of the 1952/53 season. The award is retroactive to the establishment of La Liga in 1929 so, ironically, as Pichichi predates La Liga he could not have been a candidate.

However, although the trophy has been claimed five times each by Alfredo Di Stéfano (Real Madrid, 1953–1959), Quini (Sporting de Gijón and Barcelona, 1973–1982), Hugo Sánchez (Atlético and Real Madrid, 1984–1990) and Lionel Messi (Barcelona, 2009–2018), the overall winner up to 2017/18 was Telmo Zarra, who won six trophies between 1944 and 1953. And his club? Athletic Bilbao. In season 2018/19, however, Messi equalled Zarra's record.

Around this time, in 1909, Athletic Club changed its strip from blue-and-white to red-and-white vertical stripes. There have been various reasons proposed for this fashion statement. One is that the flag of Bilbao is red and white (mostly white), and that seems reasonable. Another is that the strip closely resembles the design and colour of the Sunderland FC and Southampton FC shirts, and the switch may have been a homage to these clubs' workers and the roles they played in the establishment of Athletic Club.

Again, there is a story about a representative from Athletic visiting Southampton and discovering, in a sports shop, a bargain price for fifty red-and-white shirts. So he bought them, then passed on what was left over to the club's then-partner, Atlético Madrid.

However, the most likely explanation is also the most prosaic, which is that this particular configuration is similar to many Spanish bed mattress covers, the material is cheap, and the shirts were run up to save a few pesetas. This theory gains extra credit when one bears in mind that Atlético Madrid's nickname is 'los colchoneros' or 'the mattress makers'.

During this period, Athletic's early adoption of, and adherence to, Basque nationalism lay in its formulation of 'La Cantera'. 'La Cantera' is an unwritten, legally unenforceable, but rigid club policy which states: 'Con cantera y afición, no hace falta importación' ('With home-grown players and supporters, there is no need for foreigners'). Until then, the club had occasionally fielded English players – including, in 1903, one 'Alfredo' Mills as vice-captain – but from 1912 this all changed.

The literal meaning of the word 'cantera' is 'youth academy', but the Basque connotation is 'rock quarry', which indicates the club's perception of its fellow Basques as fit, healthy and strong. Perhaps this can be interpreted as righteously self-glorifying, although Basques, as a rule, do tend to overshadow fellow Spaniards in terms of height and physique.

In Athletic footballing terms, 'cantera' means that the club will field players only if they are born in the Basque Country or if they learned their football at a Basque academy, a policy which exists (more or less) to the present day. However, the club was canny enough to ensure that the policy does not apply to coaching staff and, over the years, Athletic's managers have been citizens of a number of different countries.

'Cantera', unlike more extreme nationalist policies, does not exclude sons of families from non-Basque countries and regions, so long as these families were born in the Basque lands. These descendants are known as 'maketos', and Pichichi was a 'maketo'.

As there is a relatively small population of around three million Basques, one might expect that, aside from nationalist and ethnic reasons, this could be considered a somewhat narcissistic, self-defeating policy. However, the statistics show otherwise: fourteen of the twenty-one players in Spain's first national team had their origins in the Basque Country; Athletic Club has always been regarded as one of the top three clubs in Spain; and the club, a founder member of La Liga in 1929, has never been relegated from the top level of Spanish football.

'Cantera' has been criticised as xenophobic, discriminatory, and even accused of promoting 'racial purity'. However, no one can accuse Athletic of prioritising Basque solidarity with its Basque footballing neighbours over its own interests. The largest and wealthiest of the Basque clubs, Athletic has often lured promising Basque footballers away from smaller Basque clubs. This 'poaching' of players, combined with the club's perceived conservative nationalistic policy, has permanently alienated several of the other clubs in the region.

The fact that coaching staff can be non-Basque meant that when Fred Pentland arrived in March 1923 as manager at Athletic, he was the third Englishman to occupy the role. Mr Shepherd had come and gone after a few months (homesickness) in 1910/11, and Billy Barnes had taken over and had steered the club to the three consecutive Copa del Rey victories.

Pentland – an ex-winger in a career which had included Blackpool, Blackburn and Middlesbrough, an internee in a German POW camp in WWI, and briefly coach at the club's rivals Real Sociedad – was to become another legendary figure at Athletic. 'Freddie', known as 'bombin' ('bowler hat'), introduced the players to the virtues of short interconnected passing, speedy movement on and off the ball, dribbling and the importance of retaining possession.

Under his management, this move away from the previously predictable 'kick and run' football, combined with the players' physical strength advantage, helped Athletic to again win the Copa in 1923. Although Pentland left to join Oviedo in 1925, he was to return in 1929 in time for the beginning of the new Liga championship. Under his eccentric but effective guidance, Athletic Club was soon to assume another period of dominance in Spanish football.

Copa del Rey

In 1902 Carlos Pedrós, the first president of Madrid FC (later to become Real Madrid) suggested to the mayor of Spain's capital city that a football competition be held to celebrate the coronation of King Alfonso XIII. The Copa del Ayantumiento de Madrid, also known as the 'Coronation Cup', was contested at the Madrid Hippodrome and was won by Club Vizcaya.

Thereafter, and until the present day, this annual, home-and-away knockout cup, with the final played as a single game at a neutral venue, is known as the **Copa del Rey** ('King's Cup'), although it became Copa del Presidente de la Repúblic (Second Republic) and Copa del Generalisimo (Franco). The Copa is one of the two major Spanish football competitions, and was regarded as Spain's national championship until the beginning of La Liga in 1929.

Fourteen clubs won the Copa between 1903 and 2018, Barcelona having claimed the silverware on thirty occasions while Arenas de Getxo and Real Mallorca have each once claimed the trophy in, respectively, 1919 and 2003.

Some sixty miles to the east of Bilbao – on today's A-8 highway which lings Galicia with the French border – sits San Sebastián, the capital of the Basque region of Gipuzkoa. Today, San Sebastián is a large, coastal holiday resort much favoured by Spaniards as well as by foreign tourists. Although lacking Bilbao's size and its neighbour's industrial and commercial infrastructure, nevertheless its inhabitants seem, to me, to exhibit the essence of what it means to be 'Basque'.

One detects here a more radical Basque spirit than that of Bilbao: a left-wing inclination in contrast to Bilbao's right-wing nationalistic spirit. Perhaps this is a function of San Sebastián's greater sense of community, or the relative absence of a profit-driven commercial-industrial imperative, but the town's 'Basqueness' is more pervasive than in Bilbao.

San Sebastián may have been less influenced by PNV than was Bilbao, but its Basque nature appears more evident and sincere. Perhaps this is simply because San Sebastián is smaller, and therefore more obvious when strolling around.

Whatever the reason, in San Sebastián football was another early starter. In 1904, local workers and students who had returned from England, and who had discovered football, set up the San Sebastián Recreation Club. In 1909 the club registered the football club as a separate organisation, so 1909 can be claimed as the foundation of San Sebastián Football Club. In 1910, King Alfonso XIII, who made the town his summer capital, bestowed on the club the honorific title 'Real', and it settled on its present name: **Real Sociedad de Fútbol**.

Wearing a distinctive blue-and-white strip, Real Sociedad was affectionately called 'La Real' and, in Basque, 'tuxuri-urdin' (the 'white and blues'). After Athletic Bilbao, it has been the second most successful club in the Basque Country's footballing history.

The rivalry between Athletic and Sociedad may not equal the intensity of, for instance, Real Madrid v Barcelona or Sevilla v

Real Betis, but it does have a special potency of its own. Over the years, there have been more than 150 Basque Derby games and, although Athletic have claimed significantly more victories, the first such Derby went Sociedad's way.

In 1909, the clubs met at Sociedad's Anoeta Stadium – where an athletics track ran around the pitch – and a capacity 25,000 fans watched as the home team won 4–2 in the semi-final of the Copa del Rey. Due to registration problems, Sociedad had temporarily adopted the name Ciclista Club de San Sebastián, but this did not stop them winning the Copa that year, with a 3–1 victory over Español de Madrid. It would be almost eighty years before they won their second Copa.

***

Inland from Bilbao and Santander, and roughly equidistant from each of them, is the town of Eibar, with a population of around 27,000. This little place, hidden in a valley sheltered by mountains, was at the heart of the Basque iron and steel industry from the fifteenth century, so much so that, at the beginning of the twentieth century, over 1,000 of the town's 6,500 inhabitants were gunsmiths. The football club **SD Eibar**, unsurprisingly, is known as 'los armores' or 'the gunners' (does this sound familiar to English readers?).

Founded in 1940, SD Eibar wears a claret-and-blue strip, which it adopted in 1943, apparently as a gift from the Catalan club although these are also the colours of the town's shield. Eibar plays in a stadium, Ipurua, owned by the local council, and the club's recent history is a remarkable one.

Eibar turned professional in 1943/44, entered the Tercera in 1950 and, for the following sixty years, the club see-sawed between Tercera and Segunda. But everything changed for Eibar at the end of season 2013/14. The club had secured back-to-back promotions from Segunda B, the Segunda and then, for the first time in its history, Eibar found itself in the top tier of Spanish football, La Liga.

By so doing, it had become the smallest club, with the smallest stadium, ever to have entered La Liga. Indeed, over half of the clubs in La Liga possessed more seats in each of their stadiums than there were residents in the entire town of Eibar. (In 2013/14 Ipurua Stadium had a capacity of 5,259, which has today increased to over 8,000.)

However, there was a problem. *Real Decreto 1251/1999*, a Spanish law, stipulated that, as the Primera and Segunda were professional divisions, the clubs who joined had to pay higher tax rates to the 'hacienda' (taxman) and increase their social capital by, in the case of Eibar, €1.7 million. Therefore, in order to maintain its newly earned, exalted status, the cash-strapped club had to pay this or accept immediate relegation.

Eibar, however, had other ideas, which did not include returning immediately to the lower league. The club launched a crowdfunding scheme – 'Defiende al Eibar' – which offered individual shareholdings, each share valued at €50. The campaign went viral on social media, and the response far exceeded Eibar's hopes. When the scheme ended, the club had raised, from over 10,000 people in seventy countries, from China to the USA and Britain to Brazil, a sum far in excess of what was required. Triumphantly, Eibar paid the money due to La Liga and entered the Primera for the start of the 2014/15 season.

Eibar began this first season well but finished in eighteenth place, and the club was technically relegated. However, Elche, who had finished La Liga in thirteenth place, could not pay its debts of around €15 million and, under the new laws, went down to Segunda in Eibar's place. The small Basque club was, therefore, reinstated in La Liga for the following season. Despite all the odds, Eibar entered its fifth successive season in Primera in 2018/19.

Eibar had reached the top echelon of Spanish football by operating within its means, and by fielding a team comprising mainly young Spanish players, on-loan signings and free transfers, who were imbued with determination, team spirit and strong ties to the community. There is surely a lesson here for other Spanish football clubs.

'Eskozia La Brava'

Without the support, enthusiasm and general bedlam of loyal fans, football matches involving clubs anywhere in the world would be very dull places. Spanish clubs are no exception, and all clubs have their own 'peñas', or 'supporters' clubs'. These committed, volatile and frequently highly inventive fans go a long way to creating the atmosphere at games, and their voluble support can often act as an added incentive to their players, toiling away on the pitch.

Earlier in this book, I refer to the happy-go-lucky fans of Cádiz CF, but there are several other eccentric and entertaining 'peñas' in Spanish football. The activities, chants and singalongs of the 'Eskozias' at Eibar and the 'Bukaneros' at Rayo Vallecano have few equals in this respect.

Eibar had good reason to celebrate in July 2015. Not only was it the club's seventy-fifth anniversary, it was also the end of the club's first-ever season in La Liga. Eibar decided to ask Scottish League champions Celtic to play in an anniversary match at the club's Ipurua Stadium.

There were existing links between Eibar and Scotland, as the previous Eibar supporter group, 'la bombonera', had been frequent visitors to Hearts, Hibs, Celtic and other Scottish club games. The connection had been reinforced in 2001, with Eibar then resident in Segunda B, when a group of supporters formed 'Eskozia La Brava' (translation unnecessary) and travelled to Edinburgh's Murrayfield Stadium to support Scotland in an international rugby match.

John Stewart, bagpiper at the 2015 anniversary game, said: 'The guys from Eibar came home with some souvenirs of Scotland: kilts and ginger "See You, Jimmy" wigs,' and probably also whisky, shortbread and Irn-Bru. The 'Eskozia' peña were instrumental in helping the club to organise the anniversary match.

Before the Celtic game, there was a parade of nineteenth-century-attired Basque soldiers carrying the Scottish saltire flag, accompanied by bagpipers playing 'Scotland the Brave'. Celtic won the game, as they normally do in Scotland, by a 4–1 margin, but the result didn't matter. By all accounts, the bonhomie between the two sets of fans was wondrous to behold, and no doubt continued well into the night fuelled by local 'Txakoli' (rough white wine) and 'Patxaran' (an equally rough sloe liqueur).

It is entirely possible that, as occurred in the aftermath of Celtic's 2–1 defeat of Inter Milan in the 1967 European Cup final in Lisbon, there are a few Celtic fans still living in Eibar, as they liked the place so much that they decided to remain. (One Celtic supporter had flown back to Glasgow after celebrating that famous 1967 victory, to be told by his wife when he reached home that he'd driven his car to Lisbon. But there is no record of this having happened in Eibar.)

Although, with the exception of Eibar and a couple of others, this chapter is mainly about the early years of Spanish clubs, I guess the question is how one defines 'early'. In Part Two of this book, I look at how the Spanish football scene developed from the formation of La Liga in 1929, and I end the chapter with the inauguration of the European Cup in 1955/56. The story then covers Spanish clubs in La Liga and in Europe until the present day.

However, over the years so many Spanish clubs have bounced between the various leagues, have known success and failure, have hibernated for many years and then reappeared, have only recently begun their journey in the Spanish game, or were once leading clubs but are today either venerable or have virtually disappeared from sight, that occasionally I feel it churlish to ring-fence them all in a strictly chronological framework.

Many of the clubs I mention are still with us, and playing their hearts out. Some are enduring hard times, while others are experiencing a period of success which will almost certainly be brief. There are, however, a number of clubs whose historical record, reputation and ability to bring out the best in players will never make them world-beaters, but will continue to reserve for them the better seats at, or close to, the Spanish league high table.

Deportivo Alavés is a case in point. Regarded as the third best team in the Basque lands, the club was founded in 1921 as 'Sport' Friends Club, in Vitoria-Gasteiz in Álava. The city today is the capital of Álava and also the capital and seat of government of the entire Basque Autonomous Community. It lies forty or so miles south-east of Bilbao, heading towards La Rioja.

Alavés has never won La Liga but, in 1929/30, it gained the honour of being the first club to be promoted from the Segunda to the Premier, although it remained there for only three years. The club then entered a long period of relative anonymity, until it came storming back to national and European success during the early twenty-first century.

In 1998/99, Alavés returned to La Liga after a forty-two-year absence, qualified twice for Europe (*see later in this book*) and stayed at the top level for five seasons. Currently it is in La Liga, where it returned for 2016/17 and where it remains. In 2017 Alavés also reached the Copa del Rey final for the first time in its history, but it was beaten 3–1 by Barcelona.

It lays claim to ownership of Spain's third-oldest professional football ground in the Mendizorrotza Stadium, built in 1924. Sporting de Gijón's Molinón came into use as far back as 1908, while Valencia's Mestalla, a formidable cauldron, was erected in 1923.

Interestingly, although the official epithet for Alavés is 'el glorioso', this probably reflects a Spanish-language grandiloquence on the part of the club. A more common nickname among fans and the media is 'babazorro', which in Spanish roughly implies 'a clown' or 'an ill-bred man'. 'Zorro' can also be translated as 'foxy, cunning and sly', and indeed Alavés uses a fox as its mascot.

However, in Basque 'babazorro' means, or can be interpreted to mean, 'one who eats broad beans as poverty food'. So the word 'babazorro' appears to be, at the same time, an acknowledgement and rebuttal of the disparagement visited upon Alavés by larger, metropolitan clubs, with more than a hint of admirable self-mockery in the adoption of the sobriquet by the Alavés fans. Good for them.

***

Nicknames

The discussion of 'babazorro' is probably a good time for a brief digression on Spanish clubs' nicknames generally.

As a rule (though there are exceptions), fans of the large, successful clubs in football countries tend to eschew amusing and interesting nicknames, leaving irony, humour and invention to supporters of the smaller perennial underachievers. Thus in Scotland, for example, we have Rangers ('Gers'), Celtic ('Hoops'), Aberdeen ('Dons') and so on – fairly predictable – while nestling in the lower divisions we discover Arbroath ('Red Lichties'), Cowdenbeath ('Blue Brazil'), Ayr United ('Honest Men'), Clyde ('Bully Wee') and a good many more entertaining and intriguing handles of affection.

However, in Spain, compared to Scotland's two or three dominant clubs, there has been until recent years a good many more clubs entering the national footballing consciousness and sharing the rewards offered by inclusion in La Liga and Copa del Rey, so their epithets flourish in the public mind. Also, even the conquistadorial giants, Real Madrid and Barcelona, retain quirky diminutives alongside the more magisterial 'blancos' and 'blaugranas'. I have already explained Sevilla's 'palanganas' and Atlético Madrid's sobriquet of 'colchoneros'. Here are a few more examples (including another popular name for Atlético Madrid):

Albacete: 'Queso Mecánico'. The football club from Albacete, the largest city in Castilla-La Mancha, has, like many of the other clubs in the region, achieved little in the way of success. However, in season 1991/92 Albacete Balompié reached the highest-ever position in its history, ending the Liga season in seventh place. Coach Benito Floro modelled his tactics on Cruyff's early-1970s Ajax, the team known as the 'clockwork orange'. Manchego cheese is Albacete's main export, so Alba was nicknamed 'queso mecánico': the 'clockwork cheese'. (Reus, in Catalonia, is known for its hazelnuts, and so CD Reus became the 'clockwork hazelnuts'.)

Athletic Bilbao: 'Leones'. St Mammes of Caesarea was a third-century child martyr who was thrown to the lions by the Romans, but the lions sat docilely by his feet, seemingly charmed by his Christian devotion. Then he was killed by a Roman soldier. The cult spread to Bilbao, where a church was named after him, by pilgrims on their way to Santiago de Compostela. Athletic named its stadium of San Mamés in his honour, and the fans adopted the name 'leones' ('lions').

Atlético Madrid: 'Indios'. As well as 'mattresses', fans have another name for Madrid's 'other' team. Since the 'relaxation' in the 1950s of the constraints on foreign players joining Spanish clubs, increasing numbers of Latin American footballers began to make their way to the more moneyed clubs. During the 1960s and 1970s, Atlético were particularly prone to purchasing players, known patronisingly as 'Indians', from South America. 'Indios' they became.

Barcelona: 'Culés'. As well as the colloquial 'Barça' and 'blaugrana', the term 'culés' has been adopted by club fans. The word 'cul' is Catalan for 'arse', and the term arose because the club's first stadium – Campa de la Indústria – was too small to contain their considerable support (and arses). So, many fans had to sit on a narrow wall, with their backsides drooping over the wall, affording passers-by views they did not particularly wish to see. But 'culés' they remain.

Celta de Vigo: 'Olivicos'. Vigo is the furthest west of all the leading Spanish clubs, its home town perched on the rocky coast of Galicia just north of the Portuguese border (this geographical proximity gives rival fans the opportunity to describe Celta fans as 'Portugueses'). Formed in 1929, the club has spent most of its existence in the top division of La Liga. As well as the club's support being known as 'Célticos', for Galicia's Celtic origins, Vigo is celebrated as 'the city of the olive', due to the planting by the Knights Templar of an olive tree in a local churchyard, as a symbol of peace. Hence 'Olivicos'.

Córdoba CF: 'Califas'. In the tenth century, Córdoba was the capital of Moorish 'Al-Andalus' which was under the stewardship of the Omeyas Caliphate (AD 921–1031). Córdoba was one of the Western world's most populous, sophisticated and intellectually progressive cities. Its liberal regime saw Muslims, Jews and Christians co-exist in relative peace and mutual dependence, although it was run on Islamic principles. Today, this period is still seen as a model of inter-faith harmony. Thus the popular name for the local football club: 'Caliphs'.

Deportivo de La Coruña: 'Herculinos'. La Coruña's main landmark is 'La Torre de Hércules' (The Tower of Hercules), a lighthouse built on a hill by the Romans in the second century AD. It is located on the mythical grave of a local despotic giant who was slain by Hercules. It is the oldest working Roman lighthouse in the world, and is a UNESCO World Heritage site. Dépor's fans are proud to be called 'Herculinos'.

'Turcos' was a pejorative term for Dépor supporters, and is another example of fans adopting chants of derision and turning these insults to their own advantage. Fans of Celta de Vigo, their long-term local rivals, called La Coruña supporters 'Turcos', as so few of their fans were apparently natives of the city. La

Coruña supporters now proudly describe themselves as 'Turcos', and even wave Turkish flags at games.

Espanyol: 'Pericos'. FC Barcelona's rivals played their football, from 1923 to 1997, in the Estadi de Sarrià which was situated in a pleasant, middle-class area of Barcelona. The trees in the nearby streets were popular with numerous colourful birds, such as budgies and parakeets. 'Perico' is Spanish for 'budgie'.

Granada CF: 'Nazaries'. As with Córdoba (page 43), this refers to the Moorish occupation of Spain, in particular to the Nasrid ('Nazaries') Dynasty which ruled the Emirate of Granada from 1230 to 1492, the year the Alhambra complex fell into the hands of the Christians. Thousands of 'moriscos' (Islamic converts to Christianity) remained in Spain, but they were all expelled in the early seventeenth century. Anyway, this explains 'Vamos, los Nazaries'.

Las Palmas: 'Los Canarios'. There is also an avian connection (cf. Espanyol above) with this Gran Canaria club. In the 1980s, a fan named Fernando 'La Bandera' Gonzalez began, on a whim, to sing and whistle bird (particularly canary) sounds during the team's home games. Las Palmas supporters were clearly amused by this, and adopted what (to them, anyway) sounds like a whistling canary. 'Pio-Pio' or 'the canaries'.

Leganés: 'Pepineros'. Before Leganés, whose football club was founded in 1928, became more or less absorbed into a suburb of Madrid, it was an agricultural village which specialised in the growing and exporting of a number of crops, in particular cucumbers ('pepineros'). So, it's only appropriate that they are nicknamed 'los pepineros': 'the cucumber growers'.

Levante: 'Granotas': One of the oldest surviving clubs in the Valencia Community – established in 1909 – Levante merged in 1939 with the now defunct Gimnastico FC to form Levante UD. Levante had the players and Gimnastico had the stadium, this being the Estadio de Vallejo which was located in an old working-class area beside an old river bed, and which was home to a large number of frogs. Since then, the symbol of Levante has been the 'granota' which is, of course, the Spanish word for 'frog'.

Málaga: 'Boquerones'. This Andalucian port on the Mediterranean had by 1904 established its own club. After frequent name changes and mergers, the current club was established in 1941, and again in 1993. One of the many culinary delicacies for which the Málaga area is rightly famed is the anchovy, so it seems only fitting that the club is known as 'los boquerones': 'the anchovies'.

Mérida: 'Romanos'. Mérida AD is the latest club to have emerged from the city of Mérida in Extremadura. It was founded in 25 BC by the Romans, and its name is a corruption of the Latin 'Emerita Augusta', meaning 'discharged veteran soldiers of the army of Augustus'. Mérida was one of the most important Roman cities in the Iberian Peninsula, and it contains more Roman monuments, including a triumphal arch, a theatre, a bridge and a temple, than does any other Spanish city. So what is a more appropriate nickname for the club than 'the Romans'?

Numancia: 'Numantinos'. CD Numancia is based in the city of Soria, in the Castile and León autonomous region, and is usually to be found in the Segunda División. The club's name (and nickname) also dates from the Roman occupation of Iberia, when Soria was a Celto-Iberian settlement named Numancia. The inhabitants, after a serious dispute with their Roman colonisers, withstood a siege by 50,000 Romans for twenty years, until they had little choice but to surrender. The club's name celebrates the people's courage and determination in the face of what should have been an overwhelming victory for the Romans.

Real Madrid: 'Merengues'. The flagship galleon in the Spanish footballing armada, Real Madrid is one of the world's wealthiest and most successful football clubs. The epithets aimed at, and claimed by, the club are many, with a few being unprintable in a family-friendly book such as this. 'Merengues ('meringues'), however, must be among the silliest, with its connotations of a lightweight, crumbly sweet cake. Obviously, it refers to the club's all-white strip (why, then, not 'icebergs' or similar?). The name was popularised by a Francoist radio sports commentator, the fans like it, and it has stuck, as meringues tend to do.

Real Murcia: 'Pimentoneros'. The capital and most populous city of the eponymous autonomous region in the south-east of the country is home to Real Murcia. The region is agriculturally abundant, and it is known as 'Europe's orchard'. Although I have never encountered nor heard of a 'pumpkin orchard', one probably exists, which is why this perennial 'yo-yo' club is affectionately nicknamed by its support as 'los pimentoneros': 'the pumpkin men'.

Sporting de Gijón: 'Marcona'. Gijón, the main port of the Asturias region, has a long history of trade with Britain, so it is little surprise that its football club, founded in 1905, is one of the earliest established in Spain. It is a large city, with a correspondingly sizeable club fan base, and is normally some geographical distance away from the competition. So when the Gijón support arrives in another Spanish city for a game, it feels like a tsunami has hit the place. Which is why Gijón fans are known as 'la marcona': 'the tidal wave'.

Valencia: 'Chés'. Most countries/large cities have their own, frequently dialect-based and often unfathomable word for 'friend', 'mate' or 'pal' (the last being of Romany origin). In the UK, think of 'Jimmy' (Glasgow), 'geezer' (East London), 'boyo' (Wales) and so on. 'Ché' is one of these friendly, hand-over-the-shoulder, blokeish terms, deriving from the Valenciano or Catalan language, used by Valencians and, by extension, is the word applied to the city's leading football club. It has nothing to do with Guevara of That Ilk.

'Murciélagos': Valencia has another unusual nickname: 'murciélagos', meaning 'bats'. A bat is also on the city's coat of arms. The reason (other than that there are many bats to be found in Valencia)? In 1238 King James I was attempting to enter the city to retake it from the Moors, as part of the 'Reconquista'. As he and his troops were about to charge the Moors, a bat landed on the king's flagpole. He saw this as a good omen and reconquered Valencia. (As a coda, in 2014 DC Comics attempted to sue Valencia CF for breach of copyright, as the club's bat logo was suspiciously similar to that of their comic hero Batman. Valencia CF was born in 1919. The first Batman comic appeared in 1940. Go figure.)

Valladolid: 'Pucelanos'. One of Spain's more successful smaller-city football clubs, Real Valladolid has spent over forty seasons in La Liga despite its adoption of a particularly noxious violet-purple strip. One theory is that 'pucelanos' derives from this, for want of a better word, 'puce' colour. Another opinion is that Valladolid was the only Spanish town which distributed cement, bought from the Roman Italian town of Pozzuoli. So 'Pozzuoli' gradually mutated into 'pucella', which then became the name for inhabitants of Valladolid. Yet another explanation is that knights from the town went to France in the fifteenth century to defend the Maid of Orleans from the English. In old Castilian, 'maid' is 'pucella', hence 'pucelanos'. This is the most plausible theory, but take your pick.

Villarreal: 'Submarino Amarillo'. Although founded in 1923 in the Valencia Community, Villarreal have achieved national and European success only since 2000. Since then, the club have been permanent residents of La Liga, apart from one season. Originally kitted out in white and black, it was not until 2003 that Villarreal adopted their all-yellow strip, although the yellow shirts (with blue shorts) dates from 1947. Their nautical nickname was acquired round this period, particularly when Los Mustangs were riding high in the Spanish pop charts with a cover version of the Beatles' 'Yellow Submarine'. The club's mascot, then a twelve-year-old named 'Groghet' ('little submarine'), made his debut in October 2001. (Interestingly, Cádiz, currently in the Segunda, are also known as 'los submarinos amarillos'. Cádiz's shirts are aslo yellow, but the poignancy of the nickname dates from the period 1985 to 1993, when the club managed to remain in La Liga by 'sinking down' towards relegation throughout each season and contriving to 'come afloat' at the very end. But nothing lasts for ever . . .)

The town of Pamplona, capital of the eastern Basque province of Navarre, is best known for its July Festival, 'the running of the bulls'. It has also been home, since 1920, to **Osasuna** football club which plays today in the town's El Sadar Stadium.

The club's name is Basque for 'health', as in 'strong, vigorous and disciplined'. Although there are many inhabitants of Navarre who do not consider themselves to be Basque, particularly in the south of the region, Osasuna's supporters tend to adopt a 'Basqueness' of a more radical, left-wing nature than what they perceive as the conservative, nationalist Basque character of, for instance, Athletic Bilbao, one of their main footballing rivals. The fact that Athletic are inclined to help themselves, from time to time, to Osasuna's best players is another underlying source of the rivalry.

'Los rojillos', 'the little red ones', were promoted to the Segunda in 1932 and to La Liga in 1935. As Navarre was not slow to ally itself with Franco in the Civil War, so Osasuna spent the War under Francoist organisation. Although it has won neither La Liga nor the Copa del Rey, it has come close, and season 2005/06 found the club playing its 1,000th game in La Liga. The following season, Osasuna reached the semi-final of the UEFA Cup, having eliminated some of Europe's leading sides, only to lose to holders and eventual winners Sevilla. Osasuna is also one of the four Spanish clubs, the 'socios', which under law is owned by its members, a controversial piece of legislation passed in 1990 by the Spanish parliament.

Two other Basque clubs – Real Unión and Arenas de Getxo – are examples of successful origins but also, and almost inevitably, of contemporary obscurity. Both clubs were founder members of La Liga in 1928/29, spent a few short years in Primera before being relegated, and have never returned to La Liga. Most of their history has been in the Tercera, and they both currently play their football in the third tier of league football, Segunda B.

Based in Irún, close to the French border, **Real Unión Club** won the Copa del Rey three times in the 1920s, including its defeat of Arenas de Getxo in the 1927 final, the only all-Basque final in the tournament's history. It also has the dubious honour of being the first club in La Liga history to concede a goal. This was scored by an Español player, 'Pitus' Prat. The club's relegation came in 1932.

Arenas de Getxo is today part of greater Bilbao, and was a middle-class enclave on the Bilbao Estuary when the club was founded in 1909. It is not unlikely that being next door to Athletic Bilbao, and not far up the coastal road from Real Sociedad, were predictable factors in Arenas' decline.

In its memorable year of 1914, Arenas beat FC Barcelona in friendlies on three occasions, and topped this in 1919 by again defeating the fast-emerging Catalan side 5–2 in the Copa del Rey final. After seven continuous seasons in Primera, however, Arenas was relegated, and over sixty seasons in the third tier was its reward for a brief dalliance at the highest level of Spanish club football.

***

NORTHERN SPAIN

As we are in the north of Spain, other early clubs – such as Barcelona, Español, Real Madrid, Atlético Madrid, Levante et al. – can wait until our investigation of this intriguing northern area is complete. There is still a good deal of footballing interest to discuss in this area before heading east and south.

GALICIA

Galicia – in terms of its geography, culture and language – is quite unlike the rest of Spain. Its name derives from the Celtic 'Gallaeci' people who settled here in the middle of the first millennium BC, and its language, Gallego, is a Castilian/Portuguese hybrid which is the first language of the majority of native Galicians. The region is mountainous, misty and coastal, with a history of deprivation, rural poverty and emigration, both within Spain and to Latin America.

Since the early years of the twentieth century, several clubs have come and gone in Galicia. A few remain, but are largely ensconced in the lower reaches of the Spanish league pyramid. These declining powers include Racing de Ferrol, SD Compostela and Pontevedra.

Racing de Ferrol is one of the oldest clubs in Galicia, dating from 1909. (Ferrol is also the birthplace of General Franco, although this is not a fact which today is generally or willingly volunteered by the local citizenry.) Ferrol was a beneficiary of the shipbuilding yards and dry docks established by the British in the early twentieth century, and from whom the original club members learned the game. Although the club has played continuously since joining the league's third tier in 1929, it has never played in La Liga, and it was relegated to Tercera at the end of 2017/18.

SD Compostela reached La Liga in 1994 and stayed there for four years, but the club now also finds itself in the Tercera. **Pontevedra**, founded just after the Civil War, was regarded in the late 1960s as Galicia's third club. Known as 'los granates' after its deep maroon colours, from 1965 to 1970 in La Liga it regularly defeated the larger clubs. Its supporters' motto became 'hai que ruelo', roughly meaning 'you have to bite the bullet when you play Pontevedra'. This warning was finally understood and acted upon by the club's La Liga competitors, which is why Pontevedra currently resides in the third tier, Segunda B.

A relatively recent addition to the Galician football roster is **CD Lugo**, established in 1953. The eponymous city, also known as Lucus Augusti, is the only city in the world to be surrounded by intact Roman walls, and Lugo is a World Heritage site. Located inland and equidistant from Santiago and La Coruña, CD Lugo drifted between the Tercera and Segunda B until, in 2012/13, it was promoted to Segunda, which is where it is to be found today.

However, two of the older clubs – Celta de Vigo and Deportivo de La Coruña – remain as prominent national contenders and, in recent years, have been leading players in the Spanish game.

The oldest – and, in recent years, the most successful – club in Galicia is **Deportivo de La Coruña**, 'Coruña' meaning 'Crown' in Gallego. La Coruña is situated on the far north-west coast of Spain, only a few miles east of Finisterre ('the end of the world') and a similar distance north of Santiago de Compostela. Santiago de Compostela is the culmination of one of Europe's most-travelled pilgrimage routes. Here is supposedly buried the remains of the venerated St James ('Iago'), the mythical warrior-saint whose bones were a symbol of the Catholic 'Reconquista' against the Moors over 1,000 years ago, although he appears to have done little to help his 'home' football club.

'Dépor' was founded in 1906, after a local student named José Maria Abalo returned from England enthusing about the game, and the club was granted 'Real' status the following year. It moved into its stadium, the beachside Old Riazor, which is close to its current home ground, Riazor, built in 1944.

The success of Spain in the 1920 Olympics encouraged Dépor, like many other clubs, to turn professional in the 1920s and, along with local rivals Celta de Vigo, it attempted to gain entry into La Liga in 1928/29, although both clubs made it only as far as the Segunda. Until the early 1990s, Dépor moved regularly between Primera and Segunda, but thereafter its profile in La Liga and European football grew more prominent, and its most successful period was from the 1990s until the early years of the twenty-first century.

Vigo, situated south of La Coruña and just north of the Portuguese border, is a city of around 300,000 people. Vigo is the industrial and fishing heart of Galicia, and its harbour is claimed to be the largest in Europe. Its football club, **Celta de Vigo**, was formed later (in 1923) than Dépor, but it has spent more seasons in La Liga, although Celta has never won La Liga or the Copa del Rey. However, as with Dépor, Celta also discovered Liga and European success on the cusp of the twentieth and twenty-first centuries.

Within Galicia, the 'Derby' between these last two clubs is as passionate as anywhere else in Spain, with the possible exception of 'El Clásico': Real Madrid v Barcelona. In fact, it's difficult to think of any football rivalry anywhere which would compare with these Spanish heavyweights.

Along with 100,000 others, I've stood in Glasgow's old Hampden Park and endured the mutual fan hatred as Celtic played Rangers in the Scottish Cup final, which is the closest experience that European football can provide to equal 'El Clásico'. But in Scotland, a game of football is ultimately just that: a game of football. In Spain, and not only between Madrid and Barcelona, football is often much more than simply a game, as this book will make increasingly clear.

***

ASTURIAS and CANTABRIA

Yet again, there have been clubs in these two regions who were founded early in the Spanish footballing calendar but who have now disappeared or are languishing, probably quite happily, in the lower leagues. However, there were three early starters in Asturias and Cantabria who are still very much in evidence in the upper levels of Spanish football.

The oldest of these footballing outposts is **Sporting de Gijón**, a club from the Asturian seaport of Gijón. Facing the Bay of Biscay, its distinctive name stems from the Latin word 'gigias', meaning 'giant', and refers to the high stone wall which the Romans built around the city. Today, it is a city of around 300,000 people, with its urban development having been aided by the exploitation of the abundant coal and iron ore deposits in its surrounding area.

In 1905, when the club was founded as Sporting Gijonés, the city's population was around 50,000. In 1915, under royal patronage, it changed its name to Real Sporting de Gijón, and in 1929 it joined the embryonic Segunda División, finishing in fourth place in its first season in the second tier. Its stadium, El Molinón, is the oldest (1908) professional football ground still in use in Spain. Originally built on the site of an old watermill ('molinón' means 'big mill' in Asturian), it was formally acquired by the club in 1924.

Sporting Gijón has never won the Copa del Rey or La Liga, but its progress in the league is an interesting story, particularly in the later years of the twentieth century in Spain and in the UEFA Cup, as we shall discover in Part Four.

Sporting's main rival, and competitor in the 'Asturian Derby', is **Real Oviedo**, some twenty miles south of the city, founded over twenty years after Sporting but with an equally intriguing backstory and, in recent years, a near terminal threat to the club's existence.

Oviedo, like Sporting, entered Segunda in 1929, reached La Liga in 1933, and remained in Primera until 1950. The club was renowned for its fast-moving possession play and passing skill, traits which were instilled in the club during the brief managership of Fred Pentland in the late 1920s. In the early 1930s, the effectiveness of Oviedo's attack was exemplified by the three 'Pichichi' trophies collected by lead striker Isidro Lángara.

After the Civil War, Oviedo was relegated to Segunda, as their 30,000-seater Carlos Tartiere Stadium had been used during the conflict by Francoist forces as an ammunition dump, and the pitch was unplayable (and probably potentially dangerous).

Further east along Spain's northern coast, between Gijón and Bilbao, lies the seaport and ferry terminal of Santander, capital of the autonomous region of Cantabria. Founded in 1913, **Racing de Santander** was the tenth and last club to have been a founding member of La Liga in 1929. Racing laid claim to this honour by defeating, in a play-off, Valencia, Real Betis and Sevilla, and it ended the 1930/31 Liga season as runner-up in Primera.

Ironically, given that today the club currently resides in Segunda, Santander was the original home of Banco Santander who are the main sponsor of La Liga Primera. Since its relegation in 1940, the club has bounced between Primera and Segunda.

However, Racing was a respected figure in La Liga virtually continuously from 1993 until 2012, and has spent well over forty seasons of its history in Primera. It has spent the last four seasons in Segunda B. Despite its financial problems of recent years which, as in the case of Oviedo, nearly saw the club disappear, it is regarded as one of Spain's most respected football clubs.

***

LA RIOJA

The small city of Logroño is the capital of the La Rioja region, which is squeezed between the Basque Country and Castile. La Rioja is Spain's least populous region, with around 330,000 inhabitants, and it won't surprise you to know that the local economy is dependent on the growth and sale of the eponymous wine.

SD Logroñés was established in the city shortly after the Civil War, in 1940. Ten years later it was promoted to Segunda, and the club oscillated between the national league's second and third tiers until 1986/87. On the final day of that season, Logroñés defeated the already promoted Valencia 1–0, and finally entered Primera.

The club remained in La Liga for nine, largely impressive seasons – its highest position being seventh in 1989/90 – =but then things began to go wrong and, by 2004, Logroñés was in Tercera, where it remained until 4 January 2009, a day which turned out to be its last national league game. The club had been suffering major financial problems, and on that day only nine players turned up, in protest at non-payment of salaries. The club then withdrew from Tercera and was relegated by RFEF to regional football.

A new club – **UD Logroñés** – was formed for season 2009/10, and so far it has remained in Segunda B, where it began. But the club is still young, and who knows what may happen? And even if the club fails to prosper, its location in a region which is, in reality, a very large vineyard should keep its supporters happy enough.

***

EASTERN SPAIN
ARAGON

'It is an error of geography to have assigned Spain to Europe: it belongs to Africa. Africa begins at the Pyrenees.' (Attributed to Alexandre Dumas)

Today's community of Aragon was once a powerful medieval kingdom, and its topography can be rather forbidding. Its position, nestling under the security of the towering Pyrenees, does little to diminish its one-time claim to regal authority.

The capital, largest city and home to the region's most successful club, is Zaragoza, which sits in the centre of the region on the banks of the River Ebro. Aragon, and neighbouring Navarre, were Francoist strongholds during the Civil War.

Towards the end of the War, the Ebro witnessed some of the cruellest and most vicious actions of the conflict, as the Republicans and International Brigades retreated from the Nationalist machine guns and crossed the river (many didn't make it) to the temporary safety of Barcelona.

The city's first club was founded in 1932, and played its early football in the Tercera and Segunda. **Real Zaragoza** was formed in 1939. The club zigzagged between the Segunda and the Primera until the late 1950s, but the 1960s was its first 'golden era'. Since then, it has been a near-permanent resident of La Liga, it has won six Copa del Rey trophies and, in season 1994/95, the club claimed the European Cup Winners' Cup. Later in this book I will be returning to Real Zaragoza.

Twenty miles to the north of Zaragoza, and even closer to the Pyrenees, is the town of Huesca and its football club, **SD Huesca**. In common with several other similarly sized Spanish clubs, Huesca has had a chequered, roller-coaster history since its establishment in 1910 as Huesca FC. The club folded in 1926, changed its name in 1940 to Unión Deportivo, and in 1956 folded yet again. Increasingly dejected by the city's inability to sustain its own football club, a number of local Barcelona supporters made a final effort in 1960, and SD Huesca was the result.

Bedecked in its heroes' 'blaugrana' strip, the fledgling club veered between the second and third tiers of Spanish league football until, at the conclusion of season 2017/18, Huesca's second place in the Segunda table was sufficient to gain entry to La Liga for season 2018/19.

Huesca was promoted to the Primera for the first time in its history, and it became the sixty-third team to join La Liga since the league's establishment ninety years ago. First Eibar, and now Huesca: the small clubs are fighting back – although Huesca ended second-bottom in La Liga and was relegated at the end of the 2018/19 season.

In George Orwell's *Homage to Catalonia* – a book which is required reading for all interested in this period – the Republican forces are laying siege to Falangist-held Huesca. A Republican officer attempts to raise his men's morale, in what to them increasingly appears to be a forlorn struggle, by cheerfully declaring 'tomorrow we'll have coffee in Huesca'.

The siege failed, but in season 2018/19 all the major Primera clubs were having their pre-match coffee in the Aragonese town of Huesca.

TWIN TOWERS

It was early in the 2001/02 football season. I have been a supporter of Arsenal since the mid-1970s, and I vividly recall sitting in front of the TV in my local bar in Stoke Newington, accompanied by my wife and son, to watch 'the Arse' play in Spain in the opening game of that season's Champions League.

Normally the bar would have been crammed with 'Gooners', but that evening it was eerily quiet and virtually empty. This was no reflection on our opponents, whose success in La Liga the previous season had gained them entry into European football's major competition. Rather, only a few hours earlier – the date was 11 September 2001, or '9/11' – two airliners had flown into New York's Twin Towers, and the subsequent events, broadcast on TV throughout the day, had considerably dampened the usually boisterous, expectant atmosphere in the bar.

I felt strangely guilty to be sitting there on such a horrifyingly momentous day. The players seemed to be simply going through the motions, as if they felt that day that a game of football was irrelevant, and they all appeared to be waiting for the final whistle, which finally concluded a 1–0 defeat for the Arsenal. This was an excellent result against England's leading club side, but the Spanish supporters' enthusiasm sounded muted on the TV, and the stadium quickly emptied. Such was my introduction to Real Mallorca.

For the last six years, my wife and I have spent up to six weeks each year in north-west Mallorca, only one hour's drive north from Palma but entirely different to the south of the island's brash touristic lifestyle. It is a ruggedly beautiful island, and is at the centre of the Balearic autonomous community, which also includes Formentera, Ibiza and Menorca. The local dialect – Mallorquí – is based on Catalan, as it is a region which is historically linked to mainland Catalonia, just over 100 miles to the north-west. So Mallorca is where I begin my exploration into the origins of football on Spain's eastern coast.

To say that **Real Mallorca** is one of Spain's 'yo-yo' clubs is seriously to understate the case, as the club's history has been as vertiginous in both directions as is the sharply mountainous landscape of the island's north-west coast.

The club, the oldest in the Balearics, was founded by a local engineer in 1916, and it is based today in the Estadio de Son Moix in the Mallorcan capital city of Palma. Over the hundred years of the club's existence it has adopted various name changes: originally Real Sociedad Alfonso XIII Football Club, it finally settled on its current name, Real Club Deportivo Mallorca, in 1949. By this time, the club had journeyed round regional leagues, Tercera and Segunda, and it was not until the 1960s that Mallorca reached La Liga, in which decade it was promoted and relegated three times from Primera.

Due to a rapid turnover of owners, poaching of its better players by larger mainland clubs, and a conveyor belt of managers and coaches, the club almost disappeared in the 1970s and 1980s. However, by the final decade of the twentieth century things had picked up significantly: so much so that, in 1989, Mallorca were narrowly defeated by Lazio in the very last Cup Winners' Cup final. Between 1997/98 and 2012/13, the club was a constant member of La Liga, achieving third position in two seasons, and it won the Copa del Rey for the only time in its history in 2003.

However, Mallorca does not appear to embrace consistency, such that, four years after relegation from La Liga, it was back in the third tier (Segunda B) of the league. However, in season 2017/18 the club was in Segunda and had rediscovered its old style and vigour. When I wrote this in late 2018, Mallorca was in Segunda, or second tier, but was playing well and had made a strong start to the season. In the event, Real Mallorca ended the 2018/19 season in a play-off position and were one of the three clubs promoted to Primera for 2019/20.

Meanwhile, it is time to catch the ferry to Barcelona, and to explore the roots of football in the mainland region of Catalonia, many of whose inhabitants are, in the splendidly appropriate words of Phil Ball in his book *Morbo*, 'besotted by their own creative triumphalism'.

CATALONIA

As this book is concerned with football in Spain, I will not devote much space to the cultural, political and linguistic anomaly that is Catalonia, other than how this has impinged on the development of the Spanish game. In any event, there is little I can, or wish to, add to the books which are currently available.

Football clubs, particularly in Spain, do not exist in isolation from their social contexts and, similar to the Basques, many inhabitants of Catalonia consider that they possess a different historical and cultural identity to that of Spaniards.

From as early as the ninth century, the Kingdom of Barcelona was a flourishing, successful independent state, organised around its seafaring and mercantile skills. It merged with the Kingdom of Aragon in the twelfth century but retained many of its rights and its independence.

From then until the mid-fifteenth century, when it was united with Castile and became part of the nascent Spanish state, it experienced its 'Golden Age'. During this period, the kingdom ruled the Balearic Islands, Valencia, the French border regions and Sardinia, and in 1359 instituted the Catalan Generalitat, the first parliamentary government in Europe.

Over the following centuries, its attempts to regain its autonomy from central state government have led to continual disputes and conflicts, and its distinctive language, Catalan – best described as an ungainly cross between medieval French and contemporary Castilian – has been suppressed, most notably under the Franco regime, although it is still widely used across the region today.

Catalonia's regional sense of 'otherness', most obvious in its major city of Barcelona, and its frequent divergence from Madrid-centred direction and rule, have been crucial factors affecting the development of football in Spain since the game first arrived in the region, as later pages in this book will reveal.

***

Although there are reports, dating back to 1882, of football games involving British expats and Catalans, the Football Associació de Catalunya, founded in 1900, was the first football association in Spain, and it organised the Campionat de Catalunya which was Spain's first football championship.

Club Gimnàstic de Tarragona (Nàstic, for short), from Tarragona to the south of Barcelona, was established in 1886, and for this reason would otherwise be considered 'El Decano'. However, the wealthy young Spanish originators did not form a football team until 1914, so their claim is out the window. Nevertheless, the club forged its intrepid way through the lower divisions and assumed residency in Segunda. Nàstic managed one season in Primera in 2006/07 but were relegated to Segunda B in 2018/19.

Just a bit inland from Tarragona is the town of Reus which was another early starter as a sports club (CD Reus) in 1909. **CF Reus**, an exclusively football-oriented spin-off, was established in 1951 and, until recently, resided mainly in Tercera. But in 2015/16 Reus finished top of Segunda B (Group 3), defeated Racing de Santander 4–0 in a promotion play-off, and reached Segunda for the first time. However, although the club was in its third season in Segunda, in January 2019 it was expelled for three years due to non-payment of its players' salaries. As the town is famed for its hazelnut production, the club possesses the zany nickname 'avellana mecánico' ('clockwork hazelnuts'). Beat that, anyone.

On the Costa Brava, north of Barcelona, sits the small coastal town of Palamós. Today, it is popular with tourists, attracted by its large beach, peaceful atmosphere and the tasty gambas (prawns), or 'gambes' in Catalan, from its busy harbour. Its main football club, **Palamós FC**, was founded in 1896, which makes it the oldest football club in Catalonia, and also the oldest club in Spain to have been established solely by Spaniards.

After it had undergone the usual name changes, it became Palamós Club de Fútbol in 1973. In the early 1990s the club was acquired by a wealthy, eccentric Ukrainian businessman (now departed), and for a few seasons thereafter it spent a few seasons in the dizzy heights of Segunda B. One will not come across Palamós much these days, as the club is to be found in Tercera.

Just a few miles inland from Palamós is the historically fascinating small city of Girona, with its carefully preserved, medieval Jewish quarter being a major touristic and scholarly attraction. Close to Palamós it may be, but Girona's contemporary importance in Spanish football is significantly greater than is that of the Costa Brava town.

Girona FC, founded in 1930, was a relatively late starter. It reached the Segunda in 1934/35 but, with occasional exceptions, remained in the lower tiers for most of its existence. Girona returned to the Segunda in 2008, after a forty-nine-year absence, and in 2016/17 the club was promoted to La Liga for the first time.

The club celebrated its first season by defeating European Cup holders Real Madrid 2–1 and finishing in tenth place in La Liga. It is, of course, more than possible that Girona's Primera status was assisted by its recent de facto acquisition by Manchester City, with the other major investment company, Girona Football Group, being headed up by Pere Guardiola, brother of City's current manager Pep Guardiola. Perhaps this fraternal link is just a coincidence, and anyway, what's wrong with keeping it in the family? However, despite this relationship Girona ended season 2018/19 in eighteenth place in La Liga and was relegated to Segunda.

To reinforce the importance of Catalonia in fostering the development of football in Spain, there are other clubs in the region – indeed, in the province of Barcelona – which cannot be overlooked in terms of their contributions to the early days of the Spanish game. The principal old boys are Europa and Sabadell (who are not owned by Manchester City).

Club Esportiu Europa, which today plays in Tercera, was one of the ten founder members of La Liga in 1929, and was included, along with Atlético Madrid and Español, as one of the three runners-up in the Copa del Rey. During the 1920s, Europa was the second-strongest team, after Barcelona in Catalonia. It was founded in 1907 and, although it remained in La Liga for the competition's first three years, it never again played in Primera.

The other elderly club, **Sabadell FC**, was established in 1903, and it has proven itself to be one of the more enterprising smaller clubs in the region. 'Los arlequinals' (named after its blue-and-white checked shirts) was the first Spanish side, in 1912, to play under floodlights, and it is a respected and well-supported club.

Sabadell entered the Segunda in 1933, reached its only Copa del Rey final the following year (losing 3–0 to Sevilla), and it has spent fourteen seasons in La Liga, the last being in 1987/88. In 1969/70 Sabadell competed in the Inter-Cities Fairs Cup, but lost to Club Brugge in the first round. However, today the club can be found languishing in Segunda B.

Some fifty or so miles inland from Sabadell, close to the region's western border in the Catalan Central Depression, is the oldest remaining settlement in Catalonia, this being Lleida. Today a city of around 130,000 people, it is home to **Lleida Esportiu**, known for geographical reasons, as 'the flatlanders'.

Formed in 1939, the club was named UD Lerida until 1978 and, although its natural homes seem to be Segunda B or Tercera, it attained Primera status in two seasons: 1950/51 and 1993/94. The club was dissolved in 2011, the same year it was reborn as

Esportiu. This remodelling and serious refinancing appears to have made little difference to its on-pitch fortunes, as it is today back in Segunda B.

However, the two Catalonian clubs which, in national and European terms, are today totemic of the region's footballing contradictions are implacable long-standing rivals who are both based in Barcelona, the capital of the region. These clubs are Espanyol and FC Barcelona.

FC Barcelona

An informal football match was held on 24 December 1899 at a racetrack in the Bonanova district of Barcelona. The opposing teams were FC Catala, which was composed entirely of local Catalan players, and FC Barcelona, which consisted mainly of British players.

This is generally considered to have been **FC Barcelona**'s first-ever game – although a match against Hispania in 1900 is often cited as the club's first official fixture – and, in what would become over the years a familiar story, they emerged victorious from the encounter.

Although today perceived by themselves, and by many other football observers, as the proud symbol of the Catalan 'nation', Barcelona's original founders, players and managers were predominantly 'foreigners', with the prime instigators being British and Swiss nationals.

As well as the British travellers, sailors and others who passed through this fast-expanding trading port on the north-east Mediterranean coast, there were several British local residents, businessmen, students and traders who were developing an increasingly affectionate attachment to Barcelona which is, after Madrid, the second-largest city in Spain.

For example, two English brothers, Arthur and Ernest Whitty, were members of a family-owned shipping company which set up business in Barcelona in the mid-nineteenth century, and they were both keen football supporters and players.

The Swiss connection to the embryonic club was one Hans Kamper, a well-travelled entrepreneur whose colourful career and his business and sport interests had included being a founding member of FC Zurich, a club established in 1896 and which today continues to compete in the Swiss Super League. Attracted by Barcelona's and Catalonia's lifestyle and commercial opportunities, Kamper focused his mind on the establishment of a football club in the city.

In November 1899 the Whitty brothers, Walter Wild (the club's first director), eleven players and other interested parties attended a public meeting arranged by Kamper, who was instrumental in ensuring that FC Barcelona was formally registered as a football club. This was ten years after a Scottish doctor had formed Spain's first club, Recreativo de Huelva, in the southern tip of Spain in Andalucia.

The blue and maroon colours of the FC Barcelona strip were also decided at the inaugural meeting. But why select blue and maroon? Several theories exist for this decision, including one that insists that accountants' pens at the time had both blue and red nibs, while another is that these were the colours adopted by Robespierre's First Republic during the French Revolution, and therefore worthy of emulation.

However, the most probable reason is that, as the Whitty brothers had attended Merchant Taylors', one of the earliest English public schools, and the school's rugby strip at the time had been blue and maroon, homage was due to the alma mater. Equally plausible is that, although Kamper's Zurich had opted for sky blue, his favourite Swiss team was FC Basel (for whom he had briefly played) and they had sported, and still wear, blue and red colours (and are known as the 'rotblau'). So FC Barcelona became the 'blaugranas', the colours by which they are today immediately recognisable.

Although Barça, as they quickly became known in Catalonia, reached the first Copa del Rey final in 1903, they lost 2–1 to Vizcaya. Over the next few years the club began to dominate most of the other clubs in the Catalonian regional competitions and in the Copa del Rey. Meanwhile, Kamper, who had been appointed club president, had been using his considerable contact list and business sense to steer the club through a rocky financial patch and, in 1909, to acquire its first ground in the city, at Camp de la Indústria.

By now, he had changed his name to the Catalan 'Joan Gamper', and in 1917 he appointed the club's first full-time manager, Englishman Jack Greenwell. Greenwell was to become the longest-serving manager in Barcelona's history, spending a total of nine years in the role. With players like the young prodigy Josep Samitier directing play and hammering in the goals, and the goalkeeping heroics of Ricardo Zamora, Greenwell managed two of the finest players in the club's history.

In 1922, due largely to Gamper's efforts and with the 'socio' membership having now reached 20,000, Barça moved to a larger stadium, Camp de Les Corts, with a capacity of 30,000.

On 14 June 1925 at Les Corts during a friendly match against Catalan side CD Jupiter, when a visiting English marine band played the Spanish national anthem 'Marcha Real', the fans booed and whistled. When the band, understandably confused by the locals' reaction, played 'God Save the King', the British anthem was enthusiastically applauded.

This mass protest was aimed against the centralising, dictatorial role assumed by Primo de Rivera, an opponent of regional autonomy and independent cultural expression, who had earlier banned the Catalan language and closed down the region's local government. This act of defiance by the fans resulted in the closure of Les Corts for six months and to the forced resignation of Gamper as club president.

Barça won the first La Liga title in 1929, but this success and consequent buoyant mood was deeply overshadowed by Joan Gamper's suicide the following year. It was the start of a new era for FC Barcelona, one which witnessed the club's temporary decline in national influence. It did not win La Liga again until 1945, although its victory in the 1942 Copa del Rey was some consolation. But thereafter, FC Barcelona was to become one of the leading clubs in Spanish and European football.

'El Sami'

In 1919, a seventeen-year-old working-class kid named Josep Samitier joined FC Barcelona, and he was to become one of the finest and most revered players in the club's history.

By the time of his departure from the club in 1932, 'El Sami' had scored 333 goals (he remains today the club's third-highest goalscorer) and helped to bring five Copa del Rey trophies and the inaugural La Liga title to Barcelona.

Samitier was the youngest member of the 1920 Spanish Olympic squad, and his remarkable talent was far in advance of his years. Initially a defender, he created the role of playmaking central midfielder, was a dazzling dribbler and possessed a powerful shot. His speciality was the flying kick, launching himself into the air to connect with the ball and earning himself the nickname 'home langosta' ('lobster man'). He was a 'total footballer' half a century before the phrase passed into general footballing parlance.

He moved to Real Madrid in 1932 but age had caught up with him, and early in the Civil War he escaped 'the reds' (he was a friend of Franco). He then joined Nice, where he remained until he returned to Barça in 1944 as coach and, latterly, as chief scout, in which capacity he was instrumental in bringing to the club the legendary Hungarian, Ladislao Kubala.

Despite his admiration for Franco and, one assumes, the Nationalist cause in the Civil War, when 'El Sami' died in 1972 thousands of fans lined the streets of Barcelona, where he received the Catalan equivalent of a state funeral.

Español (Espanyol)

Founded in 1900 in the city's middle-class Sarrià district by an engineering student at the University of Barcelona, the football club which in many respects represented the antithesis of FC Barcelona's cultural and political aspirations, was registered in 1901 as Club Español de Fútbol.

After Palamós, it was the second Spanish club to be formed exclusively by Spaniards. Español was proudly nationalistic, and the club and its fans adopted what was to become an enduring antagonistic attitude to its city rival. Indeed, Español publicly proclaimed that its *raison d'être* was to challenge and compete with 'the foreigners of FC Barcelona'.

Although the club folded in 1906, it was reborn in 1910 as CD Español, and with the blessing of King Alfonso XIII it became in 1912 **Real Club Deportivo Español**. The stricture on foreigners, however, did not apply to the club's managers, as three of its first six coaches, between 1922 and 1935, were British nationals.

Although the club claimed to be politically independent, throughout its early history its allegiance was to the central Spanish authorities, in contrast to the developing Catalan nationalist stance of its neighbour. As an indication of the club's sympathies, the 'blanc-i-blaus' (Español's white-and-blue strip) displays the medieval crown of Aragon prominently on its badge. The club played its first few seasons in a bright yellow strip but this was changed along with its name in 1910. It adopted the blue-and-white strip to honour the colours of a legendary Aragonese naval commander.

The early distant relationship between the two clubs, however, was not confined to matters off the pitch. As a sixteen-year-old goalkeeping prodigy, Ricardo Zamora began his career with Español but three years later, in 1920, he was enticed away to Barcelona, having apparently fallen out with one of Español's directors.

Along with Barcelona, Español was a founder member of the Spanish League, and in 1923 the club moved to its new stadium in Sarrià, a stadium which was to be its home until 2009. The 'Barcelona Derby' ('El derbi Barceloni' in Catalan) between the two clubs has become the most-played derby game in the history of La Liga. Today, Barça's victories in this needle match significantly outstrip those of Español, and their first encounter in La Liga in 1929 ended 1–0 in Barcelona's favour, although Español beat Barcelona by the same margin in that year's Copa del Rey final, the club's first national title.

(In 1995, the club changed its name to the Catalan 'Reial Club Deportiu Espanyol de Barcelona'. Although 'Esportiu' is the correct Catalan translation of 'Deportivo' [a Castilian word], the club wished to retain its name RCD Espanyol. So it substituted a Catalanised version – 'Deportiu' – of the Castilian term. [In this book, I use the name 'Español' and replace it, when the time comes, with **Espanyol**.])

VALENCIA

South of Catalonia lies another of Spain's autonomous communities, the Community of Valencia, presided over by Spain's third-largest city, the trading port of Valencia.

The city is home to two major clubs: Levante and Valencia. However, there are other clubs in the Valencian Community, four of which are today of lesser stature than they were at their peaks, while one has in recent years become widely known in the context of European football. The five clubs I mention here were all formed during the post-Olympic footballing enthusiasm of the 1920s.

The story of **Alcoyano**, from the town of Alcoy which lies roughly halfway between Valencia and Murcia, has had its intriguing moments. The club enjoyed twenty years in the lower leagues before arriving in La Liga in 1947/48, and was relegated at the end of the following season to return to the third tier, Segunda B, where it continues to exist.

However, Alcoyano has always been a battling side, with its supporters coining the somewhat ambiguous observation 'tener mas moral que El Alcoyano' ('to have more morale than Alcoyano'). This ironic chant derives from a 1950s game when, although Alcoyano were 0–13 down at home, the players strained every sinew to score a goal before the final whistle, but their efforts were in vain (even one goal would have helped). This obsessive, if futile, determination obviously struck a wider chord, and one must admire the resolve of these players.

The other three clubs have been relatively more successful. **CD Castellón** entered the pioneering league season of 1929 in the Tercera, and achieved a five-year run in La Liga in the early 1940s, with their final Primera season being 1990/91. The club was relegated from Segunda to Tercera in 2011/12, as it did not have sufficient funding to pay its players, but today in 2018/19 it is back, head held high, in Segunda B.

Elche also had recent financial problems. Although between 1959 and 1977/78 it revelled in a virtually unbroken run in La Liga, in 2015 it became the first club ever to be relegated from La Liga to the Segunda due to debts and financial instability. However, season 2018/19 finds Elche where it probably belongs, in Segunda. If Elche were to drop down one tier in the league, it would encounter fellow Valencians **Hércules**. Based in Alicante, the club spent twenty intermittent seasons in La Liga but, as is the case with many older, smaller Spanish clubs, it now nestles in Segunda B.

Villarreal, whose Estadio de Cerámica holds 25,000 spectators, is in the Castellón province and is a tough, successful small club. It fought its way through regional competitions, then lower leagues, and arrived in La Liga in 1998/99. Since then, Villarreal has been absent from the Primera for only two seasons, but since it arrived in Primera it has been a near-constant presence in European competition, as I will relate in Part Four.

The city and Mediterranean seaport of Valencia – from the Latin 'Valentia', meaning 'strength' or 'valour' – was colonised by the Romans in the second century BC, and it is one of the oldest cities in Spain as well as being the country's third most populated urban area. Valencia's trading links, in particular its citrus fruit trade with the UK, led to the early arrival of football on the Spanish eastern seaboard, and the game was enthusiastically adopted by the city's inhabitants.

The oldest club in the Valencia Community, and one of the city's two league teams, is **Levante**, a working-class organisation founded in 1909. Its name derives from the Latin word for the point on the horizon where the sun rises, and is also the term for the damp, mild wind, the Levant, which sweeps down from southern France, along the Spanish east coast and out into the Atlantic at Gibraltar.

'Los granotas' entered the Tercera in 1929. The club merged

in 1939 with neighbours Gimnástica FC. Levante's ground had been badly damaged during the Civil War, while Gimnástica had lost some of its best players during the conflict. So the merger made sense for both parties.

Levante played for most of its history in the second and third level tiers. However, between 2004/05 and 2018/19 Levante spent eleven years in La Liga. The club was and is 'financially constrained', and who wouldn't be, given La Liga's self-protective financial conditions of entry? In vivid contrast to the larger clubs' gargantuan transfer budgets, Levante happily existed in La Liga on a shoestring, spending only £400,000 on players over four seasons in the top flight.

If one for the moment ignores, as do the Spanish football authorities, the club's performances in the Civil War's Mediterranean League (although I will shortly be mentioning this episode), Levante's most successful period was brief, and lasted for the first nine games in La Liga season 2011/12.

At this point – the end of October 2011 – the club was top of Primera for the first time in its history, but an away defeat by Osasuna on almost the last day of that month saw 'los granotas' tumble to third, although Levante ended the season in a more than respectable sixth place. The *Guardian* headline, on the day after the loss in Pamplona, said it all: 'Levante are finally dethroned and La Liga becomes a more boring place'. There is little room for fairy stories when Real Madrid and Barcelona come gunning for you. Or when even your own city rival reaches for his holster.

This city rival is, of course, **Valencia CF**. Although it was not established as a football club until 1919, Valencia soon began to attract the talented footballers in the region, particularly when the club's 55,000-capacity Mestalla Stadium was built in 1923. The original Mestalla remains today, although plans have been drawn up for a 75,000-seater replacement, and it is, so far as visiting team supporters are concerned, one of the country's most intimidating and daunting stadiums. The Mestalla was inaugurated with a 1–0 home win against Levante, a result which both initiated and gave an early warning of Valencia's impending domination of the city's footballing future.

Valencia joined the Segunda in 1929, and by 1931/32 the club was in La Liga, where it won its first title in 1941/42. The 1940s saw Valencia establish itself as one of Spain's top five clubs, as the forthcoming chapters of this book will reveal.

***

MURCIA

Murcia is a relatively small Spanish region. The word 'fertile' is often associated with the region's soil, but it is not a term normally encountered today when discussing the quality and, indeed, fecundity of Murcia's national league football clubs.

Cartagena CF began life in Cartagena, a seaport and major naval station a few miles south of Murcia on the Mediterranean. An ancient city, it was established in the second century by the Carthaginians (no prizes for guessing this). The club, which rose no higher in its unglamorous history than Segunda B, was dissolved in 1952. In 1995, **FC Cartagena** was formed as a continuation of the former old club and, to date, it has also failed to extend its activities much beyond Segunda B.

Lorca CF started its footballing life in 2003 as La Hoya Deportive, and became La Hoya Lorca CF in 2010. Although then nestling in lowly Segunda B, the club received national attention by deciding to pay tribute to the verdant vegetable gardens of the Murcia region by imprinting the image of a broccoli onto their blue and white strip, thus becoming 'el bróccoli mecánico' ('the clockwork broccoli').

This may well have lifted sales of the vegetable, but Lorca's promotion to the Segunda in 2017/18 lasted for only one season, as it was relegated back to Segunda B, primarily for financial reasons.

The senior club in the region is **Real Murcia CF**, who kicked off in 1919. The 'pimentoneros' were briefly coached by Ferenc Puskás (1974/75) and then by László Kubala (1986/87), but the club was unable to emulate either player's legendary international status.

Although Real Murcia has won the Segunda title on nine occasions, the club has, on its eighteen forays into La Liga, never managed to end a season in the top ten. The Segunda appears to be the club's natural home, although over the last five seasons Murcia has had to be content with Segunda B.

***

CASTILE AND LEÓN

Castile and León is the largest, in terms of geographical area, of Spain's seventeen autonomous communities. It is situated more or less to the north-west of Madrid; Portugal's border is to the west; Galicia, Asturias, Cantabria and the Basque Country are to the north; and Navarre and La Rioja lie to the east. (This brief explanation is in case you do not have immediate access to a map.)

Its morphology consists of an extensive, elevated plateau, and the plain is overlooked by often spectacular mountain ranges. This geological context, combined with the region's wide temperature range, could explain why it is home to only two and a half million people, who tend to concentrate in the major towns and cities. It may appear, particularly in the bakingly hot summer months, as arid and dusty, but much of the land is fertile, and this is why Castile and Léon is known as 'the granary of Spain'.

The population centres include Burgos, León, Salamanca, Ávila, Numancia and the region's capital city, Valladolid. It was the focus of Spain's medieval history – it includes almost as many churches as it does people – and it was Franco's authoritarian Catholic heartland. But it can be a fascinating and quite beautiful region, and its historical legacy boasts the third-oldest European university at Salamanca, the Roman 160-arched aqueduct at Segovia, the eleventh-century city wall round Ávila, and much more besides.

However, its early football clubs are, with the exception of Real Valladolid, of significantly lesser stature than the impressive culture which surrounds them, and several – such as Real Burgos CF, CF Palencia, UD Salamanca and a few others – are today defunct. Others have existed mainly in the lower tiers, with occasional bursts of promotion which normally lead back to where they began.

An example: **Zamora CF**, in the north-west of the region, is a relatively new club (1968), and has never managed to move beyond Segunda B and Tercera, where it currently exists. (I am here irresistibly reminded of an English football terrace song, to the tune of 'That's Amore' by 1950s 'heart-throb' Dean Martin, about striker Bobby Zamora – no relation – who recently played for such clubs as Brighton, West Ham and Fulham: 'When the ball hits your head, and you're sat in Row Z, that's Zamora'. Zamora's directional radar frequently malfunctioned, as you can tell.)

Similar stories of relative failure can be told about other clubs in the region. For instance, **Burgos CF**, following on in the footsteps of the deceased Real Burgos CF, is an even later arrival than Zamora, with its foundation date of 1986. Although the club reached La Liga, and remained there for three seasons between 1990 and 1993, it 'ceased trading' in 1993. The following year, the club was reborn and currently exists in Segunda B.

Gimnástica Segoviana CF, a 1920s club (from Segovia), has fared little better. One might think that sharing one's name with a world-renowned guitarist might have helped, but seemingly not. Segoviana scrambled round the Tercera and regional leagues, until in 1999 it reached Segunda B (pause for guitar arpeggio). Alas, it went straight down again at the end of that season. Since that high point in its low-key history the club has twice repeated this trick, but today Segoviana is back in the Tercera, and probably doomed to remain there.

Again, the town of León, close to the northern Asturias region, was in 1923 the birthplace of **Cultural y Deportiva Leonesa**, a club which played in La Liga for one season, 1955, in its history. After forty-two years meandering between Segunda B and Tercera, it arrived in Segunda in 2017, forged an 'official relationship' in January 2018 with Leeds United, and is now in Segunda B. This is what happens if you team up with Leeds United.

Real Ávila CF, another club originated in 1923, has also spent its life stumbling around the lower tiers of the Spanish league system, and is currently happy enough in Tercera. And one more: **CD Mirandés** has spent most of its history in Tercera and occasionally local leagues. The club managed to remain in the second-tier Segunda for four years from 2012 to 2016, but is now back in Segunda B.

The city of Soria has been home to **CD Numancia** since the club's formation in 1945. Although a regular resident of the Segunda since 1997/98, Numancia has since then also enjoyed four seasons in La Liga. The club's most recent sojourn in the Primera – 2008/09 – began with a 1–0 home win against Barcelona, but ended with Numancia in nineteenth position, and relegated.

In the 1995/96 Copa del Rey, while Numancia was in the Segunda, the club astonished Spanish football by defeating Real Sociedad, Racing de Santander and Sporting de Gijón on their way to a quarter-final meeting with Barcelona, which Numancia narrowly lost.

So far, there has been little about which to rejoice in the footballing fortunes of the region of Castile and León. However, in recent years, about which you will read later in this book, there is one club which today can with justification claim to have kept the game afloat in this generally lacklustre and ill-starred footballing area of Spain.

Enter **Real Valladolid CF**, the club from Valladolid near the centre of the region, and a city of 300,000 people which was the de facto Francoist Nationalist capital during the Civil War. The origin of the city's name is (this being Spain) the subject of heated disputation, but it probably stems from the Celto-Iberian 'vallis tolitum', meaning 'valley of waters', as it lies close to the confluence of a few rivers.

A few interesting facts about Valladolid: Christopher Columbus died here; Miguel Cervantes, author of *Don Quixote*, lived and worked here; and, back in the mid-fifteenth century, Isabella I of Castile and Ferdinand II of Aragon were married in the city, thereby establishing the Kingdom of Castile and, consequentially, the final flourish of the 'Reconquista' when they kicked the Moors out of Granada's Alhambra Palace in 1492 (when, obviously, Columbus was still alive).

In keeping with regional footballing custom, Valladolid hung around the regional, Tercera and Segunda leagues from its foundation in 1928 until it arrived in La Liga in season 1948/49. However, unlike most of its footballing neighbours it remained in the Primera (with the occasional absence) until 1963/64, with its top finish being fourth in the season before it dropped back to the Segunda.

During the 1980s and 1990s, Valladolid inhabited the Primera – and played (briefly) in the UEFA and Cup Winners' Cups – before the inevitable return to the Segunda. However, in

2018/19 the club is back in La Liga, flaunting its primacy over the other clubs in Castile and Léon.

So why is it that, as a rule and exempting Madrid, football clubs from the Spanish interior perform in a less lustrous manner than do clubs from the coastal areas of Spain? Perhaps it's because the prosperous mini-economies generated by international trade tend to be on or close to the coast? Or many of the inland clubs were later adopters of the game, and therefore are still playing catch-up? Or do the more skilful footballers have a preference for the bracing sea air, and a leisurely suntan, over the hot and humid plains of the interior? Or is the simple reason that the majority of the Spanish population live near the coast?

The last suggestion is the most persuasive. When one considers the five leading clubs in Spanish football history, two are from Madrid (as you will shortly discover) and the others – Athletic Bilbao, Barcelona and Valencia – are thriving seaports. Not far behind these five are Sevilla and Deportivo de La Coruña, one of which is on the coast, and Sevilla is not a million miles from the Atlantic.

As this book progresses, I will attempt to shed more light on this geographical conundrum. For the present, and before I journey into the interior, I am about to sail south-west towards the Atlantic Ocean.

***

CANARY ISLANDS

As I've just been speculating on the subject of coastlines and the sea, and before I head to Madrid, via Extremadura, and Castilla-La Mancha, this seems like a good time to journey offshore and to consider the emergence of football in the autonomous community of the Canary Islands.

The Islands – Lanzarote, Fuerteventura, La Palma, Hierro, Gomera, Tenerife and Gran Canaria – sit in the Atlantic Ocean close to the African countries of Morocco and Western Sahara and, although part of Spain, they are around 1,100 miles south-west of Madrid but they have been in Spanish hands since the late fifteenth century.

Their name does not originate, as one may suppose, from the cute, chirping, multicoloured little birds, but rather from the Latin word 'canis' meaning 'dog'. The early Romans described the islands as being populated by 'large dogs', but it's more likely that they were seals, as seals were known by these invaders as 'sea dogs'.

Since the game arrived here, football has been a popular sport with a proliferation of small clubs and regional competitions across the islands. The two largest and most successful clubs, UD Las Palmas and CD Tenerife, are on the two largest islands of Gran Canaria and Tenerife. As one would expect, there is a serious rivalry between the clubs.

Established as late as 1949 from a merger between five Gran Canaria clubs, **UD Las Palmas** has enjoyed the hospitality of La Liga in a total of thirty-four seasons, while its Tenerife island neighbour has managed only fifteen. Indeed, kitted out in its eye-catching home strip of yellow shirts and blue shorts, in 1968/69 the club was runner-up (although, admittedly, nine points adrift) to champions Real Madrid and, as we shall see later, has also been a participant in the Inter-Cities Fairs Cup and UEFA Cup.

Las Palmas is one of the few Spanish clubs to have achieved back-to-back promotions, leaping from the third tier to La Liga between 1950 and 1952. At the end of the 1952/53 season it was relegated, but it came back in 1954 for six consecutive seasons in Primera. Since the 1970s and 1980s, when it was a near-permanent fixture in La Liga, however, it has fluctuated between Primera and Segunda, seeming to prefer the latter.

***

It is difficult to believe that the highest mountain in Spain – a country which is twice the land area of the British Isles, and which is noted for its soaring, craggy peaks and dark, moody mountain ranges – is to be found on a small rock which sticks out of the Atlantic Ocean, but it's true. 'Pico del Teide' (Teide Peak), a 3,717-metre-high volcano in the island of Tenerife's Teide National Park, can rightly claim this honour.

One of the many settlements in Tenerife, the most populated island in the Canaries, lies to the north of the island, and is the capital city of Santa Cruz, home to Tenerife's football club, **CD Tenerife**. Founded in 1912 as Sports Club Tenerife (that British influence yet again), by 1953, the club, now CD Tenerife, reached the second tier, Segunda. The club moved between Segunda and Tercera until 1989, when it was promoted to La Liga.

From 1989 until 1999, under the management of the renowned ex-players Jorge Valdano and then Jupp Heynckes, Tenerife was a permanent member of La Liga, and also performed well against tough European opposition in two UEFA Cups. In 1993/94 the club reached the last sixteen and even beat Juventus at home, but the club was knocked out by the Italian superstars, 4–2 on aggregate.

Three years later, Tenerife reached the UEFA Cup semi-final but were eliminated by eventual winners, Schalke. The 1990s was a 'golden period' for the club. Since then, Tenerife has suffered financial problems and frequent coaching changes, and entered a period of decline. In recent years it has usually played in Segunda, where today it remains, staring up at the mountain.

Although South America is on the other side of the Atlantic, the style of football in the Canaries tends more to the game as played in Argentina and Uruguay. The emphasis is on individual trickery, slick one-two passing, continual darting movements to confuse the opposition, dribbling, nutmegging and back-flicking, and general showing off with the ball. It may occasionally appear over-dainty and facile but it can be very effective, and it's more fun than watching any of Sam Allardyce's teams.

However, now it's time to head back to the Spanish mainland and travel towards the centre of the country, Madrid. And the first stop on the journey is Extremadura.

***

EXTREMADURA

An autonomous community of south-west Spain, bordering Portugal, Extremadura is an isolated, remote region of dense forests, lakes, mountains and national parks.

The region's capital is Mérida and, to its credit, it has used all its redoubtable energies in attempting to create a decent football club in the city. In 1912, CP Mérida was formed and, although it played two seasons in La Liga, it was more suited to Tercera. After the club's dissolution in 2000, a renewed Mérida UD was established, again dabbled in Tercera and, in 2013, was also dissolved. Finally, although surprisingly not dejected by the considerable efforts and commensurate lack of reward, a group of local football enthusiasts launched **Mérida AD**, which briefly enjoyed the relative luxury of Segunda but now finds itself in Tercera.

Whatever happens, I hope that Mérida AD finds life a bit easier than did **CD Badajoz**, who began as early as 1905 and had to close down in 2013, although a reformed club of the same name is currently in the Segunda. And **Ciudad de Caceres** could not have predicted the obstacles which lay ahead when it set up trading in 2006. The club folded five years later.

Also, CF Extremadura, founded in 1924 and based in the small town of Almendralejo, closed its doors in 2012 under the pressure of increasingly insurmountable financial problems. However, clearly not being people to dwell overmuch on misfortune, in 2007 some locals established **Extremadura UD** and, within three years, the club had penetrated into the Tercera. By 2018 the young club had jumped a further two tiers and today finds itself in the Segunda. The much-travelled left-winger José Antonio Reyes joined Extremadura in 2019, and he had played only nine games for the club when he died in a car crash on 1 June of that year.

To the east of Extremadura you will find Castilla-La Mancha, another inland part of Spain where football clubs, although followed as enthusiastically as in Extremadura, have been even less successful in their attempts to reach the base camps of the Spanish league peaks.

***

CASTILLA-LA MANCHA

An autonomous community, consisting of a vast plain and scattered mountain ranges, the sparsely populated Castilla-La Mancha is the backdrop for *Don Quixote*, and demonstrates that, if something can go wrong, then it will, at least in footballing terms.

No fewer than fifty clubs from this region have attempted to imprint their names on the wider Spanish national footballing consciousness. The great majority have given up the struggle and have dissolved themselves or have, by force of circumstance, made themselves at home in the regional leagues or the Tercera.

Two of the oldest clubs – **UD Secuéllamos** and **CD Toledo,** both founded in the 1920s – are in Tercera, but at least they are still alive. Other than these two trailblazing clubs, most of the others formed after the Civil War and even much later, and they have no doubt done what they could have done, but they stubbornly remain in the lower league tiers.

The main exception to this generally unhappy roster is **Albacete Balompié** from Albacete, the region's largest city. The 'queso mecánicos' began in 1940 as Albacete Fútbol Asociación in the regional leagues, but reached Segunda in 1985/86 and 1990/91. The club also entered La Liga in 1989 to 1991, and then had another Liga spell between 2002/03 to 2004/05, a season in which it managed only six wins out of thirty-eight games. Alba then found itself back in Segunda, followed by Tercera.

In December 2011, when Alba was in real danger of being relegated still further for financial reasons, the outstanding ex-Barcelona playmaker and inside-forward Andrés Iniesta – scorer of Spain's winning goal in the 2010 World Cup final – was reported to have given £400,000 to the club, which was located close to his birthplace and whom he had joined as a trainee when he was eight years old. That season the club avoided relegation, and reached the last sixteen of the Copa del Rey, beating Atlético Madrid over two games as it progressed.

In 2013 Alba was again threatened with Tercera and, again, in stepped Iniesta, this time donating £250,000 to cover unpaid wages and thereby going a long way to prevent relegation. Albacete remained in the Segunda in 2018/19 and even reached the promotion play-offs at the end of the season. And the thoroughly decent Iniesta is currently playing his football in the Far East, no doubt modestly playing down his generous assistance to his home club.

***

COMMUNITY OF MADRID

The Community of Madrid is located in the centre of the Iberian Peninsula, and it occupies the Meseta Central (Castilian Central

Plateau), which generally rises to between 600 and 1,000 metres above sea level, and which is often significantly higher. The community is bounded by mountain ranges, in particular, the Guadarrama and Gredos mountains, and by thick forests and extensive river basins.

The capital of both Castile and Spain is Madrid, with a population of around eight and a half million and, with its royal inauguration as a capital dating back only to the mid-sixteenth century, it is a relative newcomer in Spanish terms. This is the most densely populated autonomous community in Spain.

In terms of football, there are seven clubs in the community which are currently active in the upper tiers of Spanish football. Three of these – CF Rayo Majadahonda, AD Alcorcón and CD Leganés – lie close to the city, while the others – Club Atlético de Madrid, Getafe CF, Rayo Vallecano de Madrid and Real Madrid CF – are to be found within the city's Metropolitan limits.

The most recently formed club is located ten miles to the north-east of the city of Madrid. Although the club was active from the late 1950s, **CF Rayo Majadahonda** was not officially founded until 1978. It played its early football in the regional leagues and Tercera, but was three times promoted to Segunda B, the last season being 2014/15. In the final play-off game of 2017/18 against Cartagena, a ninety-seventh-minute winning goal from Rayo gained the club entry to the Segunda for the first time in its brief history.

Another recently formed club (1971) is **AD Alcorcón**, approximately ten miles to the south of the city centre and with a local population of around 200,000. (The club's preceding initials 'AD' stands for 'Agrupación Deportivo' which simply means 'sports group'.) For the first thirty years of its existence the club played in the local and regional leagues, until in 2000/01 it was promoted to Segunda B where it stayed for ten years. In 2010 it achieved promotion to Segunda, which is where the club remains today.

Alcorcón's most satisfying memory is almost certainly that of October 2009 in the first round of the Copa del Rey when, in the first leg at its home stadium – in front of a capacity 4,000 crowd – the club from the third tier humiliated the 'Galacticos' from Real Madrid by thrashing them 4–0. At the Bernabéu Stadium, Real could only manage a 1–0 victory, so Alcorcón triumphantly marched on to the next round. And elimination by Racing de Santander.

Close to Alcorcón, and slightly to its south-east, is Leganés whence originated **CD Leganés**, a club founded just over forty years before its neighbour. The club was content to play in local leagues until 1977 when it joined the fourth tier, Tercera. It gained promotion to Segunda B seven years later, and for almost thirty years Leganés remained an 'equipo ascensor' (elevator team) between the second and third tiers of the Spanish league. However, in 2016 the club achieved its first-ever promotion to La Liga, where for two seasons it scrambled into seventeenth place, the final position before automatic relegation.

Not too distant from these two clubs, and technically inside the Madrid Metropolitan Area, is located **Getafe CF**: what one might reasonably describe as 'a club of two halves'.

The original Getafe FC first saw the light of day in 1924 but folded in 1932. Twelve years later, five local citizens decided that enough was enough, and established Club Getafe Deportivo, which entered Tercera in 1970 and, by 1976, had climbed up to Segunda. Six years later, while still in the second tier, the club's finances were such that it couldn't pay the players and, facing automatic relegation, the club was again liquidated.

In 1983, the second, and much more successful part of the Getafe story began when the club was officially refounded. It moved between Segunda and Segunda B for almost twenty years, having in 1988 built its own ground, the 17,000-capacity Stadium Alfonso Pérez. However, perseverance does pay. At the end of season 2003/04 in Segunda in Getafe's final game, away against Tenerife, Sergio Pachón scored all five in the visiting club's 5–3 win, and the club secured second spot and promotion to La Liga for season 2004/05.

Getafe had played itself up from the local Madrid leagues to the heights of La Liga within only twenty years, as good a reason as any for unbridled celebration. Also, the club had become the fourth club from the Community of Madrid to play in the same season in the Primera, the first time that this had occurred in La Liga's history. And since its elevation in 2004/05, and aside from one season, Getafe has remained in La Liga till the present day, a remarkable record.

Getafe's progress in European competition has been halting, particularly when compared with the European exploits of what have historically been considered as Madrid's 'two clubs' – Atlético Madrid and Real Madrid – whose early history I'll shortly be considering. But first I want to look at the fascinating story of Madrid's 'third club', Rayo Vallecano.

Rayo Vallecano

Rayo Vallecano de Madrid, from Vallecas, a suburb just within today's Madrid M-30 orbital motorway which defines the city's boundary, is another example of an 'equipo ascensor': colloquially, a 'yo-yo club'.

The club, formed by enthusiastic local football supporters in 1924, has been relegated and promoted on nineteen occasions, and has spent eleven years in Tercera, five in Segunda B and thirty-four in Segunda. However, from season 1989/90 until the present day it has also enjoyed eighteen years in La Liga, where it ended season 2012/13 in a more than creditable eighth place.

Rayo is a 'barrio club' and Vallecas is a staunchly working-class neighbourhood, where the club is known as 'Franjirojas' and also as 'El Rayo' meaning 'lightning' (a red lightning strip runs down the centre of the club's mainly white logo).

Since its 1924 foundation the club and many of its players have identified and worked with the people of this underprivileged area of Madrid, acting generally as a focus and voice for the neighbourhood, particularly during the waves of internal immigration from poverty-stricken areas such as Extremadura and Andalucia.

The club's and supporters' adherence to multiculturalism, and its firm stand against fascism, racism and homophobia, have created El Rayo's anti-establishment status. Rayo Vallecano has a tradition of improving the lives of the people from Vallecas – for example, by involving itself and the players in local charity work and by staffing homeless shelters – and engendering solidarity and pride in local people who have suffered some hard times.

In this sense, El Rayo and its supporters are very different from the average Spanish club and, indeed, from virtually every other major club I have encountered. To the best of my knowledge, the only other European club with a similar left-wing origin, culture and politically committed support is Germany's St Pauli, the Hamburg club which currently plays in the Bundesliga second division.

As top clubs and players become ever more divorced from the game which has afforded them luxurious lifestyles, football needs more clubs like Rayo Vallecano. The game relies for its enjoyment and success on communality, local cooperation, a positive team spirit and mutual understanding. However, off the pitch, today one finds a very different mindset among the top clubs.

They compete in an increasingly febrile, financially driven atmosphere with an emphasis on individual star players, inter-club player transfers, and the primacy of the profit motive, with a corresponding decline in loyalty and commitment to one's social environment and one's roots.

So it is refreshing to discover clubs and players who retain their integrity, decency and common humanity when surrounded by greed and self-interest. Although it is a quality lacking in many football club owners, this sense of allegiance and pride in one's club is often the province of the supporters, and there are few groups of fans as admirable in this respect as the 'Bukaneros' of Rayo Vallecano.

It is perhaps difficult to reconcile this fan dedication with the fact that, since El Rayo first reached Tercera in 1949 , the club has employed over seventy managers, or around one manager per season. In fact, in a single season alone – 2016 – the club had three managers in succession. That, however, is down to the owners and not to the devoted, diehard fans of El Rayo, who are rarely slow to express their disapproval but who are unable to intervene at the upper levels of decision-making.

At the time of writing (December 2018), El Rayo were in Primera's relegation zone, having topped Segunda in 2017/18. It would have been pleasing to have seen the club remain in La Liga for a few more seasons, but this was not to be. Rayo ended bottom of Primera at the end of 2018/19 and were relegated to Segunda.

Atlético Madrid

Another club from the Spanish capital which has had to handle the slings and arrows of footballing fortune and, furthermore, one which since its inception has coped remarkably well with the stigma of being labelled 'Madrid's second club', is **Atlético Madrid**. Indeed, Atlético has overcome this enduring trauma to the extent that, in terms of the number of titles won, it is today the third most successful club in Spanish footballing history after (need I say?) Real Madrid and Barcelona.

Like Rayo, the club in its earliest days played its home games in Vallecas, at the Ronda de Vallecas, but, unlike Rayo, Atlético moved in 1921 to a slightly more upscale stadium, the Estadio Metropolitano de Madrid, where it remained until 1966.

Atlético was founded in 1903 (even then, it was beaten by the 'first club' which arrived in 1902) under the name Athletic Club de Madrid. Its progenitors were three Basque students who were joined by a few dissident members of Madrid FC, as the 'first club' was christened, and it adopted Athletic Bilbao as its 'parent club'.

The close connection between the two clubs extended to their strips – blue-and-white jerseys and white shorts, which were apparently modelled on the colours of Blackburn Rovers. The red-and-white shirts were adopted by both clubs in 1911, although Athletic preferred the blue shorts and red socks which they wear today. It is alleged that a club director acquired a job lot of Southampton jerseys, but other theories exist (*see page 31*), which is why Atlético are known as 'los colchoneros': 'the mattress makers' and, more prosaically but less controversially, as 'los rojiblancos'.

In 1921 the club severed its association with Athletic Bilbao and moved to Estadio Metropolitano de Madrid, a stadium in which it remained for the following forty years. That year, it also reached the final of the Copa del Rey, where it was defeated by none other than Athletic Bilbao.

'El Derbi Madrileño' ('The Madrid Derby') between Atlético and the 'first club' – henceforth Real Madrid – is a closely contested affair, which Real usually wins. When the clubs were formed, they possessed markedly contrasting identities. Real was the 'establishment' club, which drew most of its support from the middle classes to the north of the city. Atlético had essentially working-class roots and exuded a 'sentimiento de rebeldia' ('spirit of rebellion'). Today, the background of the two clubs and their supporters is similar, although Real still retains a 'hauteur' largely absent from the general image of Atlético.

In 1928 the club was invited to join the Primera División of the inaugural La Liga where, under the management of the peripatetic Fred Pentland, they spent two seasons before being relegated. Shortly, I will continue the story of this enigmatic club. But I cannot leave this discussion of the early days of Spanish football without delving into the origins of the main kid on the block: Real Madrid.

Real Madrid

The first football club in Madrid – Sociedad Sky Football – was set up in 1897 by Spanish and English graduates from La Institución Libre de Enseñanza (Free Educational Institute).

The Institución was free from the influence of the military and Church, and it promoted, inter alia, the emergence of post-imperial modernity, religious and secular tolerance, and the elimination of the neo-feudal class structure in Spain. So the Institute was not exactly welcomed with open arms by the aforementioned 'forces of reaction'.

The Institute viewed Britain as its sociopolitical model – the exemplar of freedom, democracy and all that was good in the world (believe it or not) – so Sky imported the English FA's rule book for guidance on a game which they believed was a character-forming, co-operative and egalitarian activity.

However, a schism developed within Sky, eventually leading in 1902 to the establishment of **Madrid FC**, the forerunner of today's Real Madrid. Brothers Juan and Carlos Padrós were the main movers behind the new club, and Juan became Madrid

FC's first president. (The inconvenient fact that the brothers were both Catalans, and were born in Barcelona, is not resoundingly proclaimed with any frequency in Real's official histories.)

Madrid FC quickly made a powerful impact on Spanish football. A young, predominantly Spanish team, bolstered by the experience and knowledge of English businessman and footballer Arthur Johnson, the club won its first four Copa del Rey finals in succession, between 1905 and 1908, as well as several local and regional titles.

From its earliest games Madrid FC's teams wore an all-white strip, which many believe was modelled on that worn by the leading English side of the time, Corinthians FC. Aside from one season's (1925) dalliance with black shorts, its home strip today remains as it was: all-white.

In 1912, Madrid FC moved to the Campo de O'Donnell Stadium. In 1923, the club, now formally known as **Real Madrid**, took on the occupancy of the 15,000-capacity Estadio Chamartin which was to be their home for the next twenty-four years. The club inaugurated the stadium with a 3–2 victory over Newcastle United.

With its largely bourgeois and relatively wealthy support, and its increasing number of 'socios' members, Real Madrid was able to secure leading players such as forward Santiago Bernabéu – who was later to reappear as the most influential figure in Real's history – and also to finance the club's expansion, with an ease denied to its competitors.

Real Madrid was one of the ten founder members of La Liga, and it remains one out of the three clubs which have never been relegated from Primera División. In La Liga's first season, Real finished in second place, behind winners Barcelona.

The first recorded game between Real and Barcelona was in 1902, when Barça emerged victors and, in the years to come, the two clubs' relationship was to become one of the fiercest club rivalries in world football, stoked by a deep and enduring historical, political and cultural enmity.

Ricardo Zamora

In today's professional game, it would be difficult to find a goalkeeper quite like Ricardo Zamora, a player considered to have been one of Spain's finest-ever custodians.

Goalies are normally regarded as pinnacles of moral probity, who guard their goalmouths as closely as they preserve their puritanical behaviour. In my experience, one of the few keepers who strayed from the path of moral rectitude was Leicester's and England's Peter Shilton ('Hand of God', anyone?) who, I recall, was caught in flagrante with a woman who was not his wife a few days before Leicester was due to meet Arsenal at Highbury.

From the Clock End terracing I watched as Shilton ran onto the pitch before kick-off, to be welcomed by the North Bank singing, to the tune of the Welsh anthem 'Bread of Heaven', 'Peter Shilton, Peter Shilton, does your missus know you're here?' To his enduring credit, Shilton smiled and waved to the Gooners in rueful acknowledgement of his misdeed.

But back to Zamora, whose lifestyle was far from that of today's model professional footballers. Born in Barcelona in 1901, the fifteen-year-old Zamora began his career with Español, but moved to FC Barcelona in 1919. His athleticism, bravery and quick reflexes formed the backbone of that exceptional side, which included his friend 'El Sami' Samitier, and led to his nickname of 'El Divino'.

He was a tall, strong keeper, and would frequently leave his penalty area to launch attacks. His quirky dress sense included the wearing, during games, of a flat cloth cap (unknown at the time in Spain but common in Britain) and a white polo-neck jumper (to provide protection from the sun).

In 1922, in possession of two Copa del Rey medals, he returned to Español who, with his formidable presence between the posts, picked up in 1929 the club's first Copa del Rey title. Zamora then spent a further six years at Real Madrid, helping 'los blancos' to acquire two La Liga titles. During his outstanding career he also collected forty-six caps for the national team between the 1920 Olympics and the 1934 World Cup finals.

As well as being universally lauded for his remarkable skill on the pitch, Zamora was known as a chain-smoking, cognac-guzzling sociable fellow who occasionally punched opposing forwards. He was also arrested for cigar smuggling (the victim of a practical joke), tax avoidance, and he served time in a Republican prison during the Civil War. He was eventually released from prison due to the intervention of the Argentine Embassy, one of the few countries which recognised Franco's Nationalist rebellion.

'El Divino' then moved to Nice to be close to 'El Sami' and, on his return to Spain, he managed a number of Spanish clubs – Celta de Vigo, Málaga and Español – before his death in 1978. He had certainly lived his life to the full.

As with *Marca*'s 'Pichichi' trophy, the newspaper initiated in 1958 the annual 'Zamora' award for the Spanish goalkeeper with the lowest 'goals to games ratio' during the previous season. Predated to 1929, the all-time record is held by Barcelona's Antoni Ramallets with five awards during the 1950s, while the man himself, Zamora, crouches in fifth position alongside several other less exalted and certainly less exuberant Spanish club goalies.

I cannot think of a more appropriate club than Real Madrid with which to conclude Part One of this book. 'Los blancos' will be featuring with an increasing frequency as this book continues, as will a number of the other clubs whose early years I have been considering.

I now move on to Part Two: the establishment of the Spanish league in 1929, football during the Civil War and in its aftermath, and the start of European club competitions in the mid-1950s. And the arrival of 'the Blond Arrow', Alfredo Di Stéfano, who, it is reasonably claimed, changed everything.

PART TWO

FROM LA LIGA TO EUROPE

Historical Context (1898–1936)

Spain ushered in the twentieth century with the coronation in 1902 of sixteen-year-old King Alfonso XIII.

One of the young king's first decisions was, at the suggestion of Madrid FC, to give his regal blessing to a football competition – the Copa de la Coronación (Coronation Cup) – which took place in Madrid in July that year. In 1903 this tournament became the Copa del Rey, the country's national football tournament until the formation of the national league in 1929.

Even at this early period in its development, football was becoming recognised as an influential and significant factor in Spanish life. However, there were wider, more entrenched political agencies, well beyond the game's existing scope and powers, which were dictating the future direction of the country.

Since the demise of the First Republic and the 1874 'Bourbon Restoration', the stated emphasis of the Spanish governments – the main parties being the Liberals and Conservatives – was on 'reforms from above', and this was to be accompanied by 'revolution from below'. However, the fact that Spain elected no fewer than ten governments between 1898 and 1923 illustrates the extent of the fluctuating political and social schisms within the country.

In 1910, the Confederación Nacional de Trabajo (CNT), an anarchist union, was founded in Barcelona and, although it joined the pre-existing socialist Unión General de Trabajadores (UGT), the two unions soon split and became rivals.

Spain's neutrality during the First World War was the main reason for the booming Spanish export trade during the War, particularly in the major cities, and these unions competed for the loyalties of the approximately one and a half million people who had emigrated in search of work from the poverty-stricken rural areas to the wealthier cities.

But all was far from harmonious. Open conflict in Barcelona in 1917 between the CNT and organised right-wing opponents led to scores of civilian deaths and generated hostility and bitterness at the national political vacillations, while many military officers also expressed their unhappiness at the army's inability to influence the growing political chaos.

The country's and the military's humiliation and loss of confidence in its government were further deepened in 1921 by the defeat of its army and the loss of over 8,000 of its soldiers in an anti-Spanish rebellion in the Protectorate of Morocco in 1921.

In 1923 General Miguel Primo de Rivera seized power, thereby ending fifty years of military non-intervention in Spain's political life. Supported by King Alfonso XIII, the authoritarian Primo de Rivera (the 'iron surgeon') initiated plans for industrialisation and public works, improved roads and reservoirs, expanded access to electricity, nationalised the telephone and oil corporations, established state-owned 'paradores' (hotels) and improved foreign trade.

In the short term, these measures appeared economically viable, but by the late 1920s de Rivera's dictatorial attitudes and centralising policies had irreparably alienated the powerful regions, had led to economic deterioration and had lost the army's support. Primo de Rivera resigned in 1930.

After a brief interregnum with an unelected government, at the country's municipal elections in April 1931 the provincial capitals voted, by an overwhelming majority of forty-six out of fifty, for republican policies, resulting in a bitter division between the cities and the rural, largely monarchist supporters. As Alfonso XIII was no longer supported by the military, the king abdicated, ending 230 successive years of the Bourbon dynasty's rule in Spain.

Spain's Second Republic, the country's first-ever genuine parliamentary democracy, was voted into power in June 1931. The Republic immediately enacted progressive liberal measures, including introduction of land reforms, reduction of the Church's and army's influence and powers, secularisation of the education system, an increase in the autonomy of Catalonia, improvements in labour legislation and working conditions, and more.

However, the new Republican government was constantly split between powerful groups representing conservatism, liberal democracy, fascism, communism, socialism and regionalism, with each grouping containing within itself its own militant factionalism. With an increasingly hostile disunity threatening Spain, Republican supporters joined together to form the Popular Front which, in the elections of January 1936, defeated the right-wing National Party by a narrow margin.

The following few months witnessed a 'collective madness' in Spain, with the country's liberal democratic beliefs and policies under attack from extremists on the left and right, as well as from disaffected regional authorities, the Church and the military, the last two being supporters of the opposition's conservative coalitions.

On 18 July 1936, a militant grouping in the army staged a *coup d'état*, organised by General Emilio Malo, against the elected

Popular Front. On 1 October 1936 General Francisco Franco was appointed leader and initiated a savage three-year Civil War which concluded with the establishment of a dictatorial regime which would rule Spain for thirty-six years and which would leave a poisonous legacy that endures to the present day.

***

La Liga: the early years

By the late 1920s, the leading football clubs in Spain were well established and possessed decent-sized stadiums, enthusiastic and growing fan bases and quality players. These big clubs – such as Barcelona, Athletic Club and Real Madrid – were ambitious and, although each could claim to be Spain's best side, as they rarely played each other these claims were untested.

The national Copa del Rey went some way towards determining an annual order of footballing merit but, like all knockout competitions, it depended overmuch on the vagaries of fortune. Also, these big clubs normally dominated their regional leagues and competitions, so a regional match was more a training exercise than it was a real game. 'Friendlies' provided a challenge of sorts, but there was no real pressure on players and little status to be gained from such fixtures.

In order to discover the best football clubs in Spain and to rank all the clubs, what was required was an annual league competition which would emphasise consistency, talent and endurance over chance and luck. This would involve an accrual of points over a predetermined season rather than a knockout system, and the league would be played on a regular basis between teams of a reasonably similar standard. At each season's conclusion, the club occupying the leadership position in the top league would be recognised as the finest in Spain, while merit would be rewarded in lower leagues by promotion to a higher standard. Failure in any league would mean relegation.

A Spanish football league arrangement of this nature was first formally proposed in April 1927 by officials of Arenas Club de Getxo. The concept was discussed, various structures were suggested, and a consensus was finally reached that the new leagues would kick off in January 1929.

The league system was to consist of a Primera División, which would become known as 'La Liga', along with two lower divisions, Segunda and Tercera. In the Primera, there were to be ten clubs. Six of these – Athletic Club, Arenas Club de Getxo, Barcelona, Real Madrid, Real Sociedad and Real Unión – had been previous winners of the Copa del Rey. Three others – Athletic Madrid, Español and Europa – had been defeated finalists at least once in the Copa. The tenth club, Racing de Santander, had won a club knockout competition to determine its inclusion.

The Segunda División was also to consist of ten clubs: Alavés, Sevilla, Celta de Vigo, Deportivo de La Coruña, Real Betis, Iberia, Real Oviedo, Sporting de Gijón, Racing de Madrid and Valencia. Eight of these pioneering clubs are still active. The two which no longer exist are Racing de Madrid, which was dissolved in 1932, and Iberia, which merged with Zaragoza Club Deportivo in 1932 to form Real Zaragoza.

***

The Spanish League

The top two Divisións are the Primera (La Liga) and Segunda (La Liga 2), both of which have been operated since 1984 by the Liga de Fútbol Profesional (LPF) (Professional Football League).

Between 1929 and 1984, the two leagues were run by the Real Federación Española de Fútbol (RFEF) (Royal Spanish Football Federation). These two divisions are recognised as being the domain of professional players. Since the start of the 2016/17 season, La Liga has been sponsored by Banco de Santander.

The third tier of Spanish league football – Segunda B – consists of four groups, each containing twenty clubs, while the fourth tier – Tercera – comprises eighteen groups, each containing twenty clubs and is organised on a regional basis. Segunda B existed for one season in 1929 and was re-established in 1977, relegating Tercera to the fourth tier.

In these two lower leagues, there is a dizzyingly elaborate system of play-offs to determine promotion and relegation. By 'elaborate' I mean both 'complicated' and 'confusing', and its details are frequently subject to change. But it all works, and the leagues are efficiently overseen by the RFEF, no easy task when one considers that no fewer than 440 clubs make up the two lower tiers.

In Segunda B and Tercera are to be found, alongside several of the large clubs' 'B' teams, some of the most historically interesting clubs in the history of Spanish football: those who have not been dissolved or have disappeared; those who have a devoted and extensive long-term fan base; those who continue to play within their often rigid financial constraints; and those who may receive cash injections from investors imbued with nostalgia and a desire to be a part of a living tradition. I mention a number of these older clubs in the early part of this book, as they were among the romantic harbingers of the modern game.

However, in contemporary Spanish club football it is difficult to compete for long with the multi-million corporations who dominate the upper echelons of La Liga. It has also become increasingly problematic to manoeuvre around the financial and legal barriers to entry which LPF has erected around the two upper tiers, particularly La Liga.

League rules

• The domestic season in Spain lasts from August to May, and each of the twenty La Liga clubs plays every other club home and away, making a total of thirty-eight games (with the usual three points for a win, one for a draw and nil for a defeat).

• The promotion ('promocion de ascenso') and relegation ('permanencia') systems are also pretty much standard. The bottom three clubs in Primera are relegated to Segunda, and the top two in Segunda promoted to Primera, with a third promotion place available to the winner of a play-off between the four third- to sixth-placed clubs. The bottom four clubs in Segunda are relegated to Segunda B.

• Since La Liga began in 1928/29, the number of clubs in Primera gradually grew in number, reaching twenty-two in 1996/97. From the following season to the present day there have been twenty clubs in Primera.

• What happens if clubs end the season level on points?
i) With two clubs: this is decided by goal difference, minus away goals.
ii) With more than two clubs: a) head-to-head points, b) home goal difference, c) total goal difference.

iii) If the tie is still not broken, then 'fair play' scales apply.

iv) If all these fail to provide a winner, a tie-breaker is held in a neutral stadium.

• One curious feature of the league system is that a club's reserve (B) team can field a side. For instance, in 2017/18 both Barcelona's and Sevilla's B teams were in the Segunda. If the A team is relegated to a division which also includes the club's B team, then the B team automatically moves down a division irrespective of its placing in that division. (Hypothetically, what happens if the B team is promoted while the A team is relegated? Does A become B, and vice-versa?)

• European competitions for the following season are currently allocated as follows: the first four clubs in La Liga enter the group stages of the Champions League; the fifth and sixth, plus the Copa del Rey winner, enter the UEFA Europa League; and if the Copa winner finishes in the top six, then the seventh club plays in the Europa League.

The first games in the new Spanish league kicked off on 10 February 1929, and this first season ended, after eighteen matches, on 23 June 1929. In the final game of the season, Barcelona beat Real Unión 4–1 and, as Real Madrid lost that day to Athletic Club, Barcelona ended two points ahead of Real Madrid and became the first Primera/Liga champions.

Athletic Club of Bilbao finished that first season in third place, but the following seven seasons, 1930 to 1936, witnessed Athletic's 'golden period'. In 1929, Fred Pentland rejoined the Bilbao club, and the English manager's continuing emphasis on ball possession and the 'passing game', coupled with his man-management and motivational talents, were instrumental in regenerating Athletic's dominant position in Spanish football. In turn, 'el bombino' was fortunate that the club's Basque-only 'cantera' policy provided him with players with the strength and skill to outplay and defeat most of the other clubs in Spain.

As a result of this happy conjunction, Athletic won four of the seven Liga titles between 1930 and 1936, and were runners-up in two of the other three. They also won four Copa trophies in a row, including two 'doubles'. Their most memorable victory was in 1931 when they beat Barcelona 12–0 in San Mamés, with prolific striker Bata, assisted by winger Guillermo Gorostiza, scoring seven of them. This remains Barcelona's worst ever defeat and is still a record score in the history of La Liga.

After Pentland's departure at the end of the 1932/33 season, Athletic won La Liga in 1935/36 under the guidance of another English manager, William Garbutt, whose first decision in early 1936 was to introduce into the first team the seventeen-year-old forward Ángel Zubieta whose performance was so effective that he became, later that year, the youngest player at the time to play for the Spanish international team. Athletic secured the Liga title on the final game of that season at its home ground, San Mamés, by defeating Oviedo 2–0.

Athletic, however, did not have it all its own way during this brief pre-Civil War period. Under legislation passed by the new Second Republic, all clubs had to drop 'Real' from their names and remove the crown from their shields. So it was that Real Madrid again became Madrid FC.

Real Madrid had embarked on pioneering overseas trips during the 1920s and had played against clubs from other countries and, having learned from these experiences, their play had become less insular and more sophisticated. Now based in their purpose-built Chamartin Stadium, in 1931/32 Madrid won La Liga, and they achieved this without the loss of a single game. The following season, they again won the title.

Although these successes, as well as securing two Copa trophies, must be attributed to the overall superiority of the entire team, Madrid's defence was exceptional. The arrival from Español of keeper Zamora, and the acquisition from Alavés of Ciriaco and Jacinto Quincoces, formed a formidable rearguard which has been described as Spain's finest-ever central defensive line-up. This legendary trio was the bedrock of the team, and permitted the more attack-minded players the space and confidence to compete on equal terms with even the mighty Athletic Club.

The only Spanish club to interrupt the Madrid/Bilbao hegemony from 1930 to 1936 in La Liga was an unexpected one. For the first four years of La Liga, Seville's Real Betis had competed in the Segunda, the league's second tier. In 1931, Patrick O'Connell arrived as the club's new manager, and he provided the players with the self-belief, determination and tactical guidance which Betis had been lacking. At the end of his first season at the helm, Betis had won the Segunda title and, in so doing, became the first club from Andalucia to join La Liga.

Under the Republic's rules, the club had changed its name back to Betis Balompié and it remained in La Liga for the following five seasons. In 1934/35 Betis played the final game of that season against Racing de Santander, whom O'Connell had managed a few years earlier, knowing that, if they won, Betis would be champions of La Liga. A comprehensive 5–0 victory secured the La Liga title for Betis, one point ahead of Madrid FC. This was the Seville club's first, and to date only, Primera title.

Patrick O'Connell

One of the relatively unsung early foreign managers in Spanish football was Dublin-born Patrick O'Connell. A stylish wing-half, he played for Belfast Celtic and a number of English clubs, including Hull City, Sheffield Wednesday and Manchester United, gaining his first Irish international cap while at United.

In 1922, in search of a new challenge, he moved to Spain, where for six years he was a popular and successful manager of Racing de Santander. He then spent two years running Real Oviedo, before switching to Betis where, as outlined in the text, he transformed the fortunes of the Seville club.

After his success at Betis, in 1935 O'Connell was lured to perform the same role at Barcelona. Because of the onset of the Civil War and the abandonment of La Liga, he coached Barcelona in the 1936/37 Republican Mediterranean League. The club was then invited by a wealthy businessman to tour the USA and Mexico, so O'Connell and sixteen players crossed the Atlantic and played such clubs as Brooklyn Hispano as well as national XI teams from both countries.

The tour was apparently a financial success and paid off Barcelona's debts, but only five players returned with O'Connell to Spain, the others preferring exile in France and Mexico, the latter country being an active supporter of the Republican cause.

The entrepreneurial Irishman then took over the reins at Betis's city rival, Sevilla, between 1942 and 1945, and he inspired the club to second place in La Liga in his first season, and to third place the season thereafter. He concluded his Spanish adventures with a final return spell at Racing de Santander in the late 1940s.

Peter Goulding wrote a poem about O'Connell, the fourth verse of which reads:

'And then he joined Betis where, just two years later,
The Championship fell to this gallant young man
By now he'd no need of a Spanish translator
Fluent in language and charm and élan'

In 1959 O'Connell died in London, but in Seville his memory lives on. In 2017, a bust commemorating 'this gallant young man' and his La Liga achievement with the club was unveiled at Real Betis's Estadio Benito Villamarín.

The final Liga matches of the 1935/36 season took place on 19 April, with Athletic yet again emphasising their dominance in Spanish football.

The last official game of the 1935/36 season was held in Valencia's Mestalla Stadium. On 21 June 1936, the final of the Copa del Rey or, as it had been retitled during the previous four seasons, the Copa de Presidente de la República, was the first 'El Clásico' final between Madrid FC and FC Barcelona. With the game almost over and Madrid 2–1 ahead, what appeared to be a certain equaliser from Barcelona's Josep Escola, shooting from the edge of the box, was superbly stopped by the initially unsighted keeper Zamora, who dived at full stretch to save at his left goalpost.

Moments later, 'El Divino' was hoisted high in celebration by Madrid fans. To this day, Zamora's 'impossible save' in that game is regarded as the finest save by any goalkeeper in the history of Spanish football.

That was the day the music died, or at least when national league and cup football went into enforced hibernation for three years. On 18 July 1936 General Francisco Franco launched a Nationalist rebellion against the democratically elected Spanish Republic, and football took a back seat during the ensuing Civil War which, for the next three years, was about to engulf Spain.

***

Civil War to Europe

The killing of a president

As his chauffeur-driven car, flying from its wing the Catalan flag the 'senyera', eased out of Madrid on the Coruña road that summer day in 1936, Josep Sunyol i Garriga gazed at the approaching Sierra de Guadarrama.

Now thirty-eight years of age, he had been born into a wealthy Barcelona family, and from his youth and throughout his training as a lawyer he had embraced the cause of left-wing Catalan nationalism and the fortunes of FC Barcelona. He had joined Barça as a member in 1925, and Sunyol's family connections and his undoubted talents had resulted in 1928 in an invitation to become a director on the board of FC Barcelona where, in 1935, he became the club's twenty-eighth president.

In the interim, and with the support of the new Second Republic, he had been appointed head of Federació Catalana de Futbol, and was elected to represent the pro-independence party, Esquerra Republicana de Catalunya, at the Cortes in Madrid.

On 18 July 1936, after the declaration of a Nationalist uprising, Barcelona was in a state of political turmoil between anarchists, communists, loyal Civil Guard members and the military and its right-wing supporters. Before Sunyol left Barcelona at the end of July, he had chaired an emergency meeting of the FC Barcelona board, had travelled to Valencia, and had then met with Republican colleagues in the capital city, Madrid.

On this particular day, 6 August, he was journeying north-east from Madrid to meet with Catalan militia who had created a line of defence against the Nationalist forces, who were attempting to surround the city. Guadarrama was on the front line of the fighting, and the line was constantly changing.

The car had wound its way through the valleys and hills, when it came to a halt at a checkpoint. Sunyol got out and exclaimed, 'Viva La Republica', believing that the troops were Republican. However, the car driver had unknowingly strayed over the front line, and the troops were Nationalists. He and his companions were searched, shot dead and dumped into an unmarked roadside grave.

Three years later, after Franco's victory in the Civil War, Sunyol was posthumously prosecuted for 'political crimes'. Although it was possible that his murderers had been unaware of or unconcerned about Sunyol's footballing status, two months after the prosecution an official report stated: '. . . he was president of Barcelona football club and he was responsible for the clear anti-Spanish line which the club adopted'. In other words, he deserved what he got.

FC Barcelona made little comment on the fiftieth anniversary of his death, and a further ten years elapsed before officials of the Catalan club attended a ceremony near to where Sunyol had been 'executed'. They erected a small stone monument to commemorate the man who had presided over the fortunes of FC Barcelona as it faced the darkest period in its history.

It is, however, quite possible that Sunyol was killed by the enemy not because he was president of Barcelona but because he was a Republican who had been caught on Nationalist territory at a time when tensions were at their most inflammatory. This is not to offer an excuse for the murder of an innocent man; rather a reason to explain what happened.

Despite this, the death of Sunyol was perceived in Barcelona as another centrist attack on Catalonia and on FC Barcelona. It served not only to inflame the passionately held, nationalist fervour of many of the inhabitants of the region, but also to cement even further the identification of the inhabitants of Barcelona with its leading football club.

When the news of Sunyol's death reached Madrid, he became a martyr to the beleaguered defenders of that city, which, unlike Catalonia and Barcelona, was on the front line of the War, which remained a communist and Republican stronghold, and which was to suffer for nearly three more years in its defence of the Republic until it became the last city to fall to the Francoists at the end of the Civil War.

Although after the War there was arguably justifiable cause to accuse influential persons in Madrid and in its leading football club (now retitled Real Madrid) of a degree of collusion with the Francoist state authorities, there is little evidence of such collusion being a prevalent factor during the hostilities. Indeed, the opposite appears to have been the case. But from this period onwards, the fragile relationship between FC Barcelona and Real Madrid began to evolve from a normal football rivalry to a state of enduring suspicion and distrust between Spain's two main football clubs and their many supporters.

***

Even in the early days of the War, many of the regions which were home to the top clubs – such as Sevilla, Real Betis, Celta de Vigo, Deportivo de La Coruña, Valladolid, Oviedo, Osasuna and Real Zaragoza – were in Francoist hands. Others – including Athletic Club, Real Sociedad, Málaga, Athletic Madrid and Real Madrid – were on, or dangerously close to, the front line of the fighting.

As the War progressed, many league footballers simply went home, into exile, or enlisted to fight in one or other of the combatant armies or militias. Also, several club stadiums were damaged by shelling and bombardment or, as was the case with Madrid FC's Chamartin, were appropriated for meetings, training or storage purposes. Consequently, Madrid FC virtually stopped playing and, until the War ended, this inactivity was replicated at many other football clubs across Spain.

National football, which had taken well over thirty years to establish itself in Spain as a popular sport, essentially disappeared almost overnight, and the football authorities had little option other than to bring an immediate halt to the national cup and league football tournaments.

The Mediterranean League

Football competitions in some areas of Spain did manage to continue at a regional level. Galicia, which was the first northern region to fall under Nationalist control, continued with its championship in 1936. Thereafter, as with parts of Andalucia, local and regional leagues became the norm, although often in a wary and infrequent manner.

However, in the Republican-held east of the country, the Campeonato Levante, normally a qualifying competition for the national Copa and comprising six clubs from the Communities of Valencia and Murcia, continued and was won by Valencia. To the immediate north, the Campionat de Catalunya, again with six clubs competing, likewise pressed on, and resulted in an Español victory.

The Republican authorities, recognising the importance of the game in these regions and football's positive effect on social cohesion, then proposed a new league competition – La Liga del Mediterráneo (Mediterranean League) – as a temporary alternative to the absence of La Liga. This tournament would involve all twelve clubs from the two Communities.

However, there were problems. The Republican authorities rejected the involvement of Madrid FC, although the city of Madrid was in Republican hands and the club's president Antonio Ortega was a communist and a colonel in the city's left-wing militias (but his brief presidential reign appears to be curiously absent from the club's records).

Madrid's new coach Paco Bru, an ex-Barcelona player and manager of the 1920s Olympic squad, had asked if his club could take part in the Catalan Championship and Mediterranean League. Some of the smaller clubs were enthusiastic, mindful of the revenue which Madrid's involvement would bring them. However, FC Barcelona felt that the club's presence would disrupt the tournament's regional character, or were worried about facing stiffer competition, so Madrid's application was not accepted.

Nor could the country's most successful pre-War club, Athletic Bilbao, join in the new league, as it was on the front line and many of its players had enlisted or escaped to France. Also, in order to reach Catalonia the club would have had to journey through Nationalist Spain.

Another problem was that Real Murcia, Hércules CT and FC Cartagena – all from Levante – had to withdraw due to fierce fighting and aerial bombardment in the area. As this left the embryonic league rather lopsided, two of the Catalan clubs, CE Sabadell FC and CF Badalona, voluntarily withdrew. To equalise numbers, the Republican organisers invited CD Castellón to be the fourth club from Levante.

There were now eight rather than twelve clubs in the Mediterranean League, but the slimmed-down competition began in January 1937 and ended four months later with, to no one's surprise, FC Barcelona, managed by Patrick O'Connell and featuring goalscoring local hero Josep Escola, coming top of the league.

It was then suggested that the top four in the league – these being Barcelona, Español, Girona and Valencia – should compete in a knockout tournament to be called the Copa de la España Libre. However, as Barcelona had been invited to visit the USA and Mexico (more on which shortly) the club would not be around to participate. Levante, who had finished the League in fifth position, replaced Barcelona and, in the Copa final, Levante beat city rivals Valencia to claim the title.

Levante has never won a major national title in its 110-year history and, as the Copa Libre was held with the support and under the auspices of the Republican government and was formally suggested as an alternative to the Copa del Rey, the club believed that its title should be recognised as such by the RFEF. In 2007, the Spanish government lobbied the RFEF to recognise the Free Spain Cup as official and Levante's claim as legitimate.

The RFEF, however, continues with its refusal to recognise Levante's title win, as the tournament was held under abnormal wartime conditions, much as the same body will not grant official recognition to Barcelona for its claim that Barça's Mediterranean League title equates to winning La Liga. 'La lutte continue', as the revolutionary Parisian students of 1968 announced. Or, rather, 'la lucha continua . . .'

The Battle of Teruel in early 1938 split the Republican area in two. This meant that no teams from Levante were able to reach Catalonia, and the prospect of a second Mediterranean League proved impossible to realise. A Catalan League of ten teams was instituted in 1938, but wartime disruption prevented its completion, although Barcelona, despite being depleted in players after the club's return from the USA, was awarded the title.

The fact that these competitions were organised, played and completed in 1937, as the Civil War was raging across Spain, demonstrates the game of football's enduring ability to survive even in the most adverse of conditions.

Barcelona 'Salvation' Tour

Survival was very much on FC Barcelona's mind as the summer of 1937 approached. The club, whose board had now become a 'workers' committee', was sinking into debt and its financial position was critical, a bleak situation not helped by a membership which was continuing to decline in numbers. From a figure of 8,000 at the beginning of the War, it was to fall to 3,500 at the end of the conflict.

When the club received in May a potentially profitable offer to tour Mexico and the USA, therefore, this was an invitation it could not turn down. FC Barcelona was approached by Manuel Mas Soriano, a Catalan-born, Mexican-based businessman, who offered to pay all expenses, to deposit for Barcelona's use $8,000 in a Mexican bank, and give the club $12,500 at the end of the trip. Such an offer could not have arrived at a more propitious time, and it was gratefully accepted. Although the trip was justified by the club as a means of raising funds for the Republican cause and also acting as an unofficial ambassador for the Spanish Second Republic, the money earned would be vital for ensuring its future. It would also give players and staff a break from the War.

Sixteen players, manager Patrick O'Connell, the club doctor and two officials set sail from the south of France on 24 May and arrived in Veracruz in Mexico on 8 June. Mexico was one of the few countries which actively supported the Republicans, and the Barcelona squad received a warm welcome. The team played its first match on 20 June in Mexico City against Club America, played several more fixtures, and contested its final Mexican game on 28 August.

In early September they travelled up to New York where their visit was being hailed in some US newspapers as the 'salvation tour', and received another friendly reception. The first game, against Brooklyn Hispano was on 6 September, followed by an American Select XI. The fourth and final match against a Jewish XI – the first game Barcelona had played under floodlights – was on 20 September, the end of the tour. They had been away from Spain for three months and had played a total of fourteen games.

The players were then given the option of staying, going elsewhere or returning to Spain. Most of the players stayed in Mexico, New York and France and, when O'Connell returned to Catalonia, only five players and the doctor came back with him. Although the tour resulted in a damaging depletion of the leading players, the money raised, which was deposited in a French bank to keep it away from Republican and Nationalist hands, totalled just under $13,000 which no doubt helped to save FC Barcelona from financial ruin.

'Republik Euzkadi'

In early 1937, the Basque Country was occupied by Nationalist forces, with the exception of Vizcaya which included the city of Bilbao.

The president of the Basque regional government decided to organise a team selected from the best Basque footballers in Spain, and invite them to take part in a tour abroad to publicise the Republican cause and raise funds for the Basque Republican fighters. Some Basque pro-Nationalists refused to join, but many Basque players were pro-Republic and gladly offered their services. As well as their belief and pride in the tour's stated purpose, most were relieved to be leaving war-ravaged Spain.

Athletic Club had won four La Liga titles and two runner-up placings in the previous eight seasons, and had been Spain's most successful club since the formation of the national league. Twenty players formed the Basque squad, of whom eight were from Athletic Club, with the others coming from Arenas, Racing de Santander, Madrid FC, Real Betis, Barcelona, Oviedo and Athletic Madrid.

The team, known variously as 'Republik Euzkadi' and 'Euzkadi Selezkioa', travelled to France, their debut game being a 3–0 win in Paris over Racing Paris on 26 April 1937. After the game, the team were told about that day's devastating German aerial destruction of Guernica, the spiritual home of the Basques, and morale was badly damaged. But the squad continued with the tour and played another four games in May in France.

FIFA had banned any affiliated nations from playing Spanish sides, due to the Civil War, and the end of May game against Holland was cancelled. But as several clubs and nations sympathised with the Republic and admired the efforts of the 'Euzkadi', the team played in Poland, Czechoslovakia and Silesia on their way to the Soviet Union.

The Basque squad was in Moscow on 19 June when they learnt about the fall of Bilbao to the Nationalists, which occurred earlier that day. In effect, this meant they could not return home.

Over that summer the Basque team played the leading clubs in Moscow, Leningrad, Kiev and Tbilisi, attracting crowds of up to 90,000, and won them all. Their final game was a defeat by Spartak Moscow.

After two and a half months in the Soviet Union, this nomadic side defeated Norway and put eleven goals past Denmark. The squad then spent the autumn and winter in Mexico and Cuba, playing games which avoided FIFA restrictions. In February 1938 they travelled to Argentina where, short of money and unable to play, they remained for three months, partially subsidised by Argentinian clubs' fundraising matches.

In May 1938 they again moved on, via Chile and Cuba, to Mexico where, under the name Club Deportivo Euzkadi, they joined a major Mexican league for the 1938/39 season and ended as league runners-up.

The Spanish Civil War had now ended, and the peripatetic team was dissolved, each player receiving 10,000 pesetas as a thank-you pay-off. Few of the team felt like returning home, and they mostly remained in the Americas where they joined Latin American clubs.

On 29 January 1939 the Nationalist army marched into Barcelona and, six weeks later, Madrid fell to Franco. On 1 April, the 'Caudillo', General Franco, announced the formal cessation of hostilities and the end of the Spanish Civil War.

***

The Franco regime: the early years

One has only to glance through the country's history to realise the truth of travel writer Jan Morris's comment that Spain is 'committed to acts of cruelty against its own kind', although this observation understates by some degree the unprecedented ferocity and internecine brutal savagery which had been unleashed by the Spanish Civil War.

After his victory, Franco declared himself 'Caudillo of Spain by the Grace of God'. It is estimated that, during the Civil War, 200,000 people were killed in battle on the front lines, 200,000 were murdered or executed, and a further 250,000 Spaniards went into exile in the War years and soon after.

The new regime enacted in October 1939 'The Law of Political Responsibility' which, in effect, gave the Nationalists carte blanche to prosecute, imprison and/or execute anyone who had committed or even considered committing 'actions or omissions that might prejudice this Movement of Redemption'. Between 1939 and 1945, at least 20,000 people were 'executed' by the Francoist regime.

The state's brutality and repression of any opposition, actual or imagined, were initially focused on the rebellious regions, particularly Catalonia, where the language was banned (Catalans were told to 'speak like Christians'), books were burned, the authority of the centralised state was reinforced and the region was run by Francoist officials.

The Catholic Church became a pillar of the state, while the regime firmly controlled the press and the education system. All political organisations were banned, apart from the state-controlled Movimiento Nacional.

At the end of the Civil War, the Spanish economy was in ruins. The devastation of agriculture led to food shortages, with food rationing in place between 1939 and 1952. The 1940s became known as 'Los Años de Hambre' ('the Years of Hunger'), and the regime's policy of 'autarky' (self-sufficiency) reflected its pariah status in Western Europe.

However, events occurring within Spain and outwith the country had, by the early 1960s, conspired to elevate the country from this disastrous nadir to a much more acceptable and less severe position of relative parity with, and wary acceptance by, many of the more liberal countries in Western Europe. And football had an important part to play in this unexpected transformation.

***

Although 'Hispanicisation' also extended into the organisation and structure of national football, the game was less affected by the state than were many other aspects of Spanish life. In 1939, La Liga and the Copa del Rey (Copa del Generalisimo, as it was now labelled) both recommenced, in a formal sense at least, in more or less their previous manner.

Franco was well aware of the power of the game to influence the behaviour and attitudes of the population, to provide a welcome distraction from repression and poverty, and to act as an effective channel for the dissemination of state propaganda, and so he instituted a new Ministry of Sport, under the direction of loyal Nationalists.

Spanish clubs were encouraged to rebuild their squads and their stadiums. Clubs were now under full Francoist control, and every club had to have a minimum of two Falange members on its board. To correspond to the 'new' unitary Spain, several clubs were retitled in 'Christian' Castilian: Athletic Bilbao became Atlético Bilbao, Madrid FC was reborn as Real Madrid Club de Fútbol and Football Club Barcelona was now Barcelona Club de Fútbol.

The two outstanding pre-War clubs, Athletic Bilbao and Real Madrid, who between them had won six of the first eight La Liga titles, emerged as champions in only one of the first fourteen post-War Liga seasons. Athletic's loss of players on their two-year overseas trip and Madrid's badly damaged stadium and meagre squad meant that both clubs had to rebuild before regaining their previous dominant status.

While Real Madrid languished, and Athletic regrouped, Valencia, Sevilla and Barcelona were also among the leading names in La Liga over the next few years. As was Atlético Aviación.

Atlético Aviación

The city of Madrid's 'second team', Athletic Madrid, had enjoyed mixed fortunes since having been invited to join La Liga in 1929. At the end of the 1935/36 season, Athletic had found itself in eleventh position, above bottom-placed Osasuna. Both teams were facing relegation to Segunda, but everything had been put on hold when the hostilities began.

By 1939 Athletic's Metropolitano Stadium was almost unplayable after the conflict, the club's financial position was precarious, and several of its best players had been killed during the War. Real Oviedo, which had ended the 1935/36 season in third place in La Liga, had asked the RFEF if it could temporarily concede its Primera place in the forthcoming season, due to the extent of the War damage inflicted on the Asturias club.

The RFEF considered the possibility of an eleven-club league, but soon dismissed this idea. Osasuna claimed that Oviedo, in return for Osasuna's help during the War, had agreed with Osasuna that the Navarre club would take its place in the upcoming season. Unsurprisingly, Athletic Madrid objected to this, as it had ended the previous Liga season ahead of Osasuna. So the RFEF decided on a two-club play-off, the winner of which would remain in La Liga.

Meanwhile, Aviación Nacional, the Spanish Air Force team, set up by the regime as a symbol of central authority with its base in Madrid, was keen to prove itself against Spain's top clubs. However, it could only do so either by engaging in the long process of starting in regional football and working its way up, or by merging with an established club. Aviación decided on the latter course, but its discussions with Madrid FC and Nacional de Madrid came to nothing.

Despite objections from a number of its pro-Republican members and players, Athletic Madrid was more amenable, and the club merged with the Air Force. The resulting team became Atlético Aviación. The merger would not only help Athletic's ailing finances, but the club would also benefit from Aviación's excellent transport links and recourse to the talents of the Air Force players.

The play-off between Atlético Aviación and Osasuna for the contested place in La Liga took place in Valencia's Mestalla Stadium in November 1939, a few days before the 1939/40 season began. Under the managerial guidance of the legendary Ricardo Zamora, Atlético won 3–1 and the Madrid club remained in La Liga.

Not only did it remain there, but also by the end of the season Atlético Aviación had won the title. After fourteen wins, seven defeats and one draw, the club's 2–0 defeat of Valencia on the final day of the season meant that Atlético were Liga champions, one point above Sevilla (whose city rival Betis Balompié, winner of the 1935 Liga title, was relegated). This was the season which technically should have seen Atlético in Segunda. In 1940/41, the club again won the title, this time ahead of Athletic Bilbao.

Over the following six seasons, Atlético Aviación finished four times in the top three Liga placings. In 1947, the club split from the Air Force and became Atlético Madrid and, under its new name, and with a much improved bank balance, stadium and squad, the club again won La Liga in the two seasons from 1949 to 1951.

Atlético's relationship with elements of the Francoist regime had saved it from possible extinction and had turned the club into champions. However, a resurgent Real Madrid was soon to take over as the dominant club in Spain, and it would be another fifteen years before Atlético again won La Liga.

***

Spain's third-largest city, **Valencia**, was the Republican government's headquarters for most of the Civil War, and its surrender to Franco's forces on 30 March 1939, combined with Madrid's formal surrender the following day, marked the end of the bloody conflict.

Valencia's coastal location, and its agriculturally productive and economically valuable hinterland, meant that thereafter it suffered less interference from Nationalists than did several other cities. It was an important port for the victors as, although the city was politically associated with the left, it had historically been Madrid's preferred trading route to the Mediterranean and beyond.

The city's leading football club, though, was in disarray. Valencia CF's Mestalla Stadium had been badly damaged by air raids, the club's senior Republican players had departed, and its presidency was briefly assumed by a Francoist army officer until the return of former club president Luis Casanova. Casanova then set about repairing, redesigning and expanding the capacity of the stadium and rebuilding the club.

Several players remained from the pre-War team, and they were joined both by promising youngsters and players from elsewhere in the country. The club won its first-ever national trophy, the Copa, in 1941 in a 3–1 final defeat of Español at the Chamartin in Madrid, and the second Copa came in 1949. Valencia also won three Liga titles in that decade: in 1941/42 (scoring eighty-five goals in twenty-six games), 1943/44 and 1946/47.

Valencia's managers, in particular Luis Pasarin and ex-Real Madrid formidable defender Jacinto Quincoces, fielded one of the finest forward lines in La Liga. Known as the 'delantera eléctrica' ('electric attack'), it included Basque centre-forward Mundo (who picked up two Pichichi awards), inside-forwards Asensi and Amadeo, and wingers Epi and Gorostiza. Supporting these outstanding forwards were midfielders Vicente Segui and local stalwart and key player Antonio Puchades, who each spent more than a decade at the club.

In 1954 Valencia won its third Copa, beating rivals Barcelona 3–0 in front of 110,000 spectators at the Estadio Chamartin. I use the term 'rivals' because, although the Valencian 'dialect' had long been regarded as a form of Catalan, arguments were increasingly being put forward by local linguists that 'Valenciano' could be considered as a language in its own right.

The Catalan refusal to acknowledge the validity of this claim was creating an extra competitive edge to encounters between the two ports' leading football sides, so this comprehensive footballing defeat of Barcelona was a particularly welcome victory for the club and for many inhabitants of the wider Valencian community.

**

Meanwhile, **Athletic Bilbao** had reorganised and had adapted to its new Francoist stewardship. Indeed, the following decade from 1940 to 1950 was to become one of the most successful periods in the club's history.

The club's 'cantera' policy had unearthed three young players – midfield playmaker José Luis Panizo, inside-forward Agustin Gaínza and centre-forward Telmo Zarra – whose talents were to bring the Basque club one La Liga title, as well as four top-three La Liga finishes, and four Copa del Generalisimo trophies during this ten-year period. And young Zarra was to prove himself a legend in Spanish football.

A Basque superstar

Considered by many observers to have been the greatest-ever Spanish-born forward, Telmo Zarraonandia – known as 'Zarra' – played for Athletic Bilbao from 1940 until 1955. A tall, skilful centre-forward, Zarra was a goalscoring phenomenon at Athletic. He scored 355 goals, of which 251 were in La Liga games (a record for sixty years until broken by Lionel Messi), a still unbeaten 81 in the Copa del Rey, and he was the leading scorer in six Liga seasons.

He was particularly adept and dangerous with his head. One of his opponents said 'he plays with three legs, the third being his head', and was described admiringly as having 'the second best head in Europe after Winston Churchill'. He once headed the ball against a crossbar with such ferocity that it bounced all the way back to the halfway line. He was also devastatingly effective with his feet.

His talents contributed markedly to one of Athletic's most successful periods. In his debut game in September 1940, a 2–0 win over Valencia, he scored both goals. In Athletic's first post-Civil War Copa final, Zarra scored the winner against Real Madrid, enabling the club to win the Spanish 'double' in 1942/43, the first season of three back-to-back Copa championship victories.

In the 1950 Copa final against Valladolid, Zarra scored in the game, which ended in a 1–1 draw after normal time. He added another three in extra time, for a 4–1 victory for Athletic. Also in that year he scored what was probably his most famous goal in Spain's 1–0 World Cup victory which eliminated England, but a 6–1 defeat by host nation Brazil denied Spain further progress in the tournament.

Zarra stands supreme at the top of *Marca* newspaper's Pichichi annual listings for the highest goalscorer in Spain. This apparently modest and self-deprecating man collected six Pichichi awards in his career. Behind him on five apiece are Hugo Sánchez, Alfredo Di Stéfano and Quini. Although in 2018/19 Lionel Messi equalled Zarra's record, Zarra's remarkable scoring legacy will continue to outlast some of Spain's finest ever players.

Humiliation in Madrid

For most of the 1940s, FC Barcelona appeared to have lost confidence in itself as a football club. Although the number of its 'socios' had significantly increased since the end of the War and its financial position had improved, the club and players seemed unable to come to terms with the Francoist central authority and its strict suppression of Catalonian autonomy.

However, in season 1944/45 Barcelona, under coach Josep Samitier, had won the La Liga title for only the second time in its history, and were to win the title twice more at the end of the decade. But in the Copa of 1943, they played Real Madrid in a game which many Barcelona fans perceived as incontrovertible proof that Real Madrid had forged links with the central Francoist state.

Indeed, some observers believe that it was in the aftermath of this game that the growing enmity between the two clubs reached its full flowering. Prior to this, there had been wariness and mistrust. But, in the eyes of many members, officials and supporters of the clubs, in particular those of Barcelona, the relationship had now become one of hatred.

No one really knows the truth about what happened at Real Madrid's Chamartin Stadium on 13 June 1943 in the second leg of the semi-final of the Copa del Generalisimo, other than that Real Madrid beat FC Barcelona 11–1.

This astonishing destruction of Barcelona, by a team who had been beaten 3–0 in the first leg at Les Corts and who, in terms of talent and footballing ability, were little different to the Catalonian side, remains inexplicable. It is also the highest ever defeat in the history of 'El Clásico'.

In the first leg in Barcelona, the whistling and booing at the Real Madrid team from the hostile home crowd was such that the local authorities issued fines to those they could discover were the guilty parties. Real Madrid officials complained about what they regarded as the loutish behaviour of the undeniably partisan Catalan fans, and that the referee had favoured Barcelona players throughout the match. Consequently, Barcelona supporters were banned from attending the second leg at Chamartin.

Before the second leg, there is little doubt that the club and the local press, in particular *Marca* – the newspaper set up by Francoists in 1938 to promote Spain as a unitary, Madrid-led state, and to discredit aspirations for regional autonomy in football matters – did its utmost to stimulate among the Real Madrid fans a toxic atmosphere of fevered frenzy aimed at the players of Barcelona. Considering that whistles were handed out before the game at the gates of Chamartin, and these were used to punctuate the swearing, threats and insults from the crowd of 20,000, it is unsurprising that the Catalonian players found the atmosphere intimidating.

It is also possible that warnings, implicit or explicit, were directed by match and Francoist officials to the Barcelona players, a number of whom had been Republican supporters in the War, against their winning the match. One of these threats is said to have come from the Director of State Security who visited the Barcelona dressing room before the game. This gentleman apparently said: 'Do not forget that some of you are playing only because of the generosity of the regime in forgiving you your lack of patriotism.' This pre-match 'pep talk' did little to allay their growing trepidation.

Whatever the cause, the increasingly beleaguered Barcelona players put up little resistance to Real, and they were 8–0 down by half-time in a deliberately bruising encounter, which was not helped by one of their team being sent off early in the game by a biased referee. The crowd's hysterical abuse continued, and the Barcelona keeper, Lluis Miró, rarely ventured into his penalty box, owing to the objects, coins and threats being hurled in his direction.

At the interval, there were several Barcelona players who were reluctant to return to the field for the second half, but what remained of their pride overruled this potential capitulation. Real eased off a bit in the second half, and the game was eventually over. The Barcelona team bus could not leave Madrid quickly enough.

Even the Francoist authorities, who had no wish to antagonise further the troublesome regions, were embarrassed by the incredibly one-sided score, and they circulated newspapers to tell them not to print reports of the game. Four months later, in a contrived attempt to demonstrate the mutually respectful relationship between the clubs, a 'Peace Cup' two-leg match was staged, but this fooled no one.

By now, the president of Barcelona had been forced to resign, due to the crowd behaviour at Les Corts, and his role had been assumed by a Francoist army officer. This served only to add to the conviction of Barcelona fans that Real Madrid was simply an agent of the central, Madrid-based Francoist regime. The conflict between Catalonia and Madrid was firmly back on the agenda.

However, although this crushing scoreline against such a major club as Barcelona suggests that, at the very least, Real Madrid were back in form, the truth is that they were a shadow of the side which won back-to-back Liga titles in 1932 and 1933.

The question of whether Barcelona were victims of a sinister government plan to show to Spain that real power lay in the capital, or whether the Catalans simply caved in and 'bottled it', is of interest to historians of the game, but the result does not reflect the state of football in Spain at the time. In the final of that season's Copa, for instance, Real Madrid were outplayed by the team of the moment, Athletic Bilbao, and limply succumbed to a 1–0 defeat.

Indeed, in the same season in La Liga, Real ended in eleventh place, one place above the relegation play-offs in the fourteen-club Primera. Throughout the 1940s, Real Madrid were normally to be found in mid-table, and again only just avoided a relegation play-off in 1947/48. Real had to be content with two Copa victories in the mid-1940s, and the club did not win La Liga again until season 1953/54.

However, after winning that Liga title in 1954, Real Madrid won three more in that decade and, by the 1960s, the club claimed eight of the ten available Liga titles, a remarkable turnaround in their fortunes. The reason for Real's re-emergence and transformation in the 1950s and 1960s can largely be credited to two men: Santiago Bernabéu and Alfredo Di Stéfano.

***

Don Santiago returns

Santiago Bernabéu made his debut in 1912 as a strapping young inside-forward with Madrid FC, spent several years as club captain and retired from playing in 1927.

A right-wing Nationalist supporter during the War, Bernabéu enlisted as a volunteer, and he was with the Francoist troops when they entered Barcelona in January 1939. After the War, he returned to Real Madrid, where he had been director of football and manager, and he was appointed president of the club in September 1943, shortly after the fiasco of the 11–1 Copa game.

The organisation of the club was chaotic, its status had plummeted from the pre-War days, and its expectations and morale were at a low ebb when Bernabéu took over. Attendances at Chamartin had fallen, the club had just escaped relegation, and the newly formed Atlético Aviación was threatening to assume Real's dominant position in the city. So this authoritarian, somewhat severe yet principled man set to work in what was seen as a thankless task: to restore Real Madrid to its former eminence.

Bernabéu immediately began to tackle the club's ramshackle organisation and to reinstate a sense of order and determination into the running of the club. But his visionary plans for the club extended far beyond its internal structure. Taking advantage of his high-level Francoist contacts in Madrid, and aware of the Francoist plans for the post-War urban regeneration of the city, he unveiled his plans for the construction of a major stadium which would be the new home of Real Madrid.

He convinced the regime and the club members (the 'socios'), the latter being the principal financial backers, that his plans were viable and would result in Madrid being home to the country's largest stadium. He also stressed the associated domestic political status and international propaganda prestige which such a stadium would generate. In October 1944 he commissioned work to begin on Real Madrid's 'Nuevo Estadio Chamartin'.

There were sceptics who believed that it was 'too much of a stadium for so little a club', and the president was aware that the concept of 'build it and they will come' was a somewhat fanciful notion. However, he was also aware that his club, although then relatively dormant, had potentially a much larger supporter and membership base than it could then boast, and that success on the pitch could fill the stadium.

Bernabéu's project was completed, and the stadium was inaugurated in December 1947 with a game against Portuguese club Os Belenenses. The ground, one of Europe's largest, was an imposing construction with room for 75,000 spectators, and the game was played to a full capacity.

Real had won the 1946 Copa, beating Valencia 3–1 in the final, and the club had again picked up the trophy in June 1947 with a 2–0 defeat of Español. These victories, and the magnificent new stadium, signalled that Real Madrid was now very much back in business, and the number of members dramatically increased. However, Bernabéu knew that to maintain and increase the Real support he had to find the players who could bring success back to the club.

By 1955, the stadium had expanded to accommodate 125,000 spectators, and Bernabéu had in place the players he required to fulfil his vision. The player who began the transformation of Real Madrid was an Argentinian footballing genius named Alfredo Di Stéfano.

Argentinian influences

While on the subject of Argentinian footballers, the South American connection had already been established in Spain.

In the winter of 1946/47, one of Buenos Aires's leading teams, San Lorenzo, had toured Spain, and their players' technique had come as a revelation to the country's clubs and observers of the game. Their superb ball control, diagonal inter-passing, speedy attacking movement on and off the ball, dribbling ability and all-round footballing trickery was in sharp contrast to the conventional direct play of most Spanish clubs.

San Lorenzo's squad contained a number of Basques, including team captain Ángel Zubieta, who had remained in Argentina after the Euzkadi tour, as well as local Argentinians and Italians, so their delicate yet effective attacking skills were well complemented by a defensive, physical robustness.

San Lorenzo began their tour with a 4–1 victory over Atlético Aviación in the Metropolitano Stadium, but were then defeated by a resurgent Real Madrid at the same venue. The Argentinian side then beat FC Barcelona and drew with Athletic Bilbao, Valencia and Sevilla. These five clubs were at the time dominant in the Spanish game, and the Argentinian team, known as 'El Ciclon' ('The Cyclone'), exposed them to a new way of approaching the game, and they were not slow to capitalise on the lessons learned.

Galician club Deportivo de La Coruña had also fallen under the influence of the Argentinian game. In 1940/41 the club was playing in La Liga for the first time in its history and it finished its inaugural season in fourth place. During that decade Dépor moved between Primera and Segunda, and had acquired the financing to redevelop its old Riazor Stadium.

Back in La Liga for 1949/50, and now managed by Argentinian coach Alejandro Scopelli, the club finished in second place, only one point behind champions Atlético Madrid, with a group of Argentinian and other South American players such as Julio Corcuera and Oswaldo Garcia, brought to the club by Scopelli.

Under the coaching of later managers, including Helenio Herrera, and with local boys Luis Suárez, four-time Zamora winner Juan Acuña and right-winger Amancio ('El Briojo':

'The Wizard'), and striker Pahiño (acquired from Real Madrid), Dépor retained its top-flight status in La Liga for a further eight seasons before falling victim to relegation and financial problems.

When I began to write this book I had the idea that I could present a history of all the leading Spanish clubs in an entertaining, informative and inclusive manner, and attempt to include the big boys – Barcelona and Real Madrid – only when events required their attention. I now realise that this is impossible. It's rather like trying to write a history of Scottish league football by concentrating on Aberdeen and Raith Rovers, while including passing references to Rangers and Celtic. It can't be done.

Consider, for a moment, the ten years of La Liga between seasons 1950/51 (roughly the point to date in this narrative) and 1960/61 (where I begin Part Three). Real Madrid and Barcelona between them won nine of the eleven available Liga titles during this period, with Atlético and Athletic Bilbao picking up one apiece. Winning titles becomes a habit and, with occasional interruptions, their dominance in La Liga has continued until the present day.

However, the emergence of trans-European tournaments, such as the European Cup, the Cup Winners' Cup and the UEFA Cup, and the expansion of these tournaments to include more clubs from an increasing number of participant countries, has allowed me also to discuss the European fortunes (and the domestic performances which brought them into Europe) of other meritorious Spanish sides: Valencia, Real Zaragoza, Real Sociedad, Deportivo de La Coruña, Sevilla, Real Betis, Alavés and others.

One cannot but respect and admire the superiority, achievements and footballing brilliance of Real Madrid and Barcelona, but one must not forget that clubs of this standard need not only to outperform but also learn from their domestic peers. La Liga contains some of the world's finest football clubs, and they deserve the attention which I will continue to afford these other clubs in both domestic and European competition.

But first I must continue with the two grand old performers. As the 1950s progressed, they were by some distance becoming the main actors on the Spanish footballing stage.

***

From observing the club's domestic and European record, one could reasonably conclude that Real Madrid was Spain's and Europe's finest club side from the early 1950s to the early 1960s. After all, the club's record in the early years of the European Cup is unparalleled, and it fielded some of the world's top players throughout this period.

However, there are many who would argue, on equally reasonable grounds, that Real Madrid was not even Spain's best side during those years, and that this honourable status belongs to **FC Barcelona.**

Barcelona's European haul of three Fairs Cups and two Latin Cups may not stand adequate comparison with Real's five consecutive European Cups. But on the pitch, it is argued, the Catalan club's outstanding footballers at the very least equalled, and arguably surpassed, the overall quality of the legendary Madrid sides of those years.

Of course, it's impossible, and facile, to attempt such comparisons, and the only reason for so doing is to stress the depth of talent at Barcelona's disposal, something overlooked by many football fans, during what must be regarded by all lovers of the game as one of the halcyon eras of Spanish club football.

Under the direction of new coach Josep Samitier, in the middle of season 1944/45 Barcelona consigned the 11–1 defeat to the dustbin of historical freak results (or devious political machinations) when they beat Real Madrid 5–0. That season, the club claimed the Liga title for the second time in its history, one point ahead of Real. In 1947/48 Barcelona won its third La Liga, and claimed the title again in 1948/49. In 1949 Barcelona were also the first winners of the new Latin Cup, a competition between the champions of France, Portugal, Italy and Spain, beating Sporting Lisbon 2–1 in the final. The forerunner of the European Cup, the Latin Cup played its final season in 1957.

So, with its team of young, mainly Catalan players, Barcelona was again making its stylish mark on the Spanish game. However, in 1950 Samitier's signing of a Hungarian-born forward, László Kubala, was to mark the rebirth of the club's fortunes and to turn Barcelona into one of the most exciting footballing sides that Spain had ever seen.

Kubala had defected from Eastern Europe in 1948 and had ended up in Italy, where he formed a team which he called 'Hungaria' and which was composed of similarly-minded Eastern European refugees. When the team toured Spain in the summer of 1950, Kubala immediately attracted the attentions of Real Madrid and Barcelona. Although Kubala was offered a contract by Real, he was instead persuaded by Samitier, and by a handsome salary, to sign for Barcelona, which he did in June 1950.

His abrupt departure had aroused the ire of the Hungarian football authorities and had resulted in a year's suspension by FIFA, so initially he played as an 'amateur' for Barcelona. But, through Samitier's Francoist contacts, and with the agreement of El Caudillo, who was not slow to seize the propaganda value of Kubala's rejection of his now-Soviet homeland, the player accepted Spanish citizenship in June 1951.

Kubala was a prodigiously gifted footballer who was rated by contemporary observers as the most complete player they had ever witnessed. He was a speedy, strong forward with a powerfully accurate shot, and he combined his muscular leadership qualities with an extraordinarily delicate sense of ball control, trickery and passing technique, all the while aware of the requirements of his teammates. He was a naturally brilliant footballer, and he was not deflected from his gifts by his rampant womanising and heavy drinking which, in return for his stellar presence on the pitch, were largely ignored by the Catalan club.

In 1951/52, Kubala's first legitimate season with Barcelona (although his 'amateur' presence had been vital in securing the club's first post-War Copa in 1951), he scored twenty-six goals in La Liga, including five against Celta de Vigo and seven against Sporting Gijón. His overall performance was instrumental in Barcelona's Copa and Liga double that season, as well as in the club's second Latin Cup victory.

In 1952/53, although Kubala had contracted TB and was out for much of the season, his astonishingly rapid recovery from the illness allowed him to return later in the season and to spur Barcelona on to another Liga and Copa double. With the Hungarian's indefatigable and inspirational presence, during that decade Barcelona picked up two further Copa trophies – in 1957 and 1959 – and another Liga title in 1959/60 (again, a double).

However, and as you are no doubt currently reflecting, inspirationally effective and even totemic as Kubala may have been to the club's progress in this exemplary period for the Catalan conquistadores, football is a team game and other players must have at least provided some assistance on those rare occasions when Kubala did not have possession of the ball. This was indeed the case, and Barcelona had cleverly constructed a complementary supporting cast of players, several of whom have also become club legends.

Arguably, the most important player in any side's sustained dominance over its peers is its goalkeeper, who must exert an unflappably reassuring presence among his teammates. Otherwise, their efforts, superhuman though they may appear, are ultimately futile in winning games. In this respect, Barcelona was fortunate in having 'El Gato de Maracaná' Antoni Ramallets as its ever-aware custodian. Ramallets' nickname – 'The Cat of Maracaná' – derived from his tireless efforts for his national side during the 1950 World Cup finals in Brazil.

Naturally, team members change over time, but certain players stand out for their critical contributions to the club. These included the elegant team captain and centre-half Joan Segarra and the incisively creative midfielder Marià Gonzalvo. The forward line over the years was a remarkable one. In 1955, one of Spain's greatest-ever players, Luis Suárez, had arrived from Deportivo de La Coruña to play alongside Kubala, while Brazilian winger Evaristo joined the club in 1957.

This forward line was dramatically strengthened in 1958 when Kubala persuaded two of the 'Mighty Magyar' Hungarian national side, one of the greatest teams in footballing history, to join the club. These two players were Honved's striker Sándor Kocsis and winger Zoltán Czibor, who were playing in the West when the 1956 Hungarian Revolution occurred and who chose to remain where they were.

This formidable side won the Liga and Copa double in 1958/59. In La Liga, Barcelona drew on points and had the same goal difference as Real Madrid, but won the title on head-to-head count. They claimed the Copa by defeating Granada 4–1 at the Bernabéu Stadium, in which game Kocsis scored twice.

Meanwhile, the ground which was home to FC Barcelona, Les Corts, had been significantly enlarged since its opening in 1922, but its maximum capacity of 60,000 was considered too small to accommodate the club's escalating popularity. A suitable site was found and work began on a new stadium.

An important factor dictating the design and capacity of the new ground was that it had to be 'bigger and better' than Real Madrid's Nuevo Chamartin (shortly to be retitled the Santiago Bernabéu Stadium). The stadium opened on 24 September 1957, the same day as Barcelona's Lady of Mercy annual festival. Initially to be called Estadio del Club de Fútbol, this 93,000-capacity temple to the footballing giants of Catalonia was and is simply known as Camp Nou.

With this formidable stadium as the backdrop to the footballing excellence on the pitch, one might be hard-pressed to conceive of any other domestic or national club from this or any subsequent era which would be able to offer a sustained challenge to this team of all the talents.

But such competition did exist, and it could be found only 400 miles to the west, where Santiago Bernabéu had built a team which finally matched his vision for his club, Real Madrid.

Los Blancos prepare for Europe

Alfredo Di Stéfano's arrival at Nuevo Chamartin was arguably the one event which created the modern Real Madrid.

Santiago Bernabéu had rescued the club from its post-Civil War relative stagnation. His enthusiasm, his organisational talents, his contacts within the Francoist regime, his access to finance and his lifelong support for, and knowledge of, Real Madrid had created the preconditions for at least a healthy future for the club. But he required a unique player, one he could unreservedly trust on the pitch, to ensure that his vision was realised of Real Madrid as one of the world's leading clubs. And he had found his man.

The fact that Di Stéfano had signed for Real Madrid and not for his other main suitor Barcelona is a subject which has justifiably preoccupied other writers, and it is a fascinating story which well reveals the chicanery, brinkmanship and skulduggery of football, which was clearly as true then as it is today. The Di Stéfano transfer negotiations were given another dimension by the supposed interventions of the Francoist regime on behalf of Real Madrid, a club which it was beginning to regard as part of its diplomatic arm at a critical juncture in the regime's policy of improving its status in the eyes of the Western powers.

However, and for the purposes of this book, suffice to say that, at the critical moment, Barcelona blinked, while Real maintained its gaze and signed Di Stéfano on 15 September 1953. As if to emphasise his attachment to his new employer, two weeks after his signing Di Stéfano scored a hat-trick in Real's 5–0 defeat of FC Barcelona.

In 1953/54, Di Stéfano's first season with Real, the Argentine master scored twenty-seven goals in thirty Liga games, gaining Real its first Liga title since the Civil War. At Di Stéfano's urging, in time for the start of the 1954/55 season, Real bought Hector Rial, an Argentine inside-left and one of Alfredo's old amigos. Also, a speedy young left-winger named Paco Gento – 'La Galerna' ('The Gale') – had been acquired from Racing de Santander early in 1953.

Di Stéfano, however, remained the main man. His twenty-six goals brought La Liga title in 1954/55 to the Bernabéu for the second year in succession, and Real won La Liga twice more before the decade was completed.

Over the next two to three years, Real Madrid was putting together, under Santiago Bernabéu's aegis and aided by the direction of the irreplaceable 'Blond Arrow', a side which would become recognised as arguably the most complete and collectively talented set of individuals ever to play together on a football pitch.

The following season – 1955/56 – a major challenge was to be offered to Real Madrid and to all the leading clubs in Europe. An annual, UEFA-managed competition – the European Cup – was about to begin, and winning this new trophy would give the continent's national league champions the right to call themselves Europe's top football club.

This was the test for which Bernabéu and Di Stéfano had been waiting. The following five years were to justify their expectations to a greater degree than even these two hardened football professionals could conceivably have imagined.

PART THREE

LA LIGA AND EUROPE

'Spain is the problem, and Europe is the solution'.
José Ortega y Gasset

Historical context (1940–1960)

At the end of the Second World War, the United Nations imposed sanctions on Spain. In 1946 the UK and France withdrew their ambassadors from the country and refused to recognise Franco's regime. The USA's Marshall Plan of 1948, which granted economic aid to Europe, was not offered to Spain. Spain was once again a socially repressed, culturally divided and economically devastated country.

Spain remained under the firm centralised control of an authoritarian, deeply conservative, religiously doctrinal and introspective regime, with a leadership which was dominated by the military and which showed few signs of reducing its hostility to modernisation or the consideration of any attempts to modify or question its policies.

However, by the early 1950s, although the regime still considered itself to be 'a totalitarian instrument in the service of the national integrity', Spain was gradually adopting less ideologically rigid policies, as modernising elements within the state apparatus increased in number and influence. Franco and his regime were slowly being persuaded that an essential requirement for this virtually bankrupt and potentially socially implosive country was to reintegrate itself, both economically and diplomatically, with its Western neighbours.

This embryonic anti-isolationist, progressive tendency within Spain coincided with an awareness by one of its previously most powerful detractors, the USA, that it may have been mistaken in adopting its earlier rejectionist attitude towards the country. The US Secretary of State, Dean Acheson, remarked that its policy of sanctions and non-cooperation had 'failed in its intended purpose' and had 'served to strengthen the position of the present regime'.

In the context of the escalating Cold War, probably the real reasons for this volte-face by the USA were Franco's virulent anti-communism and Spain's strategically important position in the southern Mediterranean, both of which were of potential value to the USA. So it forged a rapprochement with Spain, reinstalled its ambassador in Madrid, and in 1953 signed with Franco 'The Pact of Madrid', which permitted the US to locate air bases in the country in return for the USA's formal recognition and financial guarantees.

In 1955 Spain was invited to join the United Nations, and the country was then accepted by the World Bank and the IMF. The latter pressurised the Franco regime to introduce, in 1959, a 'Stabilisation Plan', which broke with the regime's twenty-year policy of autarky and took steps in the direction of a market economy, accompanied by the introduction of low-cost housing, a social security system, the expansion of education and the production and export of consumer goods.

In 1951 the regime had established a Ministry of Tourism which in 1959 devalued the peseta, abolished entry visas for tourists and took advantage of the new package tour air flights into the country. In 1960, four million tourists per annum were coming to Spain. Six years later, the number of tourists had soared to eighteen million.

Although several coastlines and coastal villages were badly affected by the impact of this unchecked tourist invasion, tourism aroused international awareness of the country and brought in much-needed hard currency. A less quantifiable but equally important benefit was that contact with people from other countries broadened the horizons of many Spaniards and lessened their sense of isolation from the world around them.

Football was also playing an important role in this presentation of the 'new Spain'. In particular, the stunning performances and victories of Franco's unofficial propaganda club, Real Madrid, were being admired by millions of football fans in stadiums and on the new TV sets which were spreading rapidly across the continent.

Spain was re-entering Europe, Europe was giving the country an approving welcome and, in terms of maintaining and increasing its mass appeal, football was one of Spain's most valuable assets.

***

The 'Vikings' conquer Scotland

Glasgow's imposing old Hampden Park, then one of the world's largest stadiums, was host to almost 130,000 people on that Wednesday evening of 18 May 1960. This huge crowd had come to watch the first European Cup final to be held in the United Kingdom.

The European Champion Clubs' Cup, as was the tournament's official title, had been launched in season 1955/56. The Cup invited the football league winners of European countries to compete for the honour of being recognised as the top club in European football. The competition's opening match – Sporting Lisbon against Partizan Belgrade – had kicked off in September 1955, and the new tournament quickly became recognised across Europe as the ultimate test for the continent's leading footballing clubs.

However, few could have imagined that, over sixty years later, the competition – under the misleading title of the Champions League and expanded from the original sixteen to over seventy European clubs – would offer the most prestigious and lucrative prize in world club football.

In 1960, European club football remained an exotic enigma to most British football supporters, but they had already received notice that England and Scotland, who had 'invented' the game of football, were no longer the unquestioned masters, if they ever had been, in what had fast become a worldwide game.

As an example of Britain's faltering dominance, earlier in the 1959/60 competition Barcelona, Spanish Liga winners the previous season, had thrashed Wolves, the pride of English football and hailed in the English press as 'the world's best football team', 9–2 on aggregate in the quarter-finals. Meanwhile, Scottish champions Rangers had also been humiliated, this time in the semi-final, by Eintracht Frankfurt, in a 12–4 aggregate hammering by the German side. The ingrained, almost disdainful superiority of Britain's leading clubs, long taken for granted in 'the home of football', was now under serious threat.

Real Madrid had been invited into this season's European Cup as the winner of the previous year's tournament, and was to contest the final against Eintracht in Glasgow. The majority of the Scottish crowd was supporting Real Madrid, partly because of the club's reputation as superb practitioners of the game but also in the hope that Eintracht, which had imperiously dismantled Rangers, would be taught a lesson by the Spanish side. So the atmosphere on the vast Hampden terraces was one of intrigued expectation as the game kicked off.

At the final whistle, the huge crowd rose in a standing ovation for Real Madrid who, in a stunning exhibition of footballing artistry, had just demolished the German champions 7–3. The game is often described as one of the finest exhibitions of football ever displayed. Reflecting some years later on the game, David Lacey in the *Guardian* observed that it 'reminded fans on both sides of the border of the shortcomings of the domestic game'. *The Times* went further with its unalloyed praise, and summed up this all-conquering team thus: 'Real Madrid strolls through Europe as the Vikings once did, destroying everything in its path.'

The game had revealed to the awestruck spectators Real's extraordinary ball control, dazzling movement, intuitive teamwork and seemingly unstoppable goalscoring talents. Orchestrated by the Argentinian playmaker and deep-lying centre-forward Alfredo Di Stéfano, the forward line was unstoppable. The combination of Brazilian right-wing schemer Canário, deft inside-right Del Sol, Hungarian inside-left maestro Puskás, and the astonishingly speedy winger Gento overran with impunity the static German defence. Puskás scored four, and Di Stéfano settled for three.

As the game progressed, Uruguayan centre-half José Santamaria, in concert with the outstanding talents of Spanish defenders Marquitos, Pachin and Zarraga, impeccably controlled the increasingly frustrated German forwards, and directed precise, accurate passes to their rampaging forwards.

Although this was Real Madrid's fifth successive European Cup victory, many observers were astonished that football of such outstanding maturity, technique and sophistication could emerge from Spain. The country had long been regarded by the UK and other European nations as being 'in' but not 'of' Europe: distant, economically and culturally backward, feudal in its outlook, and fundamentally ungovernable.

However, a 'new' Spain was emerging from the grim austerity of the post-Civil War years. The country's image of remoteness and isolation would, in the years to come, be overtaken by its assumption of the role of Europe's holiday playground: the land of 'sun, sex and sangria'. And at this point in Spain's 'makeover', its ambassador to the people of Europe was the continent's finest football team, Real Madrid.

Santiago Bernabéu's club, however, was not the only Liga team to have played during the first five seasons of the European Cup. Aside from the first season, only league champions (and the winner of the previous year's competition) were permitted to enter the Cup. The other clubs were Atlético Madrid, Sevilla, Athletic Bilbao and, of course, Barcelona.

European football competitions

Today, there are only two annual European football club tournaments: the Champions League and the Europa League. These have evolved from pre-existing tournaments, as follows.

Champions League

In 1954, Gabriel Hanot, editor of the French sports newspaper *L'Équipe*, proposed to FIFA (world football's governing body)

---

the European Champion Clubs' Cup, a home and away, knockout competition which would decide, on an annual basis, which was the top club in Europe. The winner of the Cup would join the following year's tournament, irrespective of their league performance that year.

Ratified by FIFA, responsibility for what soon became known as the European Cup passed to UEFA and, in September 1955, sixteen clubs kicked off in the new competition. Within ten years, the competition had become so successful and popular that the number of entrant clubs had doubled. As the prestige of the competition grew, the number of clubs proliferated. From 1991/92, preliminary knockout was followed by a league system. From 1994/95, the European Cup became the Champions League. From 1997/98, runners-up in the top national leagues were also included, sounding the death knell for M Hanot's 'league winners only' vision. Today, the Champions League is by some degree the world's most important club tournament.

Europa League

The Inter-City Fairs Cup lasted from 1955 until 1971, when it came under UEFA control and was replaced by the UEFA Cup. This latter tournament, the 'second-tier' European tournament, included clubs based on their national league and domestic cup performances. The European Cup Winners' Cup, for winners of domestic cup competitions, began in 1960 and was absorbed into the UEFA Cup in 1999. In 2009, the UEFA Cup was restructured and renamed the Europa League, and the Intertoto Cup was then also subsumed under the Europa League masthead.

La Liga clubs and the European Cup, 1956–1960

Before discussing the successes of Real Madrid and Barcelona in the early years of European competition, it is revealing to discover how other Spanish clubs fared during this formative period in Spanish and European football.

Although Real Madrid were regal in their domination of the European Cup's opening seasons, and deserved all the plaudits they received, the other Liga clubs generally also did pretty well but their achievements have long been overshadowed by 'los blancos'. Although a number of La Liga clubs had in previous years participated in 'friendlies' with clubs from other countries, the element of competition had been more or less absent and performances in friendly games had been largely irrelevant. Very few observers, and even fewer players, care about the results of games which yield no measurable reward.

Therefore, these European Cup clashes had suddenly become important proving grounds for Spanish clubs, who had felt themselves marginalised from the game in Europe. They now had a much wider stage on which to demonstrate their competitive talents and to prove that they were at least the footballing equals of their continental counterparts.

***

Athletic Bilbao, under the direction of much-travelled Slovakian manager Ferdinand Daučik, had won La Liga in 1955/56, one point ahead of Barcelona. They had also beaten Atlético Madrid 2–1 in the final of the Copa del Generalisimo, so this was the club's first title win, and double, for thirteen years.

Athletic's Liga win gained the club entry to the 1956/57 European Cup where, after defeating Porto in the competition's new preliminary round, Athletic drew Honved, the Hungarian

Army team. At the time, Honved fielded six of the 'Mighty Magyar' players – with a forward line including Puskás, Czibor and Kocsis – who in 1963 had beaten England 6–3 at Wembley, England's first-ever home defeat by a foreign country. To make sure England hadn't missed the point, a few months later the 'Magyars' again routed England, this time by 7–1 in Budapest. It is little surprise that Honved was considered by many neutrals to be the best club side in the world.

The first leg was due to be played in Budapest on 7 November, but protests and riots by the Hungarian people against the USSR's occupation of their country led to savage retaliation by the USSR, and on 4 November Soviet tanks, accompanied by armed troops, rolled into Budapest to crush the Hungarian Revolution. It was now impossible, or at least highly inadvisable, to play a European Cup tie in the city. Having examined and discarded other possible venues, the clubs moved the match to Athletic's San Mamés ground. On a cold Bilbao evening in front of a 40,000 crowd, Athletic won a stirring game 3–2, although a last-minute Honved goal was disallowed by an English referee.

The Hungarian side, with the players uncertain and concerned about the Soviet crackdown in their homeland, then played a series of friendlies against Real Madrid, Barcelona and Sevilla, until a venue was found for the second leg. At Brussels' Heysel Stadium, a capacity crowd witnessed another thrilling game. The Honved keeper was injured and withdrawn from the pitch early in the match and, as there were then no substitutes permitted in football, Czibor – normally a left-winger or centre-forward – took over in goal. He could not, however, prevent a 3–3 draw and Honved's aggregate dismissal from the Cup.

In the quarter-final in Bilbao against Manchester United, United were 3–0 down at half-time but fought back to a 5–3 defeat. In Manchester, a defensive Athletic side could not prevent the English club winning 3–0. Manchester United, as with every other club side who played Real Madrid in the European Cup at the time, was eliminated on aggregate by the Spanish side, this time in the semi-final.

Athletic Bilbao's admirable performances had been against three of Europe's best clubs, and the Basque team had scored sixteen goals. But the club was out of the European Cup, and it was to be twenty-seven years before Athletic made its next appearance in the competition.

***

In 1936, the Andalucian capital of Seville had been the first major southern Spanish city to fall to the Nationalists. **Sevilla** won the Copa del Generalisimo in 1939, beating Racing de Ferrol 6–2. Sevilla's forward line – insensitively called 'los stukas', after the ground attack bombers of the Luftwaffe's Condor Division which had ravaged so much of Spain in the Civil War – scored 216 goals in four seasons in the early- to mid-1940s, and Sevilla claimed its first and only Liga title in season 1945/46.

Club president Ramón Sánchez had left the club to manage RFEF in 1941, and he returned in 1946. Sevilla lifted its second Copa in 1948 in a 4–1 defeat of Celta de Vigo, and was riding high in La Liga, achieving second place in 1950/51. In 1953, Sevilla had hired Argentinian-born coach Helenio Herrera (of whom, more later). His obsessive managerial style had laid the foundations for another second place in La Liga in 1956/57 for the Andalucian club.

Real Madrid had won La Liga but qualified as cup holders, so Sevilla entered the 1957/58 European Cup as domestic league 'champions'. The new competition's escalating appeal was such that twice as many spectators had turned up for the previous season's games as had attended during the opening season, and a further ten European countries had entered the European Cup.

Attendances had also shot up. For Sevilla's first-leg home game against Portugal's Benfica, over 40,000 people crammed into the Stadio Nervión to watch the home side win 3–1. In Lisbon, a 0–0 draw was seen by a crowd of 50,000. The European Cup was filling stadiums across Europe.

An aggregate 4–2 defeat by Sevilla of Denmark's Aarhus followed in the second round. It was all looking good for Sevilla until they had the misfortune to land Real Madrid in the quarter-final. In late January 1958 at the Bernabéu, and in front of 80,000 madrileños, Sevilla crumbled in the face of a typically lethal Real onslaught. Di Stéfano helped himself to four goals and Kopa put away two in a 8–0 humiliation of Sevilla. The thoroughly dispirited visitors, aware that they were already beaten, let in three goals in the final ten minutes of the game.

The crowd for the second leg in Seville was noticeably, and unsurprisingly, smaller than in the club's previous European games, although Sevilla managed a 2–2 draw against the mighty Madrid machine, keeping the aggregate score to 10–2 and leading to the departure from the competition of the humbled Andalucians. Fifty years were to pass before Sevilla again summoned up the nerve to compete in the European Cup.

Since then, and aside from three seasons, Sevilla has been a constant presence in La Liga to the present day. And, as Part Five will reveal, the club was to have dramatic success in the twenty-first century in Europe.

***

The following season, 1958/59, was the turn of **Atlético Madrid** to attempt to topple its city neighbour from its European Cup throne. Atlético made a more spirited effort than did Sevilla, perhaps buoyed by their 13–1 stroll against Ireland's Drumcondra in a newly instituted qualifying round. Although the following round required a play-off against Bulgaria's CDNA Sofia, Atlético won this 3–1, and followed up with a comfortable 4–1 defeat of Schalke in the quarter-final.

Atlético's opponent in the semi-final was, naturally, Real Madrid. In the first leg, with Real roared on by a crowd of 120,000 in the Bernabéu, strikes by Rial and Puskás cancelled out Atlético's opener. In the second leg at Atlético's old Metropolitano Stadium, striker Enrique Collar – who was to make 470 appearances for the 'colchoneros' in his seventeen-year stay at the club – scored the only goal in a triumphant 1–0 victory for Atlético.

With the aggregate score 2–2, a play-off was contested in Zaragoza. Di Stéfano scored early on, the goal was immediately equalised by Collar, but Puskás hit the winner. Real Madrid were again through to the final. However, the win at the Metropolitano was Real's first defeat in the European Cup and it remains Atlético's only victory over Real Madrid in any European competition.

The 'mattress makers', however, soon gained revenge on the 'meringues' in domestic competition, and Atlético had not yet finished with Europe. In 1960 and 1961, the club defeated Real Madrid in successive Copa finals, although it could be said in Real's defence that their players' minds were focused on more elevated matters.

Nevertheless, in 1961/62 Atlético were back in Europe, specifically in the European Cup Winners' Cup, a tournament which had begun the previous season, when Italy's Fiorentina were the victors over Scotland's Rangers. This new tournament, contested between European national cup winners, was similar in format to the European Cup, and it was formally recognised this season by UEFA.

Such was the success of the European Cup that UEFA may have thought that the Cup Winners' Cup would replicate the public appeal and generate the mass enthusiasm of the former. However, by their nature knockout competitions do not always reveal a country's top club, and this was the case with the new competition. Consequently, this tournament, although welcomed by European football fans, never quite attained the prestigious heights achieved by the European Cup.

However, the tournament did provide Atlético, now coached by Real Madrid ex-manager José Villalonga, with its first European trophy. The club's journey to the final was achieved by beating Sedan, Leicester City, Werder Bremen and Motor Jena, all worthy clubs but lacking the public recognition and perceived glamour of the league champions in the European Cup.

At Hampden Park on 10 May 1962 Atlético Madrid met Fiorentina in the final, watched by a crowd of under 30,000 which, compared to the 130,000 who packed into the same ground to watch Real Madrid's dazzling exhibition only two years previously in the European Cup final, indicates the lower level of public interest in the new competition. Or maybe there was a tram strike in Glasgow.

Atlético's Joaquin Peiró, an inside-forward nearing the end of a long career with the club, opened the scoring. Fiorentina equalised and the game ended 1–1. Remarkably, it took four months to organise the replay, which took place in Stuttgart on 5 September. Stuttgart did not possess a tram service, so the crowd was larger, around 38,000. Peiró scored again in Atlético's 3–0 victory, and the 'rojiblancos' became the second European club to collect the gleaming new trophy.

Atlético again reached the Cup Winners' Cup final in 1962/63, the following season – defeating, en route, solid but somewhat unglamorous clubs, these being Hibs, Botev Plovdiv and Nürnberg – but the Spanish team collapsed 5–1 in the final to a resurgent Tottenham Hotspur. However, the club's victory in the 1961/62 European Cup Winners' Cup final is of major importance to Atlético Madrid, as it is a European trophy which its illustrious city rival has never won and, given that the tournament's life ended in 1999, is never going to win.

***

If one were to ask someone who knows a bit about European club football, and has no partisan axe to grind, if he or she could list the three most memorable/exciting/revolutionary events and/or unforgettable performances in the history of the competition – the three things which stand out above everything else that has happened over the last seventy years or so – it's a fair bet that at least one of the following three will, or should, figure on every list.

These are, in no particular order:

• Celtic's exuberant 2–1 hammering of an increasingly terrified Inter Milan in Lisbon in the 1967 European Cup final, a game which, within ninety minutes, initiated the death throes of 'catenaccio' and witnessed the re-emergence of joyful, attacking football in Europe.

• Johan Cruyff's introduction of 'Total Football' into the European club game, when his Ajax team – Neeskens, Krol, Mühren, Keizer, Haan et al. – bewildered virtually every other team in Europe in the early 1970s by showing that, for all its apparent complexity, football is a simple game if you know what you're doing.

• The utter domination of club football in Europe by Real Madrid when winning five European Cups in succession from 1956 to 1960 through the obvious expedient of filling every position in the team with the finest available player, and then telling your genius playmaker to do what he wants.

As this book is concerned with Spanish club football, I will here concentrate on Real Madrid (although Cruyff and his deeds at Barcelona will appear later), and on the obvious truth that, if you have in your team a selection of the world's most talented players, who play not for themselves but for the team, and the whole shooting match is led by Alfredo Di Stéfano, then you will, barring occasional accidents, be unbeatable.

This is essentially what happened at Real Madrid during their magical era all those years ago. As many readers will be aware of this, I will try not to dwell overlong on the team and its players. But, as any discussion of Spanish football would be woefully incomplete without at least a brief description of Real Madrid's golden era in European football, here is what happened.

Real Madrid: the greatest?

There are some commentators who argue that, in relation to today's game, the general pace of football was more relaxed and slower at that time, that defences were poorly organised and porous, and that the tactical development of the game was relatively primitive.

This being so, continues the argument, today this particular Real Madrid team would be regarded as a no-more-than-average European side, so it is invidious to claim that, over this period, Real can be described as 'the greatest-ever club football team'.

The first thing I would suggest to these commentators is that they get hold of a video of that 1960 European Cup final and marvel at the speed, intelligence, passing talents and all-round footballing vision of Real Madrid, as these players bewildered

---

Eintracht Frankfurt while managing to score seven goals. This should make critics rethink the points they make. If not, I answer their observations below.

There may be an element of truth in the observation about the game being more 'relaxed', but most of the top European sides beaten by Real were of at least a sufficiently high quality to give any of today's leading European clubs a more than decent game. So what does this say about Real Madrid?

Defensive formations in the 1960s were probably less rigidly organised than is the case today – and that's far from being a criticism, given how frequently tedious is much of today's defensive game – although it would be difficult in modern football to find as complete and effective a defender as, for example, Real's José Santamaria. And there were plenty of other tough and intelligent defenders, in Real Madrid and in other teams of the time, who would have been able to confound and disarm, with ease, many of today's superstar 'galacticos'.

I agree that, in the 1960s, in most football teams, forwards assumed and were granted a priority over their defenders, and there were usually five forwards in a side. However, isn't attacking play and scoring goals the whole point of football? Old-style wingers and dribbling, elusive inside-forwards may be considered a luxury in today's game but, at their best, they were mesmerising and could create and score plenty of goals. A stout rearguard can frustrate the opposition but I, for one, have rarely felt elated when watching a nil-nil draw.

As for tactics, it is fair to say that top European club football then was at least twenty years ahead of the British game – and often involved British managers – and the leading coaches certainly knew what they were doing. Whoever it was who said, 'They are playing a game with which I am not familiar,' was betraying his/ her own lack of knowledge and grievously underestimating the tactical nous of players with such clubs as Real Madrid, Athletic Bilbao and Barcelona, and most other leading clubs in Spain and Europe, who were well aware of what was required of them on the pitch.

Even if one accepts these criticisms, one can confidently state that Real Madrid was virtually unbeatable in Europe over this five-year period. In the club's home ground, the Santiago Bernabéu Stadium, which sometimes had 125,000 supporters waving white handkerchiefs, Real was undefeated in all sixteen of its European games between 1955 and 1960, an enviable record.

There is one question mark which could possibly be raised at Real's unrivalled status, and that concerns the format of the system. In a knockout tournament such as the European Cup, it was then entirely possible for a top club to reach the final by defeating three significantly weaker clubs, while stronger clubs often had to face each other before arriving at the final.

This would not only ensure the former club a relatively easy journey to the final, it would also eliminate some of the stronger competition. For instance, in the 1956/57 season, as we have seen, Athletic Bilbao had to play against Porto, Honved and Manchester United (by whom Athletic was narrowly eliminated). In the same season, Real had a preliminary round bye, Rapid Vienna (on paper, a win for Real although, in practice, it required a play-off) and Nice (a 6–2 win for Real), although Real had to face Barcelona in the semi-final. So, one could argue that Athletic were unlucky and that Real's final appearance required less effort.

However, fortune favours the brave and, over time, the disparate nature of the opposition tends to level out. And to win the Cup for five consecutive years requires a club to possess a degree of quality and talent which is well above the vagaries of chance.

In an era which produced many memorable, and occasionally brilliant, European club teams, Real Madrid over those five seasons was ultimately supreme over them all. That's good enough for me.

Real Madrid: European Cup, 1956 to 1960

None of it could have begun without Santiago Bernabéu's hiring in 1952 of a business manager, Raimundo Saporta, who was instrumental in overcoming the shenanigans involved in acquiring Di Stéfano. And none of it could have happened without Di Stéfano.

Real Madrid's manager, José 'Papa' Villalonga, joined the club in time for the first European Cup season, 1955/56. An ex-military man and a tough character, he was fortunate to inherit in his 1955/56 squad the Spanish defenders Miguel Muñoz, Juan Zarraga and Marcos Marquitos, and the two Argentinians Di Stéfano and Hector Rial, with Cantabria's own 'Paco' Gento on the left wing.

Real scored eleven goals on their way to the semi-final and, in a tough two-legged tie against Italian champions AC Milan, made it sixteen goals in their 5–4 win. The Spanish team faced France's Reims in the final in Paris's Parc des Princes, and an eightieth-minute Rial goal proved the winner in the 4–3 victory, Real's first European Cup. Reims' star forward, Raymond Kopa, had previously agreed to join Real Madrid for the 1956/57 season and, after the final, he remarked, 'After what I have seen in this game, I don't know why Real want me.'

The inaugural season had been even more successful than UEFA had imagined, with over one million spectators having attended the 1955/56 ties and with the spectacular tally of 127 goals scored.

In the following season, 1956/57, with Kopa in electrifying form on the right wing, Real met a defensive Fiorentina in the final, held at the Bernabéu, and, in a rather dull and unadventurous game, won 2–0. Real's captain Muñoz picked up Real's second European Cup, from General Franco.

By the start of the third European Cup season, Muñoz had retired (but was shortly to return as manager), Luis Carniglia had taken over as coach, and commanding centre-back José Santamaria had joined from Uruguay. In Real Madrid's canter to this, their third successive final, in the three aggregate ties they rattled in twenty-two goals, ten of which were against fellow Spaniards Sevilla (so much for national solidarity). In the final, held in the Heysel Stadium in Brussels against a resilient and well-matched AC Milan, the game remained 2–2 at the final whistle. In extra time Gento scored the winner for a 3–2 Real victory, and title number three was in the Bernabéu trophy cabinet.

Over the summer of 1958, Real's forward options were immeasurably strengthened by the arrival of Honved's and Hungary's ex-captain, Ferenc Puskás. The overweight, thirty-one-year-old political refugee silenced any possibility of sizeist or ageist criticisms by scoring twenty-one goals in his first twenty-four Liga games for Real Madrid. Although in appearance an unlikely sportsman, the 'Galloping Major' was the possessor of a remarkable footballing brain and of a left foot which was lethal when close to goal which, because of his brain's positional sense, was a frequent occurrence.

Again, Real Madrid reached the European Cup final in 1958/59. Having somewhat fortunately disposed of Atlético Madrid 2–1 in a semi-final play-off, Real found itself again facing Reims in the final, this time in front of 70,000 spectators in Stuttgart. The coach had dropped Puskás for this vital match but, in another lacklustre and uninspiring final, Real edged the game 2–0 to win the fourth European Cup. Reims was to be the last French finalist until St Etienne reached this stage seventeen years later.

Soon after the game, Kopa returned to Reims, and Muñoz returned to Real as the club's new manager. Other arrivals included Didi and Canário, both Brazilians. Didi, the star of Brazil's 1958 World Cup squad, returned to Brazil before the 1960 European Cup final perhaps because of homesickness but more likely because of his doomed attempts to outshine Di Stéfano, a man who was most unwilling to tolerate dethronement.

Muñoz, who was the first man to win the European Cup as a player and manager (after claiming the 1960 final trophy, Real's magnificent swansong), and who was to remain as Real Madrid's manager for almost fifteen more years, decided to go shopping. Before the Hampden game, he acquired from Osasuna the Cantabrian left-back Enrique Pachin to team up with Marquitos and to allow Santamaria more opportunity to roam upfield. He also acquired from Real Betis a creative, Andalucia-born inside-right, Luis Del Sol.

These two players were acquired by Muñoz just in time to make their mark, along with the other nine Real Madrid players, in the epic 1960s European Cup final. For the record, the 1960 fifth European Cup-winning Real Madrid team was laid out in a 2–3–2–3 formation (which is remarkably similar to the 2–3–5 system of my youth): *Dominguez – Marquitos, Pachin – Vidal, Santamaria, Zarraga – Del Sol, Puskás – Canário, Di Stéfano, Gento*

***

Barcelona resurgent

In the 1958/59 season's La Liga, Real Madrid had finished in second place behind Barcelona. Under new coach Helenio Herrera, Barça were mounting a challenge to Real's hegemony. Herrera was an Argentinian-born French national, who was an obsessive disciplinarian but also a charismatic motivator. In Spain, he had managed, with a good deal of success, Valladolid, Atlético Madrid, Málaga, Deportivo de La Coruña and Sevilla.

As Liga champions, Barcelona were making their debut in the European Cup, and began the campaign in style with an 8–4 win over CDNA Sofia and a 7–1 thrashing of AC Milan. The club was drawn in the quarter-final against English champions Wolverhampton Wanderers, a powerful, hard-running and direct team.

However, Wolves had no answer to Barcelona's superiority. Wolves lost 4–0 at home and 5–2 in Catalonia, Czibor scoring four in the latter game. Once again, a leading British club had been outclassed by the footballing quality and tactical sophistication of a top European side. Wolves manager Stan Cullis ruefully admitted, 'If we had to be beaten, I'm glad it was by a club like this.' The footballing lesson handed out by Barcelona demonstrated that English clubs had still to confront the glaring inadequacies of English 'kick and run' football and the long-ball game.

Before the semi-final against Real Madrid, a row between Herrera and Kubala over bonuses resulted in the manager dropping crowd favourites Kubala and his ally Czibor from the first-leg game. Real won both ties 3–1, and Barcelona were eliminated. Shortly after the games, a disappointed Herrera, blamed for the defeat, moved to Inter Milan, a club where he was to become a legend.

Barcelona, however, again won La Liga in 1959/60, having the same number of points and the same goal difference as Real

Madrid, but ahead by one goal in head-to-head matches. This is about as tight as it gets, even in La Liga. However, both clubs were back in the European Cup: Barcelona as Spanish league champions and Real Madrid as reigning holders of the trophy which, in recognition of the club's five in a row, was presented by UEFA to Madrid in perpetuity.

This gift of the trophy to Real by UEFA was the least the organisation could have done, given that a total of just over two million spectators had attended that season's European Cup games. The first six seasons of the tournament had far exceeded UEFA's expectations in terms of public enthusiasm and revenue earned, and Real Madrid's performances had been crucial factors in the establishment, critical recognition and mass appeal of the competition.

Real Madrid, however, were an ageing side, and this would inevitably have a negative impact on the pace of their game and on the quality of their football. Also, as well as a resurgent Barcelona, other quality clubs were emerging as potential champions, including Portugal's Benfica, the 'Eagles of Lisbon', managed by the much-respected Hungarian coach, Bela Guttman.

Many observers were predicting that Real would struggle to make the 'six in a row', for which Bernabéu, the eternal optimist in footballing matters, had hoped. And so it proved in the 1960/61 season, when Real's dominance finally came to an end.

In the first round, Luis Suárez scored both Barcelona's goals in the first-leg 2–2 draw at the Bernabéu, while in the return tie at Barcelona a dramatic flying header from Evaristo in the last few minutes gave Barcelona a 2–1 win. In what was to become a recurring and self-righteous litany from both clubs of 'biased' refereeing, chairman Bernabéu claimed that the presiding English official in the latter game was responsible for 'one of the greatest injustices in the history of Spanish football'. Meanwhile,

Evaristo simply stated the obvious: 'Madrid complained because they lost.'

It was inevitable, and had to happen sooner or later. Real Madrid had been eliminated from the European Cup, the competition the club until then had made its own.

Barcelona reached the final in Berne and faced the commanding defence and lightning attack of Benfica. Although Czibor and Kocsis scored for the Catalan side, the 'Eagles' won 3–2 and claimed the 1961 European Cup. For the first time, the Cup had left Spain but, to look on the positive side, it only went next door.

Inter-Cities Fairs Cup

I have referred earlier in this book to the 'Fairs Cup', and you may be wondering what exactly was this oddly named competition, what was its origin and what became of it.

Originally known as The International Industries Fairs Inter-Cities Cup (you can see why they shortened it), the Fairs Cup was the grandparent of today's omnivorous Europa League, although the Fairs Cup was never in its existence sanctioned by UEFA.

Under the organisers' stated aim of 'juxtaposing commerce and football' the tournament was open to all European cities which hosted an international trade fair. As there were sixty such fairs held annually in the continent, the Cup was potentially both inclusive and, importantly, highly profitable.

The Fairs Cup, initially set up as a league system followed by knockouts, kicked off in June 1955, three months before the European Cup, and was the first trans-European football tournament. (The Mitropa and Latin Cups don't count, in this respect, as they were geographically limited to particular areas within Europe.) A London XI, featuring various players including Fulham's Johnny Haynes and Arsenal's Cliff Horton, played the first match against a Basel XI (in reality, FC Basel) in Switzerland, and won 5–0, Horton claiming a hat-trick.

A Birmingham (Birmingham City FC) XI was eliminated by Barcelona in a play-off, and Barcelona, in the second leg of the final, beat London 6–0, thereby becoming the first holders of the Inter-Cities Fairs Cup. It was also the first European trophy in what is now FC Barcelona's bulging trophy room or, more likely, rooms. The fact that the tournament's first final was played almost three years after the commencement of the competition did not seem to bother the organisers.

In 1960 Barcelona also won the second Fairs Cup, which had now dispensed with a league stage. The number of potential entrants increased in 1961/62 when three teams were permitted to join from each European country. From then until 1967, Spanish clubs were dominant, featured Valencia (twice) and Real Zaragoza as winners, and then, in 1966, Barcelona won for the third time, beating Chelsea 5–0 in a final play-off.

The tournament was won by English clubs from 1968 to 1971, as Spanish clubs were busy competing in La Liga and more 'glamorous' competitions. From season 1971/72, the Fairs Cup became the UEFA Cup and finally came under the control of UEFA.

The Fairs Cup may have enjoyed a short, rather truncated existence, but it was the first donkey on the beach. It also, in 1966, introduced to football competitions the 'away goals' rule and, in 1970, the penalty shoot-out, the latter not making a World Cup appearance until Argentina in 1978.

If for no other reasons than these innovations, the tournament deserves credit. After all, fair's fair.

La Liga clubs, Europe and the 1960s

It occurs to me that, with my current concentration on Real Madrid and Barcelona, you may already have forgotten that there are, in La Liga, clubs which are not 'blancos' or 'blaugranas'. However, as I have mentioned before in this book, on occasion it's difficult to switch from Hamlet and Polonius to Rosencrantz and Guildenstern, as the last two make only fleeting appearances on stage during these particular years.

Nevertheless, it would be an affront to these splendid clubs if I continue to neglect them. So, before I return to the two big boys and their 1960s' adventures, here is an account of what the (temporary) supporting cast was up to in the 1960s and early 1970s. These clubs will soon come into their own, well before the final curtain falls.

***

Although Real Madrid won La Liga from 1960/61 to 1968/69 (except for Atlético Madrid's impertinent intrusion in 1965/66), Real picked up only one Copa del Generalisimo in the same period. Not even 'los merengues' could win everything, and anyway its attention was diverted elsewhere (as the club would no doubt say).

This decade saw the welcome return of Valencia and Atlético Madrid, the re-emergence of Español, Real Betis, Sevilla and Athletic Bilbao, and the arrival in Spain's footballing elite of Real

Zaragoza, Real Oviedo, Elche and Las Palmas. (I discuss the early years of these clubs in Part One, and their post-1929 domestic development, where applicable, in Part Two.) Between 1960 and 1970 these clubs featured in domestic or European finals, and/or they finished at least one season in La Liga's top three.

Despite the two aforementioned clubs, who were alternating the roles of school captain and head prefect, there were the glimmerings in Spain's footballing classroom of what one might tentatively describe as 'democratisation' within the Spanish club game.

The growing visibility and relative success of 'other' La Liga clubs between the mid-1960s and the present day was and is a function of several factors: the establishment and expansion of European tournaments, and Francoist Spain's encouragement to the clubs to take part; the increasing number of clubs, and not only national cup and league winners, who were invited into, or qualified for, these tournaments; the external corporate investments and sponsorships which were becoming available to larger clubs; the fact that clubs were becoming used to playing the larger European clubs, and their earlier feelings of inferiority were diminishing; the European successes of Real and Barça had raised the profile of Spanish club football in Europe and had shown to other Spanish clubs that, with enhanced self-belief and quality players, they too could achieve greater domestic and continental rewards; and, finally, the incontrovertible fact that Spanish clubs were fast becoming very good football teams.

***

After its successes of the 1940s and the free-scoring 'delantera electrica', **Valencia** had entered a period of relative decline which was arrested in 1970 with the appointment as coach of Alfredo Di Stéfano. Somewhat curiously for a once-lethal striker, as a coach

Di Stéfano had developed into a cautious, defensively inclined tactician. Nevertheless, in his first season the Argentinian legend managed Valencia to its first Liga title since 1946/47, and in the following season of 1971/72 the club was runner-up in La Liga behind Real Madrid.

In European competition, Valencia were early achievers, at least in the Fairs Cup. In 1961/62, having destroyed MTK Budapest's chance of reaching the final with an emphatic 10–3 aggregate win in the semi-final, a final 7–3 defeat of Barcelona brought Valencia its first European trophy. Its second European silverware arrived the following season, when the club dispatched Yugoslavia's Dinamo Zagreb in the final.

In 1963/64 Valencia again reached the Fairs final and almost made it 'three in a row', but a revitalised Real Zaragoza claimed the title. The club's 1970/71 Liga win gave Valencia its first taste of the European Cup competition the following season, but it was eliminated in the second round 3–1 by Budapest's Ujpest Dozsa, possibly in revenge for the damage Valencia had inflicted on Dozsa's Hungarian city neighbour ten years previously.

But all was far from lost. Within a few years Valencia was to distinguish itself not only domestically but also in the European Cup and the Cup Winners' Cup, as this book will later reveal. Valencia is regarded, with good reason, as one of the enduring top five clubs in Spain.

***

Sitting beside the River Ebro in north-eastern Spain, Zaragoza is the capital city of the community of Aragon, once a medieval kingdom.

'Zaragoza' derives from 'Caesaraugusta', as the existing settlement was named 2,000 years ago by its Roman occupiers. The nickname of the city's football club, **Real Zaragoza**, is further evidence of the city's Roman influence, as the club is known as 'Los Maños', from the Latin '*magnus*' ('great').

Having sampled top-tier football but almost immediate relegation in the first five seasons from the club's foundation in 1932, when Real Zaragoza was again promoted from Segunda in 1956/57 it became virtually ever-present in La Liga from then until 2012/13. Today, however, it resides in Segunda, the club's home for the previous six seasons.

Despite this no-doubt temporary lapse, in recent years Real Zaragoza has become a familiar name in Spanish and European football. Although in 1956 it professed few claims to footballing celebrity, this all changed in the club's first era of domestic and European renown, the 1960s, when Real Zaragoza won two Copas and the Fairs Cup. Also, between seasons 1960/61 and 1968/69, Zaragoza ended each season in La Liga's top five but, perhaps surprisingly, the club never landed the ultimate title during these years.

It is said that if you remember the 1960s then you couldn't have been there. But Real Zaragoza was most certainly there, and remembers the decade as one of the finest periods in its history. In 1960/61 Zaragoza ended the Liga season in third place, and the following season the club managed fourth, with the club's Peruvian striker, Juan Seminario, winning the Pichichi award for his twenty-five goals in thirty games in the then sixteen-club Primera División. Zaragoza also reached the final of the Copa del Generalisimo in 1963 but lost 3–1 to Barcelona.

Season 1963/64, in particular, was unforgettable. Under the initial managerial guidance of ex-Barcelona keeper Antoni Ramallets, and having signed from Sevilla the ex-Real Madrid Brazilian forward Canário, Zaragoza won the Fairs Cup and the Copa. The club's forward line – Eleuterio Santos, Juan Villa, Canário, Marcelino and Carlos Lapetra – was dubbed 'Los Magnificos'. Zaragoza defeated Atlético Madrid 2–1 (Lapetra,

Villa) in the Copa final and Valencia 2–1 (Villa, Marcelino) in the Fairs Cup final.

Winning both cups was a remarkable performance by Real Zaragoza, and the club were also Fairs Cup finalists in 1966 but lost to Barcelona over two legs. However, the club secured its second Copa in 1965/66, beating Athletic Bilbao 2–0 (Villa, Lapetra).

This was effectively the end of the 1960s triumphant period for Real Zaragoza. In the 1966/67 Fairs Cup the club was knocked out by Glasgow club Rangers, after a dogged 2–2 stalemate was decided by the simple expedient of tossing a coin. This then-common method of settling a game was and is as accurate and as fair a method of deciding on a winner, as is today's penalty shoot-out. (Why should one player – the keeper – be blamed if he misses a crucial save in what is a team game? What about the mistakes made and opportunities lost by the other ten players over the previous 120 minutes?) Also in those days of strict alcohol licensing, with coin-tossing there was the added benefit that one could leave the match before the pubs shut.

However, as with Valencia, 'Los Maños' would soon be back in contention, and the club were to add another European cup to their trophy cabinet, as we will shortly discover.

***

If the Spanish football authorities ever decided to offer a prize to the most unpredictable club during the first thirty years of the national league, then it's a safe bet that **Real Betis Balompié** would walk away with it. Betis could keep the award in its boardroom cabinet which currently contains its Tercera, Segunda and Primera titles, as well as its two Copa del Rey cups. A haul such as this well demonstrates a club's battling credentials.

However, since 1959 Betis has more or less settled in La Liga, but it took some while to get used to the Primera. From time to time the club still wanders downstairs, but it normally clambers quickly back to La Liga, where its distinctive green-and-white strip is easily recognisable.

Although green and white is an unusual colour combination for a European league home strip, it is favoured by, among others, Celtic, Feyenoord, Ferencvaros, Rapid Vienna and even Racing de Santander. Indeed, Betis say that it adopted Celtic's 1911 strip, and that the green was maintained as homage to the club's 1930s Irish manager Patrick O'Connell. However, most of these other clubs wear hoops (one of Celtic's nicknames is 'the Hoops') or horizontal bands of some type, and I cannot think of any senior European club, other than Real Betis, which today wears vertical green and white stripes.

However, putting these observations to one side, when last I mentioned Real Betis in this book the club had secured its only Liga title in 1934/35 under O'Connell's managership, just three years after it had won Segunda. The Civil War then intervened and, shortly after the conflict's conclusion, Betis had managed to retain only two players from its 1934/35 Liga-winning side. Betis remained in La Liga for one season (1939/40) and its footballing fortunes then entered into a slow but steady decline.

The club was relegated to Segunda in 1940/41 and, apart from one season back in La Liga, the Segunda was where it remained until the end of 1946/47, when it slid down another tier into Tercera. For the following seven years the Seville club existed in the third tier. This was an era in which Betis endured much troubled soul-searching, as well as patronising ribaldry from Sevilla fans.

But with the support and determination of club president Manuel Ruiz Rodriguez, Betis was back in Segunda for 1954/55. Then Rodriguez, wearied by the struggle, resigned that year and was replaced by Benito Villamarín. Clearly a man of some substance, Villamarín steered the club back into La Liga for 1958/59. Betis then enjoyed a relatively successful eight successive years in Primera, finishing in third place in 1963/64.

In 1961 Villamarín had bought for the club its stadium, the Heliópolis – the ground Betis had been using since 1929 – and embarked on a series of improvements. The ground was then rechristened the Estadio Benito Villamarín, shortly before the chairman resigned in 1965 and the season before Betis was again relegated. It was time for another period of self-examination.

By the early 1970s, however, Betis was establishing itself, albeit with some initial setbacks, as a regular member of La Liga. The club won its first Copa del Rey in June 1977, defeating Athletic Bilbao at Atlético Madrid's Vicente Calderón Stadium. However, as one might expect from Betis, it was a nail-biter of a finish. With the final score tied at 2–2, Betis won 8–7 on penalties, with twenty-one penalties required before it was declared the winner.

The following season, Betis found itself in European competition for the first time in its history, and celebrated with a first-round 3–2 aggregate defeat of mighty AC Milan in the Cup Winners' Cup, only to lose to Dinamo Moscow in the quarter-final. At the end of the season, 1977/78, the club was relegated to Segunda, but it bounced back up again to La Liga the following season. And so on it went. The stubborn determination of this remarkable club is wholly admirable and, as one would expect, Real Betis will be back in Part Four of this book.

***

Through the 1940s and 1950s, La Liga was the province of Spain's top five clubs – with Sevilla making an occasional guest appearance – who dominated the top three positions. It was a similar story in the Copa del Generalisimo, which was claimed every season by the same big five, except in 1940 and 1948 when **Español** and then **Sevilla** picked up the trophy. (Español, incidentally, holds the record, if such it can be called, of being the club which has spent most seasons in La Liga [eighty-one] without having ever won the title.)

However, the losing Copa finalist during these years was not quite so predictable, although Español was beaten on three occasions in the final. Other clubs which shared this second-placed Copa 'honour' were Celta de Vigo, Real Valladolid, Real Sociedad and Granada.

***

Celta de Vigo met Sevilla in the 1948 Copa final and, although the Galician side opened the scoring, the game ended 4–1 in Sevilla's favour. Otherwise, it was Celta's most successful season to date, as the club finished in fourth place, its highest-ever position in La Liga, and Celta striker Pahiño was the highest Primera scorer that season. The club was to equal this fourth place in the opening years of the twenty-first century, during the brief period it also became a respected force in European football.

***

Champion of Segunda in 1947/48, **Real Valladolid** found itself for the first time in La Liga where, coached for its inaugural Primera season by the ubiquitous Helenio Herrera, the club from Castile and Léon was to lodge itself for ten successive years. At the end of its second season, 1949/50, it lost 4–1 to Athletic Bilbao in the Copa final at Real Madrid's Chamartin Stadium. At the end of its tenth La Liga season Valladolid was relegated, and bumped up and down for the next few decades, although it did play in Europe towards the end of the twentieth century. (In 2018, Brazilian ex-international striker Ronaldo, who had played for Barcelona and Real Madrid, acquired a 51%

shareholding in Real Valladolid, so one can probably expect some positive developments from this 'yo-yo' club.)

***

During the Second Republic, San Sebastián's **Real Sociedad** had adopted the name 'Donostia', the Basque name for the city. Until the early 1980s, the club operated a similar 'cantera' policy regarding player selection to Athletic Bilbao.

Real Sociedad had won the Copa del Rey in 1909, and had been runner-up in 1910, 1913 and 1928. It became a losing finalist in 1951 for the fourth time, having put three past Real Madrid with no reply in the semi-final, but suffering the reverse scoreline from Barcelona in the final.

In the decade prior to this – the 1940s – the club was relegated and promoted between Primera and Segunda on no fewer than seven occasions. However, from then until the present day, aside from two relatively brief sojourns in Segunda, Real Sociedad has been a permanent fixture in Primera. Later in the book I will relate the club's 1980s successes in La Liga and its adventures in three European competitions.

***

What may be regarded by larger, self-regarding clubs as a mundane and even embarrassing conclusion to a tournament may be, for others, an aspiration, and one devoutly to be wished, with its achievement a landmark in the club's history. The latter was the case with Andalucia's **Granada** when it reached, for the first time, the final of the Copa del Generalisimo in 1959.

On its way to the final, Granada beat Elche 9–6, Cádiz 10–3, AD Plus Ultra 7–2 and, in a semi-final tie-breaker, Valencia 3–1, all scores being aggregate, but impressive nonetheless. Granada's

4–1 defeat by Barcelona (Kocsis scoring two of them) in the final probably did little to dampen Granada's enjoyment at the prestige of parading its players' talents in front of 90,000 spectators at the Santiago Bernabéu Stadium.

You may be wondering about the above-mentioned AD Plus Ultra. This was a Madrid-based club – Agrupación Deportivo Plus Ultra – which took the Latin 'plus ultra' meaning 'further beyond', from the Spanish national motto. In 1952 it became Real Madrid's reserve team, and it folded in 1972. Real Madrid Castilla then took over as 'los blancos' reserve team, and Castilla played in the 1980 Copa del Rey against its senior team, Real Madrid, having the good grace to lose 6–1. Reserve teams are no longer allowed to play in the Copa del Rey.

***

As this story now appears to be moving inexorably and unavoidably back to Real Madrid, Part Four will consider the club's virtual domination of La Liga during the 1960s. Between 1960/61 and 1968/69, 'los blancos' won every Liga title aside from one season – 1965/66 – when Real finished second to Atlético Madrid. Barcelona finished in second place in only four seasons, and the Catalan club managed only two Copa wins during the period.

However, other Spanish clubs were making their presences felt in the Copa and in European competitions in the 1970s and early 1980s, as we shall see in the following section of this book. But the 1960s in La Liga was effectively the story of Santiago Bernabéu's men.

PART FOUR

'TIME FOR CHANGE'

Historical context (1960–1986)

In the 1960s, Spain experienced an 'economic miracle', due mainly to the 1959 Stabilisation Plan and the rapid growth of the tourism industry.

The economic boom during this decade began to make modest inroads into narrowing the gap between rich and poor, and assisted in the growth and political influence of a professional middle class. There was a significant move away from economic dependence on the unreliable agricultural sector towards a greater emphasis on an industrial and service-based economy. This in turn accelerated emigration from the countryside to the fast-growing towns and cities which, although unemployment remained high, offered work in such successful industries as shipbuilding.

This increasing prosperity was accompanied by state investment in Spain's infrastructure, including the building of roads, railways and reservoirs, and the higher per capita incomes encouraged the emergence of a 'consumer society' in the country. More was spent on education, illiteracy rates fell, women were assuming a greater percentage of the workforce, state censorship of the press was abolished, and the power of the church was waning and was slowly evolving into a more secular society.

In 1970 the country signed a trade agreement with the EEC. Only eight years previously Franco had denounced moves in the direction of economic relations with the EEC, so times were changing, at least insofar as the state's position on international trade was concerned.

However, this apparently healthy economic background did little to appease the growing opposition factions within Spain to the Francoist regime. Politically, the most active and effective opponent was the Spanish Communist Party, which in 1948 had abandoned its armed struggle as a 'rupturista' (change from outwith the system) in favour of an 'aperturista' stance (change from within).

From the early 1950s, the CP began to ally itself with trade unions, and a series of strikes and workplace protests between 1962 and 1964 provoked violent reactions from the regime, the effects of which resulted in an even stronger opposition to Francoism. The Party was also instrumental in the creation of Comisiones Obreras ('Workers Commissions'), today's leading Spanish trade union with over one million members. Meanwhile, the Socialists preferred to wait and bide their time.

ETA emerged in the Basque Country in 1959 and was committed to regional independence through violent means. Before its renunciation of violence in 2011, ETA's 'war' against the Spanish state resulted in the deaths of hundreds of people, most notably in 1973 when it planted the car bomb which killed Admiral Luis Carrera Blanco, Spain's prime minister and Franco's political heir.

By the late 1950s, the Catholic Church, increasingly influenced by younger priests with no personal experience of the

Civil War, was beginning to distance itself from the regime. The Vatican also was becoming aware of demands for human rights, was concerned about an increasingly pervasive secularism, and was issuing encyclicals to accommodate these changes in social attitudes. Many Spanish priests and several bishops were inclined to apologise for the Church's role in the War, and 'curia priests' were involving themselves in trade unions and in workers' movements.

By early 1975, the opposition to Franco's rule had coalesced into Platáforma de Convergencia Democrática (Democratic Convergence Platform), a loose anti-Francoist coalition which included Basque and Catalan separatists but which had no room for the Communist and Socialist parties. The non-violent overthrow in Portugal of Salazar's dictatorship in April the previous year also concentrated minds on the possibility of establishing democracy in Spain.

The regime, however, continued with its brutal methods – including enforced exile, lengthy prison sentences and execution by firing squad – of dealing with certain opponents, protestors, activists and militant workers' groups. This incited further strikes and protests across Spain, as well as the withdrawal from Madrid of ambassadors from eight EEC countries.

However, attempts at reform by the ailing Franco would no longer be possible, as he died in his bed on 20 November 1975.

***

Prince Juan Carlos, whom Franco had designated in 1969 as his successor, was aware of the need within the country for sensitive and diplomatic action in the immediate aftermath of Franco's death. The monarchy is popular in Spain, and it was formally impartial during the Civil War so, although Carlos came under criticism from various groups for his caution, in 1976 his appointment of Adolfo Suárez as prime minister was generally regarded as a positive forward step.

As the regime had been a dictatorship by a military man rather than a fully structured military dictatorship, the state bureaucracy required minimal adjustment in a transition to democracy. In 1977 the Communist Party was legalised and the National Movement was dissolved. Parliament also approved non-governmental political activity, as well as the adoption of parliamentary democracy and a constitutional monarchy.

Spain's first general election for forty-two years was held in February 1978, and was narrowly won by a coalition of twelve centrist parties, the Unión del Centro Democrático (UCD). Compromise between left and right was now seen as essential for the establishment of a democratic Spain. In order to prevent a return to previous insurgencies and to minimise future vengeful activity, the Cortes passed the 1977 Amnesty Act which included the controversial 'Pacto de Olvido' ('Pact of Forgetting').

Such a policy was deemed necessary to promote 'national reconciliation', and it was designed to ensure that responsibility for the suffering and crimes committed during the Spanish Civil War and in its aftermath was not placed on any political or social groupings.

Partly as a result of the 1974 oil price rise, the country's economy plummeted, with inflation and unemployment soaring and the peseta again devalued. A solution had to be agreed by all political parties in the overall Spanish interest, but constitutional interests were, in the meanwhile, paramount.

The 1978 Constitution consolidated the role of the monarchy, established universal suffrage and a two-chamber Cortes, created Spain as a unitary state but one subdivided into seventeen quasi-federal Autonomous Communities and, importantly, declared 'there shall be no state religion'.

The February 1982 general election was a turning point in

Spanish modern political history. As the election approached, the UCD coalition collapsed under the burden of its internal contradictions and factionalism. With a voter turnout of more than 80%, the left-reformist Partido Socialista Obrero Español (PSOE) (Spanish Socialist Workers' Party), led by Felipe González, won 48% of the vote.

The PSOE electioneering slogan – 'Por el cambio' ('Time for change') – had struck a chord with the weary and jaded voters. Democracy had finally been achieved in Spain, and the PSOE was to govern the country for the following fourteen years.

***

Real Madrid in Europe, 1961–1966

While all these profound developments were occurring in the real world, back on the football pitch it was more or less the same old story.

Although the 1960s was a domestic league virtual walkover for Real Madrid, the club was beginning to encounter problems in the European Cup. In 1961/62 – the season following the club's embarrassing first-round elimination by Barcelona – things perked up a bit. Putting twelve past Odense in the first round raised spirits, as did overcoming Juventus in a Paris quarter-final play-off. A semi-final 6–0 stroll past Standard Liège found Real in another final, this time in Amsterdam against the Benfica 'Eagles'.

In a fast, fluid and exciting game, described as 'the night of the long shots', Puskás scored three in the first half, becoming the only player to have scored two hat-tricks in separate finals, but Eusébio's two goals for Benfica within three second-half minutes brought a second successive title back to Lisbon in a 5–3 win. Season 1962/63's European Cup ended abruptly for 'los blancos', knocked out 4–3 in the preliminary round by Anderlecht, but Real reached another final the following season after having won 1963's La Liga by twelve points.

Kidnapped

In 1963, if I had been running Venezuela's Armed Forces of National Liberation (FALN), I'd have thought of someone else to kidnap other than Alfredo Di Stéfano. His predilection to self-absorption and to running the show would have made him an uncomfortable roommate. The FALN had first considered Igor Stravinsky who was also in the country, but an octogenarian might have died on them and they didn't want that. So Alfredo it was.

Di Stéfano was in Venezuela with Real Madrid who were competing in a pre-Liga season tournament against Porto and São Paulo. At 6 a.m. on 25 August, four members of the left-wing revolutionary group, in the guise of anti-narcotic police, led Di Stéfano from Caracas's Hotel Potomac to a waiting van where they revealed their true selves, pointed a gun at him, and took the world's greatest footballer to a small hotel room.

Unsurprisingly nonplussed and not a little scared by this kidnap ('I thought they'd shoot me at any minute'), nevertheless Alfredo went along with it, as there appeared little else he could do. The leader, twenty-year-old Paul del Rio, explained that they wanted publicity and not a ransom (the snatch became world front-page news that day, so they achieved that), described FALN's aim (to protest against the authoritarian government of Venezuela's Rómulo Betancourt), and promised Di Stéfano that he would soon be released unharmed. The Real Madrid superstar then relaxed and played cards and dominoes for two days with his captors, after which he was given a clean shirt and released on the Avenida Libertador (appropriately) from where he hightailed it back to his fellow madristas. Jaunty as ever, Di Stéfano turned out for Real Madrid the following day and was given a standing ovation by the crowd.

In 2005 del Rio, by then a well-regarded artist and forgiven by Real Madrid, was flown to Spain in an attempt to film the captor and captive in a conversation about the good old days and to mark Real's continuing centenary celebrations, but Di Stéfano refused to play the game. I can't say I blame him.

Coach Miguel Muñoz, aware that Puskás and Di Stéfano were no longer in the first bloom of youth, began to rebuild his team after the Benfica game. Out went Del Sol to Juventus, and incomers included defender Ignacio Zoco (Osasuna), midfielder Lucien Muller (Reims) and inside-forward Amancio Amaro (Deportivo de La Coruña). Muñoz tried to acquire Pelé from Santos but was rebuffed, perhaps partly because of Didi's brief, unhappy experience at the club.

Having scored twenty-seven goals in reaching the 1964 final in Vienna, Real had the bad luck to line up against Herrera's Inter Milan, the prime exponents of 'catenaccio', a system where a sweeper played behind four full-backs and which was ultra-defensive in intent and in practice. Although blessed with such quality, attack-minded players as Jair, Suárez and Mazzola, Inter scored what they needed and then withdrew into defence. The Italian side efficiently and effectively closed down Real, and emerged 3–1 victors. However, ever the realist, Madrid captain Gento commented, 'There was no doubt Inter deserved to win.'

This was the last game Di Stéfano ever played for Real Madrid. Following a disagreement with Muñoz and Bernabéu's rejection of an extension to his contract, the relationship between the president and the player broke down irretrievably. The scorer of forty-nine European Cup goals for Real Madrid moved on a free transfer to Español in the summer of 1964. To replace his departed talisman, Muñoz promoted Ramon Grosso from the reserve side, and he also acquired young central midfielder José Martinez Sánchez ('Pirri') from Granada.

Outplayed and defeated 6–3 by Benfica in the 1964/65 quarter-final, yet another Liga title found Real Madrid back in the 1965/66 tournament. In the second round Real returned from the first leg in Scotland with a 2–2 draw against Kilmarnock, the Ayrshire club's only season in the European Cup. Santamaria and Puskás were dropped before the second leg, and that Scottish away game had been the final appearance in the European Cup for them both.

Madrid-born Manuel Velázquez replaced Puskás, and tough-tackling centre-half Pedro de Felipe arrived from Rayo Vallecano to take over from Santamaria. The two legendary players' advancing years had become a handicap to the team, and the club also had to bow to RFEF's ruling that only foreign players of Spanish parentage were permitted to play.

That season, Real Madrid reached the final with a young, all-Spanish eleven, which had Amancio to thank for his second-leg semi-final winner against Inter in Turin. Opponents Partizan Belgrade opened the scoring in the Heysel 1966 final but, with twenty minutes remaining, Amancio and young right-winger Serena each scored, to ensure Real Madrid claimed its sixth European Cup trophy. This game marked the end of an era, as it was not until 1981 that Real reached another European Cup final, and thirty-two years were to pass before the club again won the European Cup.

***

Real Madrid's 1960s domination of La Liga came to a halt, appropriately enough, in 1969/70, when La Liga title turned left at the traffic lights and ended up in the hands of **Atlético Madrid** for the first time in four years.

On the final day of that season, away to Sabadell, Atlético had to win to ensure that Athletic Bilbao would not overtake them. Around 15,000 fans travelled to Catalonia from Madrid, and 'los colchoneros' rewarded them for their support with a 2–0 win and La Liga title. Atlético had now embarked on its most successful period of the twentieth century.

Atlético was the only team other than Real to win La Liga that decade, and 'los rojiblancos' also ended three other seasons as runners-up. Real Madrid's exploits had seemingly worn out its players, and Real finished sixth in La Liga, behind Atlético, Athletic Bilbao, Sevilla, Barcelona and Valencia.

Atlético had won the Copa in 1965, and had beaten Real Madrid by a single point to claim La Liga in 1965/66. In Atlético's first appearance in the following season's European Cup, the club was knocked out 3–2 in the second round by Yugoslavia's Vojvodina after an extra-time play-off in Madrid.

Atlético Madrid were again in the tournament in 1970/71 but this time reached the semi-final, under the midfield direction of the long-serving Adelardo and with an attacking trio of Luis Aragonés, Javier Irureta and José Gárate. Aragonés, known as 'Zapatones' ('Big Boots') for his prowess at free kicks, was to end his playing career as the highest scorer in the club's history. Irureta and Gárate were Basques (Gárate was Argentina-born to Basque parents), with the former going on to become a successful manager and the latter winning three consecutive Pichichi awards between 1969 and 1971.

In Madrid, an Irureta goal separated Atlético and Johan

Cruyff's 'Total Football' Ajax side, but in Amsterdam for the return leg three goals from the Dutch without reply led to Atlético's departure from the tournament and to Ajax winning the first of the club's three European Cup titles in succession.

Atlético, however, had not yet concluded its 1970s' temporary resurgence, and the club entered the European Cup in 1973/74, having once more topped La Liga. New players – forward Rubén Ayala and defenders 'Panadero' Diaz (his dad owned a bakery) and Ramón Heredia – had arrived from Argentina.

The club also had a new Argentinian manager, Juan Carlos Lorenzo, a replacement for Max Merkel who had been sacked the previous summer. Lorenzo had been the Argentina manager in the 1966 World Cup in England when, after his country's game against England at Wembley, English boss Alf Ramsey described the South American players as 'animals'.

In the competition, Atlético disposed of Galatasaray, Dinamo Bucharest and Red Star Belgrade, and faced Scottish champions Celtic at Parkhead in the first leg of the semi-final. Even the most ardent 'colchoneros' fan would have found it difficult to defend the Atlético players' tactics and behaviour during that game, but the Spanish club left Glasgow with a 0–0 draw. Back in Madrid for the second leg, a 2–0 defeat of Celtic found Atlético Madrid in the club's first European Cup final.

'Battle of Parkhead'

I find it difficult to recall a more cynical and disgraceful performance by any football team anywhere than that which Atlético Madrid displayed at Glasgow's Parkhead in April 1974.

The crowd of 72,000 was incensed by Atlético's behaviour throughout the game, as the Spanish team kicked, spat at and fouled the Celtic players, in particular little winger Jimmy 'Jinky' Johnstone, on its way to a goalless draw. Seven Atlético players were cautioned and three of them sent off as the team exhibited a blatant disregard for the laws of the game and the spirit of international club football.

A disgusted Jock Stein, the Celtic manager, said: 'It was never a match. It was a shambles.' After the game he and some of his players received death threats, and he tried unsuccessfully to move the second leg of the European Cup semi-final to a neutral venue. Twelve days later at the Estadio Vicente Calderón the return match kicked off, in front of a massive police presence, with six Atlético players suspended due to the Parkhead fiasco. The negative tactics of the first game were forgotten by the home side as Atlético eased its way to the final with goals from Gárate and Adelardo.

UEFA's powers were limited when it came to dealing with on-pitch behaviour, so the organisation could only offer a rebuke to the Spanish club, rather than the suspension from the tournament which many felt the club deserved for the 'Battle of Parkhead'.

But there were more than a few neutral football followers who were supporting Celtic in the return game in Madrid.

The 1974 European Cup final was at Brussels' Heysel Stadium on 15 May against Bayern Munich, the first German club to reach this stage since Eintracht Frankfurt in 1960.

In a close, absorbing match, the score was 0–0 at full time. In the 113th minute Atlético's midfield general Luis Aragonés curved a splendid free kick past Sepp Maier in the Bayern goal. With only seconds remaining, German defender Hans-Georg Schwarzenbeck shot speculatively from forty yards, and the ball eluded the unsighted Atlético keeper Miguel Reina for a Bayern equaliser and Atlético's dismay.

The European Cup's first final replay was held two days later in the same stadium. Atlético's midfield playmaker Javier Irureta was suspended, having been booked at Parkhead and again in the first game of the final. Bayern, however, were at full strength, and two goals apiece from Gerd Müller and Uli Hoeness – the latter's second strike finishing off his solo run from the halfway line – gave Bayern a 4–0 victory and the first of the West German club's three successive European Cup titles.

Atlético had again lost out on Europe's big prize but, despite the unfairness felt by their fans at the result of the first leg, there weren't too many people crying into their beer in the East End of Glasgow.

As well as their defeat in the European final, 'los rojiblancos' had to suffer the sight of their city rivals holding La Liga title for the following two seasons, although Atlético did lift the Copa in 1976 for the fifth time in the club's history, Gárate scoring the only goal of the final against Real Zaragoza.

Season 1976/77, however, saw Real Madrid inexplicably ending up in ninth place in La Liga behind such clubs as Las Palmas and Real Sociedad. One point above second-placed Barcelona sat Atlético Madrid, proud winners of La Liga for the eighth time. Asturian midfielder Marcial had joined Atlético from Barcelona at the start of that title-winning season. Curiously, he had the distinction of being the only player to have scored against Real Madrid for four different clubs, these being Elche, Español, Barcelona and, of course, Atlético.

In the 1977/78 European Cup the club reached the quarter-final where Marcial's two goals in Madrid against Bruges were insufficient to prevent Atlético's departure from the competition after a 4–3 aggregate defeat by the Belgians. Twenty years were to elapse before the club's reappearance in the tournament.

***

While Real Madrid had enjoyed a brief break from dominating the Spanish Primera, two other leading Spanish clubs had won the title, while a third club had suddenly appeared for the first time to occupy the third, then the second place in La Liga.

This new arrival in the top three was **Las Palmas** from the Atlantic island of Gran Canaria. In its fourth season back in La Liga, in 1967/68 the club achieved its highest placing in the top division since its foundation in 1949. The following season, Las Palmas secured second place behind winners Real Madrid. The club was fourth in 1977/78, and it remained in La Liga, apart from a couple of seasons, until its relegation in 1988.

During this balmy period, Las Palmas made it to a Fairs Cup and two UEFA Cups, with little progress in either. In 1978, it reached the only Copa final in its history but lost 3–1 to Barcelona. The first season of the twenty-first century, however, saw the club back in Primera, but since then Las Palmas have spent only another four seasons in La Liga. Maybe it's a bit too chilly up there.

***

With three La Liga titles already under its belt, **Valencia** had become more familiar with the altitude at the top of Primera, as the club gained its fourth title in 1970/71 and a runner-up medal in 1971/72.

Aside from winning the Copa in 1967, 'los che' had maintained a relatively low profile since their glory days of the

1940s. Although the club's Liga form remained indifferent during the 1970s, Valencia reached, and lost, three Copa finals in succession between 1970 and 1972, but re-emerged in the 1979 Copa final with a stylish and emphatic 2–0 win over Real Madrid and qualification for the 1979/80 Cup Winners' Cup.

Valencia had expanded its international squad with its acquisition in 1976 of Argentina's Mario Kempes and, two years later, West Germany's Rainer Bonhof. Bonhof, from Borussia Mönchengladbach, was a defensive midfielder with a powerful shot, and he had been a pivotal member of West Germany's 1974 World Cup final victory. Kempes, who arrived from Rosario, was a striker with a lethal left foot, which he had employed with great effect to score twice in Argentina's 1978 World Cup final extra-time 3–1 win over Holland.

In the Cup Winners' Cup both these players were in the Valencia team which beat an off-form Rangers 4–2 in the second round. In the second leg at Ibrox, the Rangers defenders were aware of Kempes' powerful left foot so they ensured the ball was limited to his right. In the seventy-eighth minute Kempes scored his second goal of the game with an unstoppable thirty-yard shot into the top corner of the net . . . with his right foot. Valencia then defeated a strangely quiescent Barcelona 5–3 and eliminated an impressive but defensively naive Nantes 5–2, as the club reached the final, where the opposition was Arsenal.

The game was fairly uneventful and remained goalless after extra time. Kempes and Liam Brady, arguably each club's best player, opened the penalty shoot-out. With the score 5–4 to Valencia, Arsenal winger Graham Rix had to score. Rix shot, but keeper Carlos Pereira guessed correctly and saved it. Valencia had won its third European trophy. 'Los che' would have to wait twenty years for the next one. And Graham Rix would prefer that people stopped reminding him of the game.

'Derby of the Ikurriña'

When Franco assumed power in 1939, one of his first acts was to ban regional languages, culture and, in the interests of 'national unity', any activity which might promote or celebrate regional difference. This legislation was aimed particularly at the troublesome Basque and Catalan regions. Included in Franco's ban was the display of the 'Ikurriña' – the red, green and white Basque flag – which was designed in 1894 as a symbol of the Basque people.

Although under the Second Republic the Basque lands (in 1936) and Catalonia (in 1932) had each been granted a form of self-government, this was anathema to Franco. His anti-regional laws were firmly policed and were one of the main pillars of Franco's centralised dictatorship.

Just over one year after Franco's death, Real Sociedad were about to play the local 'derby' against Athletic Bilbao. One of the Real Sociedad players, Josean Uranga, who was later to be sentenced to eight years' imprisonment for collaborating with ETA, smuggled a home-made Ikurriña into Real Sociedad's old Atocha Stadium before the game kicked off.

Real Sociedad's captain, Ignacio Kortabarria, was aware and approved of Uranga's activity, as were the Sociedad players. Before the game, he spoke of his intentions to the Athletic captain, José Angel Tribar, and Tribar informed him that he and his players unanimously supported Kortabarria's plan.

So it was, then, on 5 December 1976, that the two captains carried out the flag, held high by both men, into the Atocha Stadium, and placed it ceremonially on the centre circle while the ETA anthem 'Eusko Gudariak' ('Basque Soldiers') was played on the stadium's speakers.

Among the 16,000 spectators, who cheered, applauded and wept as the flag was again on public display, there were numerous policemen. As well as the pride felt by the players, there was a sense of trepidation and even fear surrounding this act of regional defiance, which remained illegal. The police, however, allowed the game to continue and took no action.

This de facto acceptance of regional expression was generally applauded throughout Spain. As the game was screened live on national television and watched by millions, the impact of the players' symbolic gesture on national sentiment was almost immediate. The following month, Basque local authorities requested legalisation of the Ikurriña, and by the end of January the flag was flying from Pamplona town hall.

In July 1979 the Spanish Prime Minister Adolfo Suárez agreed to self-government for the Basque and Catalan provinces, and guaranteed these provinces more powers than any other Spanish region. The law was enacted in October of that year, and regional nationalism reappeared on the Spanish political agenda.

The opening four Liga seasons of the 1980s witnessed the revival of the Basque Country and its return to La Liga's centre stage.

San Sebastián's **Real Sociedad** had, throughout its seventy-year history, won one trophy: the Copa del Rey in 1909, the year in which the club was founded. Since then, Sociedad, although a founder member of La Liga, had never finished in the top three of Primera and was regarded by many as a venerable but increasingly makeweight club.

However, as the 1970s drew to a close, 'La Real' was waking from its years of slumber and making its presence felt in La Liga by winning the Primera title in both 1980/81 and 1981/82.

Unlike Atlético Madrid and Valencia, both of whom had relied to a good degree on imported foreign players for their assault on the predictable and recurring hegemony of Real Madrid, Real Sociedad grew its own.

As with Athletic Bilbao, Real Sociedad had, since its foundation, adopted the policy of 'cantera' (Basque only) in its player selection. (This policy was dropped in the late 1980s when the Republic of Ireland international John Aldridge joined the club from Liverpool, and the club now has few such constraints when it comes to signing players.) Several players grew up and spent virtually their entire careers with Real Sociedad, including captain and centre-half Ignacio Kortabarria, midfield playmaker Jesús Zamora, inside-forward Roberto Lopez Ufarte, and striker Jesús María Satrústegui who became the leading goalscorer in the club's history and formed a productive scoring partnership with Zamora.

Two other players – winger Txiki Begiristain and midfielder José Maria Bakero – began their football careers with 'La Real' and played in the club's two title-winning seasons, before moving later to become valuable members of Barcelona's 'Dream Team' of the early 1990s.

Under manager and club ex-player Alberto Ormaetxea, Sociedad gave notice of its intentions when the club finished in fourth place in La Liga in 1978/79, and then in second place the following season, one point behind Real Madrid. Between April 1979 and May 1980, 'La Real' established a Spanish record, still unbroken today, of a thirty-eight game unbeaten run. In 1980/81 Real Sociedad won its first Liga, but although there was much rejoicing in the lands of the Basques at the Primera coming 'home' after a twenty-five year absence, it could hardly have been a closer contest.

On the final day of the season, Real Madrid was breathing down Sociedad's neck and winning its last match, while Sociedad needed one point to clinch La Liga. With only a few seconds remaining of its game away at Sporting Gijón, and 'La Real' 2–1 down, Zamora achieved instant Basque sainthood, and an unlimited lifetime supply of free drinks in San Sebastián, by levelling the score just before the final whistle blew. Although both clubs had the same number of points, and Real Madrid's goal difference was better, Sociedad won the title by virtue of being one goal to the good over Madrid in head-to-head encounters.

At the end of the 1981/82 season, joy was once again unconfined in San Sebastián as Real Sociedad repeated its title win, this time with a more convincing two-point margin over second-placed Barcelona. The club's gloss had been slightly tarnished the previous autumn after a first-round elimination by CSKA Sofia in the European Cup, but another Primera title win more than compensated for this mishap. Also, the club's run in its second foray into the European Cup was significantly more impressive than the first, as the team beat Vikingur, Celtic and Sporting Lisbon before being narrowly defeated 3–2 in the semi-final by Hamburg.

Real Sociedad had not quite finished its admirable run, as the club won the Copa in 1987, and the following season, it finished in second place in La Liga behind Real Madrid and was runner-up to Barcelona in the Copa. Since then, 'La Real', aside from three seasons in Segunda in the early twenty-first century, has been a consistent member of Primera but, to date, has been unable to replicate its successes of the 1980s.

***

Perhaps around the late 1970s there was something in the air in the north Spanish coast which contained a hint of rejuvenation, or an elixir of renewed vitality, for older football clubs in the area. The club which picked up the Basque baton from Real

Sociedad, and which won La Liga for the following two years, was Athletic Bilbao, an institution to which I will shortly return.

Meanwhile, along the coast and further to the west, the Asturian club **Sporting de Gijón** was also enjoying the most illustrious few seasons in its long history. Sporting is one of the oldest Spanish clubs, but since its foundation in 1905 it has never won either La Liga or the Copa. However, during this period it was not for the lack of trying.

The club had spent most of its life in Segunda, but in the mid-1970s to the mid-1980s it turned into a serious challenger in Spain and also made several inroads into European football. Sporting returned to La Liga in 1970/71 and, after it had been relegated for a season, it came roaring straight back in 1977/78 to finish fifth in Primera and qualify for the UEFA Cup.

The club was fortunate enough to have a number of more than decent and committed players. Sporting's defence contained the reliable left-back Cundi and Antonio Maceda, a commanding centre-half who would earn thirty-six Spanish caps, while up front roamed players of the calibre of Argentinian left-winger Enzo Ferrero and, perhaps above all, the striker Quini who had joined Sporting de Gijón as a young man.

Quini: another kidnap

When an unusual and unpredicted event occurs once, it's often considered an aberration. If it happens again, it then becomes a pattern or, at least, an emulation, particularly if the event involves the kidnap of footballers.

I mentioned earlier (pp.180-181) the kidnap of Alfredo Di Stéfano. Almost twenty years after Alfredo's hijack, another revered Spanish goalscorer was abducted. The first kidnap was for political reasons, and the second was, more prosaically, for money. Either such an abductive tendency exists within Spanish football (unlikely), or it was coincidental, or it was, more likely, inspired by the Di Stéfano incident.

In 2018 Sporting de Gijón's old ground was renamed El Molinón-Enrique Castro 'Quini', in honour of Oviedo-born 'Quini' who, between 1970 and 1980, was the club's all-time top striker during its headiest era. While at Sporting, the player picked up three Liga Pichichis as well as the Don Balón award for Best Spanish Player in 1978/79. Quini moved to Barcelona in the summer of 1980 for a more than substantial transfer fee and, while at Barcelona, he picked up two further Pichichis.

In early March 1981, Quini, like Di Stéfano, made national headline news when he was kidnapped at gunpoint by two masked men, forced into a van, and held captive for twenty-five days. After extended negotiations between the authorities and kidnappers, he was released unharmed. (In his absence, his new club Barcelona managed only one point from four games and its Liga challenge evaporated.)

It has been suggested that Quini may have developed 'Stockholm Syndrome' when in captivity, as he refused to press charges against his captors and he did not claim the five million pesetas payment for personal damages to which he was entitled. Unsurprisingly, in 1984 he moved back to the relative security of Sporting de Gijón where armed kidnappers are few and far between.

Quini was a footballing hero to many at national level (he gained thirty-five Spanish caps) as well as in Gijón, where he was named in 2016 as 'an adoptive son of the city'. His funeral in

Gijón in 2018 was attended by an estimated 14,000 people, an indication of the man's popularity in Asturias and beyond.

The season 1978/79 is regarded by all 'sportinguistas' – the name adopted by the club's anarchically cheerful and largest official supporters' group – as the finest in the history of Sporting Gijón.

Sporting ended that Liga season in second place, the highest it has ever reached, and later in 1979 the club beat Torino 3–0 in the UEFA Cup first round at the old Molinón Stadium although, in round two, Red Star Belgrade progressed in the competition at Sporting's expense.

(Curiously, although in the 1980s Sporting were adept at entering the UEFA Cup, they did not seem particularly keen on remaining there. In that decade, the club qualified for four further UEFA Cups and were knocked out in the first round in all of them.)

The following season concluded with Sporting de Gijón in third place in Primera. Sporting also reached two consecutive Copa finals in 1981 and 1982, but lost them both. At the end of the 1980s the club began to run out of momentum and, after it suffered a ten-year residency in Segunda before returning to Primera at the century's end, Sporting was again relegated to Segunda at the conclusion of season 2017/18. The club's 250 'peñas' ('supporters' clubs') deserve better than this, so let's hope the club returns quickly to Primera.

***

Athletic Bilbao remained the biggest and most successful club in the Basque Country, but a glance at the club's trophy cabinet at the end of the 1981/82 season would have made one seriously question the validity of this observation.

The two Madrid clubs, Real and Atlético, dominated Spanish club football in the 1960s and 1970s, with Real in charge and Atlético grabbing what was left over. 'The Lions' of Bilbao had not won La Liga for twenty-six long years, and had won only three Copas in the same period.

However, signs of a revival in fortune were appearing. Athletic Club had reached the 1977 UEFA Cup final, and had narrowly lost on away goals to Juventus. Two Liga titles in succession had been achieved by Basque neighbours Real Sociedad. And, most promising of all, in the summer of 1981 the club had appointed thirty-one-year-old Javier Clemente as manager, and the new boss's talents had helped the club to fourth place in La Liga in his first season.

Clemente was an ex-player with Athletic Club, whose career had been cut short by injury. A committed Basque nationalist, he knew well what was expected of him, and his knowledge of the 'cantera' was already producing positive results in his selection of some of the younger players. He had inherited top-class strikers Dani and Manu Sarabia but, while he appreciated the virtues of attack, he was at heart a conservative, defensively-minded coach who was happier to win games in a brusque, efficient manner rather than risk losing them through the adoption of stylish and attractive attacking football.

Clemente had brought in a young Antoni Zubizarreta, who was to become one of Spain's greatest goalkeepers. The centre of his defence was the menacing, hard-tackling Andoni Goikoetxea, and Clemente favoured two defensive midfielders, two centre-backs and a sweeper, as well as two midfielders to feed his attack. Pretty it was not, but it worked well for that Basque side.

The tactics of 'El Rubio de Barakaldo' ('The Blond from Barakaldo'), as Clemente was known, were applauded by the

Athletic support and appealed to the younger players from the 'cantera'. At the end of only his second season, 1982/83, he won Athletic Bilbao its first Liga title for twenty-seven years, and he and his team were celebrated across the Basque Country.

'The Butcher of Bilbao'

The thundering crunch of the tackle could have been heard in the furthest reaches of the vast Camp Nou Stadium.

It was 23 September 1983, and the small, extravagantly gifted Diego Maradona had arrived in Barcelona the previous summer. Midway through the second half of the clubs' first encounter of that Liga season, Barcelona were three goals ahead of Athletic Bilbao. Maradona had the ball at his feet when, from behind, the massive frame of Bilbao centre-back Andoni Goikoetxea savagely smashed into him, almost breaking his ankle. It was one of the most disgraceful and notorious tackles in Spanish footballing history.

'Goika', as he was affectionately known by his Basque fans, had a history of such indelicate encounters. This brutal assault resulted in Maradona's absence for three months as he recovered from what was perceived by Barcelona fans as a deliberate, but effective, foul, designed to prevent the Argentinian forward's increasing influence on his teammates and to eliminate a threat to Bilbao's second Liga title in succession.

Maradona was in agony as he was shepherded off the pitch, his footballing future in jeopardy. 'The Butcher of Bilbao' had done what he was paid to do, and the hatred between the clubs only grew more intense as they battled for the top spot.

Welcome to Spanish football, Diego.

In the post-Franco years, Catalonia and the Basque Country had much in common. The language and culture of both regions had been suppressed during the dictatorship but, in order to maintain what the post-Franco Spanish state viewed as the essential unity of Spain, the two regions had been granted a significant degree of autonomy in the 1978 Constitution. Although the Basques and Catalans each saw themselves as different and somehow 'special', there existed between them a co-operative solidarity and a mutual respect. Until it came to football.

César Luis Menotti, manager of Argentina's 1978 World Cup-winning squad, had taken over from Udo Lattek as manager of Barcelona, and had acquired the young Maradona from Boca Juniors for a world record fee of £5 million.

When the little Argentinian, wearing jeans and trainers, first wandered into the Barcelona dressing room, he was met with dismissive comments and jeers from the preening Barcelona players (Barcelona players specialise in preening). Diego said nothing, grabbed an orange from a fruit bowl and produced a masterclass in keepy-uppy and control, did the same with a pair of rolled-up socks, then replaced the objects where he'd found them and ambled out of the dressing room. From that moment on, the jeering stopped.

Unlike Clemente, Menotti emphasised similar skills to those of Maradona in his players, and Barcelona's seductive, attacking style could not have been more different to Bilbao's stolid, defensive and workmanlike attitude to the game. Politically and culturally, also, the two men were poles apart. With Real Madrid about to finish a deserved break in its trainer's corner, these two clubs were slugging it out with each other for supremacy in Spain, and this was obvious on the pitch.

That season, 1983/84, Clemente's Bilbao did it again. 'The Lions' finished the campaign level on points with a re-emergent Real Madrid, but one goal ahead on goal difference and one goal to the good in head-to-heads. Barcelona were third, one point behind the other two. It can be tight in Spanish football.

Athletic Club also won the Copa, and whom did Bilbao beat 2–1 in the final? Barcelona. In front of a 100,000 crowd at the Santiago Bernabéu Stadium, Endika Guarrotxena scored in the fifteenth minute, and 1–0 was the final score. The game is best remembered, though, for the mass punch-up between the players at the final whistle. Maradona headbutted Athletic midfielder Miguel Sola, and all hell then broke loose. Eventually, it came to an end, with a few on-pitch scores having been settled.

Athletic Bilbao came third in 1984/85 and again in 1985/86, but their time was over, as Clemente left for Español during the latter season and Real Madrid had arrived back on the scene. Since its historic double of 1983/84, Athletic has to date not won another Copa nor has it claimed a further Liga title.

As for 'Goika', he departed for Atlético Madrid in 1987 and profusely apologised for his infamous tackle on Maradona, but his boots from that game featured prominently in the display case in his front room.

***

With all this excitement having more or less concluded in the north of this fractious footballing country, it's a good time to travel south and east to discover what was going on elsewhere in La Liga.

In particular, as I wrote at the end of Part Three, the adventures of the chief conquistador, Real Madrid, deserve at least a mention, if only because they won six Liga titles in the 1970s to place alongside the eight they picked up in the 1960s. Before I turn to 'los blancos', however, the ups and downs in the same period of 'los blaugranas' are worth investigating.

When **FC Barcelona** won La Liga in 1959/60, it was to be its last title for the following fourteen years, although they were runners-up in six of these seasons. It then took the club a further eleven seasons to win its next Primera, and they were second-placed for four of them. So what had gone wrong?

The most obvious reason for the Catalan club's relative subordination was the fact that the main competition was of a more consistent and higher quality than Barcelona. On the rare occasions when the old enemy Real Madrid decided to have a brief rest, along came Atlético Madrid, Valencia, Real Sociedad and Athletic Bilbao to keep the Liga throne sufficiently warm for the inevitable return of Real Madrid.

In the first few seasons of the 1990s Barcelona would be ruling Primera but, during the preceding two decades, the club was a second-class traveller attempting to enter a first-class carriage. This was all the more galling as, when Barcelona did enter the European Cup as Liga champions in 1974/75, the club made it to the semi-final. Also, over these years Barcelona reached three European Cup Winners' Cup finals, and emerged as victors in two of them.

Barcelona won the Copa in 1963 and 1968, with the final of the latter being a 1–0 defeat of Real Madrid at the Bernabéu. The club also claimed the Fairs Cup in 1966. However, the financing of Camp Nou in 1957 left the club with little money to spend on new players. Fine younger players, such as 'Charlie' Rexath and Josep Maria Fausté, did emerge, but it was a relatively bleak decade for Barcelona, by the club's own standards.

At last, in 1973/74 Barcelona won La Liga again, and the title was largely down to the galvanising effect and the brilliant footballing brain of one man: Johan Cruyff, arguably the most innovative and accomplished footballer in the history of the game.

Cruyff signed from Ajax for a world record transfer fee of £980,000, having captained the Dutch club to three successive European Cup wins and having decided against accepting an offer from Real Madrid. Although reportedly Cruyff had said he couldn't play for a club associated with Franco, the player denied that this was the reason. However, this story went down well with Barcelona fans, as did Cruyff naming his son 'Jordi', the name of Catalonia's patron saint.

The major obstacle to Cruyff's arrival was not the Castilian club but rather the Francoist authorities' ban on foreign players, which had formally been in place, although frequently circumvented, since 1962. At Barcelona's legal insistence the ban was amended in May 1973 to permit Liga clubs a maximum of two foreign players each. Cruyff signed for Barcelona in August 1973.

The Dutchman, playing alongside Juan Manuel Asensi, Carles Rexach and Manuel Pina, was instrumental in Barcelona's capture of La Liga. At the season's end, Cruyff had scored sixteen goals, the club was an extraordinary ten points ahead of second-placed Atlético Madrid, and Barcelona's goal difference was fifty-one. Atlético's was nineteen. Best of all for the Catalan support: not only had a Cruyff-inspired Barcelona hammered Real Madrid 5–0 in February 1974 at the Bernabéu but also Real finished in eighth place, sixteen points behind Barcelona.

Cruyff was named European Footballer of the Year for his efforts that season, and was awarded the title again the following season, although Barcelona could only finish third behind Real Madrid. La Liga then set up camp in Madrid for the next five seasons. Cruyff left Barcelona for Los Angeles Galaxy in 1978, but he left behind him a rejuvenated football club.

Shortly after Cruyff's departure, the Catalans underlined the importance of his legacy by securing two European Cup Winners' Cups within four years. In 1979, Barcelona, accompanied by 30,000 supporters, travelled to Basel for the first final, where the team squeezed a 4–3 extra-time win over Fortuna Düsseldorf, the highest-scoring final in the tournament's history. Then in May 1982 at the Camp Nou, Barcelona gained its second Cup Winners' Cup trophy, defeating Standard Liège 2–1 in the final.

Off the pitch, in 1978 Josep Luís Núñez had been elected Barcelona president, the first president to have been voted into the post by the club's members. He was to remain in control for a further twenty-two years, and his sharp-eyed attention to expenditure and cost began to improve the financial situation of the club.

Barcelona, even with young Diego's brief couple of seasons at the club, won only one further Liga title and three more Copas in the 1980s. However, Johan's return as manager towards the end of the decade would make the club's 1970s mini-revival appear a nostalgic but distant memory, as Cruyff's 'Dream Team' was to sweep all before it in Spanish and European football.

***

As I have mentioned, the second half of the 1970s in La Liga belonged to **Real Madrid**. Although at the tail-end of the 1960s the club temporarily ceded to others its stewardship of the title, after a few seasons Real was back in charge: of the domestic game.

Europe was a different story, as the club seemed to have misplaced its final competitive edge in continental competition. Real reached three European finals between 1971 and 1973, and was the loser in all of them.

The club made its first appearance in the European Cup Winners' Cup final in 1971, and lost 2–1 to Chelsea in a replay. Then, having been eliminated in four European Cup semi-finals since its final win in 1966, the club made it to the European Cup final in 1981 and lost a disappointing game 1–0 to Liverpool.

The 1983 Cup Winners' Cup final was held in Gothenburg against Scottish champions Aberdeen, who defeated the Spanish club 2–1 through a John Hewitt header with only eight minutes remaining of extra time.

Despite Real Madrid's European shortcomings, in Spain from the mid- to late-1970s they won five Liga titles, including two Copa 'doubles'. Pirri remained as sweeper, with midfield variously patrolled by German internationals Paul Breitner, Günter Netzer and Uli Stielike, while up front were Amancio, Santillana and Juanito. English winger and goalscorer Laurie Cunningham was added to the mix in the late 1970s, but this all-star side appeared to lose the plot at the last stage in Europe.

In June 1978, Santiago Bernabéu died at the age of eighty-two. Bernabéu, who well encapsulated the description of 'one-club man', had been associated with Real Madrid in various capacities since 1911 and had taken over as club president in 1943. His death occurred when the 1978 World Cup finals was taking place in Argentina, and FIFA initiated a three-day period of mourning during the competition. He had been a right-wing Francoist sympathiser, but he was also a visionary and ultimately responsible for the survival and then the rise of Real Madrid to the peak of the Spanish footballing pyramid.

Awaiting its turn in the Real Madrid youth and reserve teams, however, was what came to be known in the second half of the 1980s as 'La Quinta del Buitre' ('The Vulture Squad'), young home-grown players who were to add a further dimension to Real Madrid's football and, by so doing, become madrileño legends.

Talking Spanish

Spanish is the most commonly spoken language in the world, after Mandarin Chinese. If your understanding of Spanish is patchy, here are a few selected words and expressions which you may come across in match reports ('atestados de fútbol') and television commentaries, and which may help you understand what's going on.

Campo de fútbol: a football ground
Partido de fútbol: a game of football
Balompié: football (literal translation)
Gol: goal
Equipo: team
Equipo ascensor: 'yo-yo' team
Temporada: season
Peña: official supporters' association (fan club)
Vestuarios: dressing room

Entrenador / técnico: trainer / manager
Portero: goalkeeper
Defensa: defender
Mediocampista: midfielder
Centrocampista: central midfielder
Media punta: number ten
Libero (barredor): sweeper
Forzara: forward
Delantero: striker
Extremo: winger
Capitán: captain
Arbitro: referee
Cantera: youth system

Fuera de jugo: offside

Tiro libre (faita): free kick
Tiempo añadido (suplementario): extra time
Descuento: injury time
Propia meta: own goal
Linea de meta: goal line
Saque de banda: throw-in
Saque de esquina: corner kick
Tanda de penalis: penalty shoot-out
Area: penalty box
Penal: penalty
Travesaño: crossbar

Pausa: dummy
Bloquear: to block
Internada: tackle
Ataque: attack
Tirar a puerta: shoot at goal
Meter un gol: score a goal
Sombrero: chipping ball over opponent's head
Targas defensivas: defensive play
Juego de posicion: passing game
Juego sin balon: off-the-ball play
Tarjeta roja / amarillo: red / yellow card
Expulsar un jugador: send off a player
Empate a cero: score draw

What many observers found frustrating in this period – the 1960s and 1970s – was the relative absence at the top of La Liga table of clubs from outside the 'big five'. As we have seen, a few clubs – such as Real Sociedad, Real Zaragoza, Español, Sevilla,

Las Palmas and Sporting de Gijón – had their moments, but these were brief glimpses compared to clubs like Real Madrid. The same was true in the Copa del Rey, with one-off appearances in this period for Real Betis and Elche.

Although the 'big five' continued to dominate in the coming years between the mid-1980s and the present day, other clubs began to figure more prominently in the Spanish league and cup and in European tournaments. These included Deportivo de La Coruña, Real Betis, Valladolid, Osasuna, Celta de Vigo, Getafe, Alavés, Villarreal and even the welcome arrival in a Copa del Rey final of Spain's oldest club, 'El Decano', Recreativo de Huelva. However, this was the case mainly in European competitions, as there was little change in the composition of the ruling elite in La Liga. The 'big five' were slimming down and being replaced by the 'big two': Barcelona and Real Madrid.

When one considers that, in the thirty-five seasons from 1984/85 to 2018/19, these two clubs won thirty La Liga titles, the footballing duopoly becomes apparent. The reasons for the continuing success of the big clubs – across Europe as much as in Spain – are obvious, and we don't need Bob Dylan to tell us that 'money doesn't talk, it swears' nor do we have to have read *Das Kapital* to understand the commercial imperatives which drive these mega-clubs.

As the financial rewards, particularly in the European game, became increasingly astronomic in scale, the money spent on players by the larger Spanish clubs grew proportionately, and the financial qualifications imposed on clubs for promotion to La Liga became correspondingly prohibitive. The smaller, financially troubled clubs, even in Primera, were often more concerned with survival than with success.

However, since the European Cup transmuted into the Champions League in the 1990s, and opened up qualification for the tournament to clubs who were not national champions, and as the other European competitions lowered their own entrance criteria and also widened their intake, there are today more clubs than ever before who are able to experience European football. These opportunities have led middle-ranking Spanish and other European clubs more or less to abandon the remote chance of winning their league, and instead playing for qualifying positions in the leagues for these European tournaments.

National cup competitions also offer the opportunity of entering Europe and, as the leading clubs increasingly regard these cups as secondary to the leagues, the knockouts are often, for smaller clubs, regarded as another route to the financial attractions of the European club game.

Despite this rather bleak perception of modern European club football, however, every so often the unexpected and unpredictable can happen, seemingly arriving out of nowhere, and can turn everything upside down. This is the story of just such an event, and involves a 'provincial' Spanish football club – Deportivo de La Coruña – whose performances and achievements, for a few years around the turn of this century, allowed smaller clubs again to believe in themselves and in the possibility that they too could succeed against the giants of the game.

***

The rise of Super Dépor

La Coruña (A Coruña in the local Gallego language) is the largest city in Galicia. This autonomous region in the far north-west corner of Spain and north of Portugal is far from the 'sun and sangria' tourist lands to the south and east, is a frequently rainy and bleak area, and is dominated by its coastline where the Atlantic Ocean meets the Bay of Biscay: 'Costa da Morte' ('Coast of Death').

Its football team, Deportivo de La Coruña, is one of the country's oldest clubs, formed in 1906. It enjoyed a successful La Liga period in the 1940s and early 1950s, and was the launching pad for local players Manuel Pahiño and Amancio Amaro, both to become renowned Real Madrid strikers, and Luis Suárez, later with Barcelona and Inter Milan and regarded as Spain's finest-ever footballer.

Thereafter, Dépor was a quintessential 'yo-yo' club, as it flitted up and down between the Primera and Segunda Divisións. At the end of the 1972/73 season, the club was relegated from Primera to Segunda. It remained there, even spending one season in Tercera, until it reached its nadir in the late 1980s, when a combination of poor results, structural and managerial failures, lack of direction and the club's mounting debt problems seriously threatened the continuing existence of Deportivo de La Coruña.

In 1988 at an open meeting of club supporters and members of this respected but small, financially strapped club, a new board of directors, headed by Augusto César Lendoiro, was elected. Shortly after the new board settled in, the financial situation and organisation of Dépor began to improve, as did the club's on-pitch performance. Club president Lendoiro was a wealthy and engaging ex-politician, with a bulging contacts book and a determination to resurrect the club, and he was assisted in his plans for Dépor by an ex-player and then manager of Deportivo, Arsenio Iglesias.

Dépor reached the Copa del Rey semi-finals the following summer. The next season, 1989/90, the club narrowly missed out on promotion from Segunda. However, by the start of the 1991/92 season Deportivo de La Coruña was back in La Liga, and the club was to remain in the Primera División for the next twenty consecutive years.

With Lendoiro's financial investment in new players, an

increasing number of whom were Latin American (the team of the 1940s/50s also contained several Argentinians), and a team otherwise composed mainly of young and veteran Spanish players, Dépor ended 1992/93 in third place in La Liga. As a result, the Galician club entered European competition for the first time in its history, although it lost to Eintracht Frankfurt in the third round of the UEFA Cup.

Brazilian international striker Bebeto, who was to gain seventy-five caps for his country, was lured from Vasco da Gama in the summer of 1992, and in his first season he formed a productive partnership with fellow Brazilian Mauro Silva and long-serving Spanish winger/midfielder Fran. Bebeto scored twenty-nine goals in that campaign and received the Pichichi award, while the team lost only four games and ended the season third in La Liga.

The following season, 1993/94, came down to the last game, and was the most dramatic finale to a Liga season for many a year. Dépor had led the league for most of the season, and on the final day the club was, along with Barcelona, ten points clear of Zaragoza and Real Madrid. Barcelona were ahead of Dépor on goal difference and on head-to-head encounters, but Dépor would win La Liga if the team beat seventh-placed visitors Valencia.

At Deportivo's Riazor Stadium on 14 May, 34,000 'Turcos' (Dépor supporters) watched a closely contested game, as a win for Valencia could qualify 'los che' for European competition. The score remained level until, with only a few minutes remaining, Dépor was awarded a penalty. The normal penalty-taker Donato (another Brazilian) had been injured earlier in the game and was off the pitch, and Bebeto refused to take the kick. The onus fell on Serbian sweeper Miroslav Dukíc, whose nervous effort was saved, the final whistle blew and Barcelona had won La Liga. Close but no cigar for Dépor, whose second place was nonetheless the club's highest finish and equalled its placing forty-four years previously.

Bebeto concluded the 1993/94 campaign with sixteen goals, fourteen fewer than his Brazilian amigo Romário, whose employer was Barcelona. Within a few weeks, these two players were to score eight goals between them in the 1994 World Cup finals in the USA where, along with Mauro Silva, they were members of the Brazilian side which won the world title.

Deportivo was again La Liga runner-up the following season, this time to Real Madrid, and its UEFA Cup progress was halted by Borussia Dortmund. However, 1995 was a landmark year for Dépor as it reached its first Copa del Rey final. The first game against Valencia was abandoned by the referee in the eightieth minute, with the score 1–1, due to a waterlogged pitch. Three days later in Madrid in the 'eleven-minute final', Deportivo defeated Valencia 2–1 and secured the first major national trophy in its history.

British manager John Toshack was in charge in 1996/97, when Brazilian forward Rivaldo spent his first Liga season at Dépor, scoring twenty-one goals and helping the club to another third place in Primera. Rivaldo's departure to Barcelona after his single season in Galicia brought Dépor over £20 million as a transfer fee, a sum no doubt welcomed by the free-spending Lendoiro, a man of a seemingly extravagant nature but also of discernment in assessing players' suitability for his club.

Dépor sunk to twelfth place in 1997/98, but the club was continuing to bring in international players. In summer 1999, ex-Atlético Madrid player Javier 'Jabo' Irureta was appointed manager of Deportivo de La Coruña. Bebeto had left, but Mauro Silva and Fran were still in the side, and they were joined by more Brazilians – Djalminha and Flávio Conceição – as well as Dutch international striker Roy Makaay.

Irureta had introduced a 4–5–1 formation but, with two

attacking midfielders/wingers, in reality it tended to be more of a 4–3–3 layout, and Irureta's men were strong in defence but quick on the break and determinedly attack-minded.

The season 1999/2000 was Dépor's 'año estupendo', and it finally justified club owner Lendoiro's obvious belief that, by spending vast amounts of money on proven international stars and by appointing a decent manager to organise them, success would most certainly follow. Well, up to a point, Augusto . . .

At the end of this season, Deportivo de La Coruña became the first non-Madrid and non-Barcelona club to win La Liga for fifteen years, and it was and is the only Liga title which the club has won. Dépor were top for most of the season, and the team won the title five points ahead of second-placed Barcelona. It had been a curious Liga season. Real Madrid finished in sixth place, Atlético Madrid was relegated and Dépor won La Liga in spite of winning only five of its nineteen away fixtures.

However, Deportivo de La Coruña had not yet finished. In the summer of 2000 the club spent another £100 million on three new creative players: international playmaker Juan Carlos Valerón, striker Diego Tristán and central midfielder Sergio, all Spanish internationals (for a change). The squad now consisted of four Brazilians, three Argentinians, two Moroccans, a Serbian, a Dutchman and a Cameroon goalkeeper (Jacques Songo'o, African Keeper of the Year in 1996), as well as several more than useful Spaniards.

Dépor's final flourish came in 2001/02. In the final of the 100th Copa del Rey – 'el centenario' – at the Santiago Bernabéu Stadium, the Galician side had the bad manners to beat Real Madrid 2–1 to win its second Copa trophy. This unexpected defeat for Real Madrid, who were fielding such 'Galacticos' as Zinedine Zidane, Roberto Carlos and Luis Figo, was made worse for 'los blancos' by the game being played on the centenary – to the very day – of Real Madrid's foundation, and the club was much looking forward to its post-match winner's celebration. Well, gentlemen, now you know how it feels.

Then in 2002/03, Deportivo reached the quarter-final stage of the Champions League, on its way beating Manchester United 2–0, and then defeating Arsenal by the same score at both the Riazor and at Highbury. (I was at Highbury for the latter game and I was one of the many 'Gooners' who, impressed by Dépor's compact movement, neat inter-passing and scoring opportunism, applauded the Galician club off the pitch at the final whistle.) Lauded in the international football press, Deportivo de La Coruña was then ranked by FIFA as 'the fourth-best club side in the world'.

By this stage in Dépor's twelve-year admirable assault on the Spanish and European football establishment, the club was starting to lose its momentum. However, and to its great and enduring credit, during the period from 1993 to 2004 Deportivo de La Coruña had won the Liga and two Copas, finished in La Liga four times in second place and four times in third place, and had spent five consecutive years in the Champions League where it had defeated major European clubs of the standard of not only Arsenal and Manchester United, but also Juventus (three times), Bayern Munich (twice) and AC Milan (winning 4–0 at home after a 4–1 away defeat): not bad for a club which had nearly written itself off only fifteen years previously.

In 2004/05 Dépor finished in eighth place in La Liga, was beginning to sell its overseas stars, there were internal player problems, and Irureta left the club. Indications of an imminent decline were becoming apparent. In 2010/11, Dépor ended the season in eighteenth place and was relegated. It quickly returned but, in its next five seasons, the club rose to no higher than fifteenth place in Primera.

As I write these words in April 2019, Deportivo de La Coruña is in Segunda, and now appears to have reverted to its 'yo-yo' status. But the club's daredevil attitude, perseverance, talent and determination to overcome the odds was an inspiration to many other clubs outside football's elite inner circle. And it was fun while it lasted.

*****

'Real Barcelona'

My reason for writing this section on Deportivo de La Coruña is to demonstrate that so-called 'provincial' clubs, if they are prepared to work hard, play as a team, are sufficiently determined and, crucially, have access to sufficient funding, are capable of taking on and beating the big boys on the street, in this case Real Madrid and Barcelona (henceforth 'Real Barcelona') as well as establishing a respected reputation in European football.

In the current context of La Liga, however, this is difficult and happens rarely, as most clubs don't have the financing or infrastructure to maintain such a praiseworthy few seasons as Dépor's. More's the pity.

Most books written about Spanish club football end up as books about Barcelona and Real Madrid. This is inevitable, unavoidable, and is not intended as a criticism as this book will also probably fall into the 'Real Barcelona' category. It is impossible to write about contemporary Spanish football without concentrating on these two.

As an example, since 2000/01 – the first full season of the twenty-first century and the season following on from Dépor's Liga win – sixteen of the nineteen seasons to date have been won by either one of these two big clubs. From the start of La Liga in 1929 until the present day, these two clubs have won the title in nearly two-thirds of the seasons in the existence of La Liga.

Spanish club football is little different from most other

European countries which are also dominated by two or three clubs. The mega-clubs become, over time, virtually impregnable: Real Madrid, Barcelona, Bayern Munich, Liverpool, Juventus, AC Milan, Ajax, Anderlecht, Galatasaray, Celtic . . . they all occasionally lose games and miss out on titles, but they remain top clubs within their own countries.

Splendid institutions they may be and, at their best, they can be riveting to watch, as they are all capable of playing sublime football of the highest quality. However, their imperious manner and baronial status denies them access to the romance and magic of football, which is what the game is really about. Heroic losers are generally more appealing, and frequently more interesting, than are quasi-corporate winners, and football is no exception to this observation.

This being so, in the following few pages I will be examining some clubs who may lack the celebrated history and grandeur of 'Real Barcelona', but who have shown themselves capable, from time to time, of upsetting the natural order of things in La Liga.

However, I devote Part Five, the concluding section of this book, to Real Madrid and Barcelona – as well as the recent successes of Valencia, Sevilla and Atlético Madrid in Europe – and their journeys from the mid-1980s and early 1990s to the present day, when the 'blancos' and 'blaugranas' enjoy their well-earned domination of contemporary Spanish and European club football.

***

Also in Galicia, south of La Coruña and just north of the Portuguese border, is the port of Vigo, home to **Celta de Vigo**.

'Los célticos' – like several clubs in Spanish football, a 'yo-yo' team – cannot boast a major national trophy. Its highest Liga position is fourth, and the club has reached three Copa finals, losing all three.

Since its formation in 1923, Celta has spent over fifty seasons of its history in La Liga. Despite this worthy pedigree, Celta de Vigo seems to save its most laudable performances for Europe, as was evident during the six-season period from 1997 to 2003 when it was dubbed 'EuroCelta' by the Spanish press.

At the conclusion of the 1997/98 season, Celta lay sixth in La Liga and qualified for the UEFA Cup. It beat Liverpool 4–1 but Celta were eliminated in the quarter-final. In 1999/2000 Celta was again knocked out in the quarter-final, but not before it had beaten two of the biggest clubs in European footballing history: Benfica (7–0) and Juventus (4–1). In Celta's third successive UEFA Cup season, the club faced Barcelona, once more in the quarter-final, and the Catalans squeaked through on away goals after a 4–4 draw. Celta de Vigo was punching well above its weight.

The 2002/03 season was domestically Celta's finest-ever Liga finish, in fourth place. In the following season 'los célticos' made a first appearance in the Champions League and reached the final sixteen, where Arsenal, at the time England's best side, inflicted a 5–2 defeat on Celta.

The club's performance in Europe was in marked contrast to its disappointing form in La Liga, as Celta was relegated at the end of that season. This must be some sort of record: one day Arsenal, the next Málaga's B team. But Celta was quickly back in Primera, although it faced serious financial problems and entered into administration, which doomed the club to Segunda for five years.

As I write, Celta de Vigo is once again slugging it out with the heavyweights in Primera División. It's a resilient, proud club, and the top level of the Spanish league is its natural home.

***

When last we encountered 'los lobos' of **Real Betis**, the club – just like Celta de Vigo – had enjoyed a good run in Europe but was relegated in the same year, this being 1977/78. Again like Celta, Betis came straight back to Primera and for three seasons around the early 1980s it ended in the top six. After another three seasons in Segunda, back up came Betis in 1994/95 to finish third, the club's best season since its one Liga triumph sixty years previously.

The club was knocked out of the UEFA Cup in the third round, but it was again in Europe two years later, having been narrowly beaten in the Copa final by Barcelona 3–2, after Luis Figo's extra-time goal. There is no shame in being defeated by a team containing Figo, Guardiola, Luis Enrique, Popescu and Stoichkov, among others.

However, in 1998 Real Betis acquired its very own superstar. The club surprised the world of football by leapfrogging Lazio, Manchester United, Real Madrid and Barcelona and signing twenty-year-old Brazilian winger Denilson from São Paulo for a world record transfer fee.

The boy from Brazil

In the latter part of the 1990s, the outstanding performances of a young Brazilian left-winger for his local club São Paulo excited a good many of Europe's leading football clubs.

Denilson, a gifted dribbler with blistering pace and an uncanny ability to leave flat-footed even the most experienced defender, had made his club debut at the tender age of seventeen. The Brazilian media even compared the self-confident young forward to the country's legendary wingers Jairzinho and Garrincha.

Among the clubs keen to acquire Denilson's services was Real Betis, at best a middle-ranking La Liga club but one which its president, Manuel Ruiz de Lopera, hubristically perceived as potentially being a member of European football's 'super league'. De Lopera offered São Paulo what was then a world record fee of £21.5 million for Denilson who, in summer 1998, was unveiled in front of 20,000 fans as a Betis player.

The Brazilian played his first Liga game in August that year but, perhaps weighed down by unrealistic expectations and also finding Spanish football less willing than was Brazil to grant him the space he required and to tolerate his individual flair and showboating, Denilson did not score his first goal for Betis until February 1990.

At the end of Denilson's second season Betis was relegated to Segunda, the Brazilian was sent on loan to Flamengo, he returned in January 2001 and he helped the club to return to La Liga for 2001/02. However, his ball control and consistency having deserted him, he was increasingly sidelined and could not claim a regular first-team place.

Eventually, he left Real Betis in 2005, and for the following five years Denilson played in five different countries: France, Saudi Arabia, USA, Brazil and Vietnam (where he was top scorer).

Although Denilson gained sixty-one caps for Brazil, his career in Spain had been initially over-hyped, and his individualism (and over-reliance on his left foot) was incompatible with the Spanish game.

It's a pity for everyone concerned that Manuel Ruiz de Lopera jumped in with all that money before properly assessing Denilson's ability to handle the demands of La Liga.

Over the following few years Betis was, as usual, up and down, led by a succession of managers, including Serra Ferrer, Luis Aragonés and Javier Clemente. However, when Ferrer returned in 2004/05 he led Betis to fourth in La Liga and the final of the Copa. Betis claimed its second-ever Copa trophy by defeating Osasuna 2–1, the extra-time winner for Betis coming from Dani.

Since then, Real Betis has continued in its own inimitable way: dealing with lawsuits, relegation and even a defeat by local enemy Sevilla in the quarter-final of the 2013/14 Europa League, followed by another relegation. However, despite the Denilson episode, and having hired and fired twenty-one managers over the last twenty years, this perverse but persistent 112-year-old club was sitting happily in mid-table in La Liga at the end of the 2018/19 season.

Having remained more or less intact throughout its eccentric and erratic history, Real Betis appears to be a born survivor.

***

Far to the north of Seville, the Basque region grabbed the European football headlines in 2001 when **Alavés** reached the final of the UEFA Cup. In the late 1980s 'los babazorros' from Vitoria-Gasteiz had been playing their football in Tercera, but in 1998/99, the club gained promotion to La Liga for the first time for forty-five years. The following season, Alavés ended in sixth place in La Liga and qualified for the UEFA Cup.

After winning six home and away UEFA Cup rounds – in the process defeating Inter Milan 5–3 and Kaiserslautern by a stunning 9–2 in the semi-final – the club reached the final in Dortmund against Liverpool in 2001, its first-ever appearance in European competition.

By half-time in a thoroughly enjoyable game (one of *World Soccer* magazine's 'Top Twenty' best-ever football matches) Liverpool were holding on to a comfortable 3–1 lead, but within minutes of the restart Javi Moreno scored twice to level the score. Fifteen minutes remained when Robbie Fowler netted another for Liverpool, but two minutes before full-time Jordi Cruyff ('Cruyff Minor') levelled again for Alavés.

In extra time, a 'golden goal' would decide the winner. With penalties beckoning, the Basque club's right-back Delfí Geli unfortunately headed the ball into his own net for a 'golden own goal'. Liverpool, successfully riding their good fortune, became UEFA Cup champions, while Alavés' exceptional performance, in the final and in the tournament generally, came as an eye-opener to many people, probably including the players and supporters of Deportivo Alavés.

Alavés was back in Segunda five seasons later but the club was re-promoted in 2016/17 and faced another final, the Copa del Rey in Madrid in 2017, against Barcelona. After the match the *Guardian* summed it up: 'Lionel Messi inspires Barcelona to Copa triumph', and the brilliant little Argentinian scored one and made the other two in the Catalan club's 3–1 victory over a determined but, again, futile Alavés display. The game was Luis Enrique's farewell as Barcelona's manager, and Barcelona had won the Copa title three years in succession for the first time for over sixty years (the club equalled its own record set in 1953).

Alavés today remains proudly in La Liga, as does its Basque neighbour Eibar. Both recent arrivals from the region are continuing to surprise many observers of the Spanish football leagues, and the determination of these clubs shows little sign of abating.

By contrast, the two established Basque clubs, Athletic Bilbao and Real Sociedad, have in recent years struggled to recapture the performances which saw them win four consecutive La Liga titles in the early 1980s.

Athletic reached three Copa finals between 2009 and 2015 and lost them all to Barcelona. The club has failed to reach the top three in La Liga for the last thirty years. Real Sociedad has also largely disappointed, and has only two top-three appearances in Primera over a similar period.

***

Although Levante has historically been the main rival to Valencia CF in the Valencian community, in recent years **Villarreal**, from the eponymous town in the province of Castellón, has challenged Levante's role.

In common with so many Spanish clubs, Villarreal has undergone a number of guises in its history. The club known today as Villarreal CF was formed in 1956 and travelled through local and national leagues until it entered La Liga in 1998/99. Relegated after one year, Villarreal immediately returned to Primera and since then, aside from one year in Segunda, it has remained in La Liga till the present day.

Villarreal ('the yellow submarine') has never won the Copa and neither has it claimed La Liga title. However, the club has played over 150 games in Europe although it has not yet won a major European competition. In only its third season at the highest level (2003/04), the club reached the semi-final of the UEFA Cup but lost to – who else? – Valencia. In the following season Villarreal was again defeated in the tournament but achieved third place in La Liga, granting the club a place in the Champions League. Also in 2004/05, its Uruguayan striker Diego Forlán picked up the Pichichi award for his twenty-five goals for the club.

I remember being at Highbury when Arsenal played Villarreal in the spring of 2006 in the first-leg semi-final of the Champions League, and the Gunners then scraped through 1–0. In Spain, Arsenal keeper Jens Lehmann secured the London side's first and only place in a European Cup final, saving a last-minute penalty from Argentinian Juan Riquelme to save a 0–0 draw.

Arsenal then lost in the final to Barcelona, but I was much impressed by the skill, teamwork and relentless attack of that Villarreal side. Players of the stature of Riquelme and Forlán clearly flourished under manager Manuel Pellegrini, and the team's determination and will to win were obvious. In 2007/08 Villarreal finished in second place behind Real Madrid, but the club was again eliminated by Arsenal from the Champions League, this time in the quarter-final.

To date, Villarreal has reached the semi-finals of three Europa League seasons, twice won the Intertoto Cup, and played twice in the Champions League in a period of less than twenty years, a proud record for such a recent arrival in the top division.

***

In European football, one occasionally encounters commentators and observers labelling certain football clubs as 'cup sides'. This phrase is normally intended as mildly pejorative in its implications, these being an inability or unwillingness to embrace the virtues of consistency, determination and hard work in favour of a dilettantish, cavalier attitude to the game. In other words, 'cup sides' are 'fancy dans'.

This ignores the fact that a country's leading clubs usually do well in both league and cup competitions although, under the demands of contemporary European football, league success brings greater rewards. Most of the top sides, however, have continuing access to the financial resources and quality players necessary to do justice to both competitions.

The majority – the smaller, underfunded and less fashionable clubs – do not have these advantages, and are therefore less able both to grind out league points on a regular basis and also to maintain strong and reliable teams for knockout competitions. Unsurprisingly, these clubs tend to concentrate on the country's cup tournaments, where luck can play a major part and where, at least theoretically, there are more opportunities to compete on an equal basis.

These points bring me, perhaps unfairly, back to **Real Zaragoza**, a club which I last discussed in Part Three in the wake of its late-1960s elimination from the Fairs Cup. I use the word 'unfairly', as no one can accuse the club from Aragon of being content with underachievement or of lacking in ambition.

Founded in 1932, Real Zaragoza was, aside from seven seasons in Segunda, a permanent member of La Liga from 1951 to 2013: in other words, over fifty years dining at the top table. But the club has never won La Liga, with its closest finish being second place in 1974/75.

However, if one examines its record in the Copa del Rey, between 1963 and 2006 Zaragoza has reached eleven finals and has won six of them. On top of this, Real Zaragoza held aloft the European Cup Winners' Cup in 1995. Does this make the club a 'cup side' or what? At the very least, the club can lay claim to a remarkable history in knockout tournaments.

'Los maños' collected a third Copa title in 1986 with a 1–0 win over Barcelona and, following the appointment of Victor Fernandez as manager in 1991, Zaragoza's fourth Copa arrived in 1994 after a tight 5–4 penalties defeat of Celta de Vigo. In May 1995 at the Parc des Princes in Paris, Real Zaragoza faced Arsenal in the final of the European Cup Winners' Cup. A strong Zaragoza team, with Argentinian striker Juan Esnáider and midfield goalscorer Francisco Higuera, and with Uruguay's Gus Poyet controlling midfield, went 1–0 ahead in the first half, while Arsenal's John Hartson equalised in the second period.

In the 120th minute – the last few seconds of extra time – midfielder Nayim whacked in a highly speculative forty-five yard lob which somehow eluded Arsenal keeper David Seaman, and Real Zaragoza had won the Cup. The chant 'Nayim, from the halfway line' is unleashed by rival fans to taunt Arsenal supporters to the present day and, to make matters even worse, Nayim played for Spurs before he joined Zaragoza.

The fifth Copa title was won in 2001, and the club's sixth followed four years later against Real Madrid. Dani and David Villa scored for 'los maños' in reply to a David Beckham free-kick goal, and then Roberto Carlos struck to ensure 2–2 and extra time. A goal six minutes from the end of the extra period brought victory to Real Zaragoza.

Real Zaragoza was relegated to Segunda at the end of 2012/13, and has remained there since. But few 'maños' supporters will forget 'Nayim, from the halfway line'.

***

In Part One of this book I mentioned a club – **Real Mallorca** – which had never won a Copa or La Liga title but which surpassed expectations, probably including its own, in the early years of the twenty-first century.

The Balearic Island club had contested two Copa finals in 1991 and in 1998, but was defeated in the former 1–0 by Atlético Madrid and, in the latter, went down 5–4 on penalties to Barcelona. Despite these setbacks, Mallorca was enjoying one of the more successful periods in its history, and the club ended in third place in La Liga in both 1998/99 and 2000/01.

In the 1998/99 Cup Winners' Cup (Copa winners Barcelona had also won La Liga, so it entered the Champions League, which allowed runner-up Mallorca to compete in this tournament) Mallorca fought its way to the final, having defeated Chelsea in the semi-final.

This was the very last Cup Winners' Cup final as, from the following season, the competition was abolished and national cup winners were to be permitted access into an expanded UEFA

Cup. The game was played in the unlikely setting of Birmingham (I have nothing against the fine city of Birmingham, but UEFA could surely have dreamt up a rather more romantic venue for such a historic occasion).

In an entertaining match, although Mallorca striker Dani scored his fourth goal of the tournament, Italian cup winners Lazio netted twice and emerged as the Cup's last-ever winner, with a 2–1 scoreline.

As I also mention in Part One, season 2001/02 was Mallorca's first appearance in the Champions League, and it met Arsenal in the first group stage. (In case you are thinking that I mention Arsenal with some frequency in this book because it's my local club, this is not the reason. Rather, Arsenal does appear to play more than its share of Spanish clubs in European competitions. And why not? They're usually good games.)

On the unforgettable day of '9/11' (the Twin Towers attack), Mallorca won 1–0 at home, in an understandably depressed atmosphere. In the return match, goals from Pires, Bergkamp and Henry resulted in a 3–0 win at Highbury against a defensive Mallorca, and the Spanish club was eliminated from the tournament while Arsenal moved on to the second group stage.

However, spirits lifted in season 2002/03 when Real Mallorca won its first Copa del Rey. Although the match was again played in a relatively unglamorous setting (Estadio Manuel Martinez Valero in Elche), 28 June 2003 was once more an historic day, as the opposition was the daddy of them all, Recreativo de Huelva. Recre, 'El Decano', is Spain's oldest club and it was on a winning streak. It had eliminated Atlético Madrid and Osasuna on its way to the final, and it was also Recre's first-ever appearance in a Copa final. Sadly for hopeful football historians everywhere, Mallorca sealed a 3–0 win over the Andalucian side, Samuel Eto'o scoring two of them in the final few minutes.

At the end of 2012/13, Real Mallorca's sixteen consecutive La

Liga seasons came to an end with relegation. However, within seven years Mallorca would be back in Primera.

***

On the coast of southern Andalucia, below the white villages of the Sierra Nevada which gaze over the Mediterranean, there sits what was once the ancient Phoenician trading settlement and harbour of Málaga. Today, Málaga is the busy port, commercial centre and touristic hub of the Costa del Sol, and its population of just under 600,000 makes it Spain's sixth-largest city.

Málaga was in 1904 home to one of Spain's earliest football clubs but, similar to Real Mallorca's experience, it has suffered a rather dysfunctional history in the game. Unlike Spain's other coastal cities, Málaga has never quite managed to produce an enduringly successful football club, although several such attempts have been made but have largely proved fruitless.

Perhaps this is because it's such a pleasant, friendly place, with a good many other cultural and social distractions to occupy the citizenry. The restaurant-lined beach on the eastern edge of the city certainly does not encourage any tendencies to practising ball control or indeed to strenuous exercise of any sort.

The city's current club, **Málaga CF**, was formed – or, rather, re-established on the remains of the late CD Málaga – in 1993, and it has attracted national and European attention only in recent years. The new club was promoted to La Liga for season 1999/2000 under the coaching of Joaquin Peiró. In 2001/02, the popular manager guided Málaga to eighth place in La Liga and to the final of the 2002 Intertoto Cup, where it beat Villarreal to win the trophy.

The following season, playing its home games at the club's new stadium, La Rosaleda (Rose Garden), Málaga reached the quarter-final of the UEFA Cup, beating on the way Leeds

United and AEK Athens, only to be eliminated on penalties by Portugal's Boavista.

When Peiró retired in 2003, several of the best players also left the club, and Málaga's Liga performances gradually declined to the extent that it ended bottom of La Liga and was relegated at the conclusion of the 2005/06 campaign. Málaga didn't return to La Liga until 2008/09. The club was suffering from severe financial problems, which were to a degree alleviated by the arrival of a new owner, a Qatari businessman, in the summer of 2010. The Chilean manager Manuel Pellegrini, who had acted the previous season in a similar capacity at Real Madrid, took over as coach early in 2010/11 and Málaga ended that season in an unexpectedly decent mid-table position in La Liga.

Before season 2011/12 kicked off, in came Dutch international striker Ruud van Nistelrooy and, from Villarreal, playmaking midfielder Santi Cazorla, the latter for a club record €21 million. Other arrivals included winger Isco and left-back Nacho Monreal. This injection of fresh talent and experience saw Málaga finish the season in fourth place in La Liga, its highest-ever placing, and affording qualification for the following Champions League.

Cazorla left for Arsenal and van Nistelrooy retired from the game at the end of this season, both decisions perhaps partly influenced by the continuing perilous financial situation of the Andalucian club. During the 2012/13 season Monreal joined Cazorla at the Emirates Stadium, and in summer 2013 Isco joined Real Madrid.

Nevertheless, despite these departures, in the 2012/13 Champions League, Málaga emerged unbeaten and top of its group which contained Zenit St Petersburg, Anderlecht and AC Milan, worthy opponents all. In the quarter-final first leg at La Rosaleda, Málaga drew 0–0 with Borussia Dortmund. In Dortmund, the Spanish side was 2–1 ahead after ninety minutes, but Borussia scored twice in injury time and a devastated Málaga was eliminated from the competition.

After the Borussia game the club made a formal complaint to UEFA, arguing that both injury-time goals had been offside. The goals were deemed valid, and there appeared to be a faint aroma of sour grapes wafting around Málaga. In another respect, however, UEFA did pay attention to the Andalucian club. The organisation excluded Málaga from the Europa League for the following season on account of the club's debt-ridden status.

Pellegrini, after three arduous but reasonably effective seasons at the club, was lured away by Manchester City, and the ubiquitous Bernd Schuster took over in the summer of 2013. Five managers later, at the end of the 2017/18 campaign, Málaga once more propped up La Liga in twentieth place and was again relegated.

It remains odd that a city the size of Málaga clearly finds it difficult to sustain a serious and consistent challenge in Spanish football, with its main club in Segunda. But, as of mid-February 2019, and coached by the sixth post-Schuster manager Juan Muñiz, the club occupied second place in Segunda, one point behind league then-leader Granada, so perhaps there will be a return to La Liga in the near future?

**

From the year 2000 to the present day, La Liga clubs have dominated European football.

Between the two of them Real Madrid and Barcelona have claimed ten European Cups over these eighteen seasons, while Atlético Madrid and Valencia have been runner-up finalists on three occasions. In the UEFA Cup / Europa League over the same period, Sevilla have won the trophy five times, while Atlético Madrid have claimed three titles. Espanyol, Athletic Bilbao and, as we have seen above, Alavés, have each been runners-up in the tournament final.

When one considers the quality of the competition from other European countries, this is a remarkable record which re-emphasises the pre-eminence of La Liga in recent years. However, a glance at the names of these clubs reminds one of the dominant presence of only a few Spanish clubs, mainly Barcelona and Real Madrid, with Alavés being the only Spanish 'outsider' to reach a European final.

In Part Five of this book, I concentrate on Real Madrid, Barcelona, Atlético Madrid, Sevilla and Valencia: big names in Spanish football and the leading contenders in Europe since the turn of this century.

However, before so doing, I'd like to draw your attention to the words of Juande Ramos, then-manager of **Rayo Vallecano**, whose club made its first and, to date, only appearance in European football when the Madrid-based outfit reached the quarter-final of the 2000/01 UEFA Cup.

'Los Vallecanos' ended ninth in La Liga in 2000 and had qualified for Europe by winning the Fair Play draw. (This had been established by UEFA in 1993, and permitted entry into the UEFA Cup for three domestic 'fair play' winners in Europe each season.) On its journey into the European unknown, Rayo had beaten four club sides, including such heavyweights as Lokomotiv Moscow and Bordeaux. Inevitably, Rayo was eventually eliminated. It's a pity, though, that Rayo's conqueror was the Basque Country's Alavés, who won 4–2 on aggregate, as it was also celebrating its first taste of the European game that season.

After his team was knocked out of the tournament, the Rayo Vallecano manager Ramos said: 'For us, this has been an unforgettable experience, and it was great to see two modest sides have a chance of reaching the UEFA Cup semi-finals. It was a shame that someone had to lose.'

This was a heartening and sincere statement from an obvious lover of the game. However, it's also a poignant and rather depressing reminder of the gulf which has developed in the modern game between the super-wealthy mega-clubs and all the rest of us, toiling away to little avail in the footballing undergrowth.

PART FIVE

WALKING SPANISH

The Vulture Squad

It was early February 1984 on Andalucia's Atlantic coast and the game was not going Alfredo Di Stéfano's way.

Thirty years previously, Alfredo had been instrumental in regenerating his club, and he had recently returned as its manager. However, that day his team were trailing 2–0 at half-time in a Liga match at Estadio Ramón de Carranza in Cádiz. This was not supposed to happen to **Real Madrid**.

Although Real had failed to win the Primera División for the previous three years – almost an eternity by Spanish standards – it was that season engaged in a top-of-the-table tussle with Athletic Bilbao and Barcelona, and every Liga point was vital. Meanwhile, Cádiz CF was playing in only its third season in Primera in its forty-five-year history and, although doomed to relegation that year, it was enjoying its fleeting superiority over one of the big boys.

During the interval, a concerned Di Stéfano decided that a substitution could only improve matters. So he brought on a seemingly nervous young forward, making his debut in the first team, to replace Carlos Santillana. In the remaining forty-five minutes, the substitute – Real youth academy graduate Emilio Butragueño, whose slight, boyish appearance belied his twenty years of age – scored two goals and created the third in a 3–2 victory over the Cádiz side.

Butragueño's performance that day must have hastened notions of early retirement in Santillana, one of Spain's most respected centre-forwards and a 'los blancos' regular for the past fourteen years. The young forward's remarkably assured awareness and trickery on the pitch came as a revelation to the seasoned veteran but less so to Di Stéfano who had earlier that season watched the player impress 60,000 club fans at the Bernabéu when Emilio had starred for Real's reserve side, Castilla.

By the end of this particular Liga season, Real Madrid would finish level on points but with one goal fewer than the winners Athletic Bilbao, and Di Stéfano, would leave the club. However, Butragueño was to become a Real Madrid hero. He and his audacious posse from Real's youth and reserve teams were about to redefine the club's footballing culture and restore its primacy in Spanish football after several relatively bleak years for 'los blancos'.

***

In the early 1980s, Madrid was home to a countercultural revolution – 'La Movida Madrileña' – in the wake of Franco's death.

The 1982 election victory of Felipe González and the arrival of leftist social democracy had unleashed in Spain an invigorating sense of freedom and modernity which was pervading the major cities, in particular Madrid. The focus of artistic attention and experimentation was moving from Barcelona to Spain's capital, and this was celebrated in the city with the ubiquitous slogan 'solo se vive una vez': 'you only live once'.

This hedonistic reawakening of creative expression, and its accompanying revival in the self-belief of madrileños, were understandable reactions to the Francoist years of conservatism, austerity and grim authoritarian rule. This was complemented by an equally dynamic and innovative shift in attitude to the game of football which was being initiated by a generation of younger players at the city's leading club, Real Madrid.

At the Bernabéu there was emerging the nucleus of a team which would become regarded as the club's finest side since the late 1950s, with the difference being that these players were local lads who had developed their talents at La Fábrica, the club's youth academy, under the direction of head coach and Real Madrid and Spanish international ex-winger, the famed Amancio Amaro.

The inspirational heart of the team, which was to win five consecutive Liga titles between 1985 and 1990, was 'La Quinta del Buitre' ('The Vulture Squad'). This enduring nickname was coined by an *El País* journalist in late 1983 when the Quinta played for Castilla, which in 1983/84 won Segunda, with Athletic Bilbao's reserve side, Bilbao Athletic, in second place. Under RFEF rules, neither club could be promoted as both first teams were in Primera, so the Quinta was gradually 'transferred' to Real's first team.

These were five precociously talented young footballers. Butragueño, whose nickname 'El Buitre' defined the quintet, was a charismatic personality, an inventive goalscorer and the group leader. The other four comprised Manuel Sanchis, a stylish sweeper/centre-back; Rafael Martín Vázquez, a technically gifted attacking midfielder; Michel, a winger and uncannily accurate passer and crosser of the ball; and Miguel Pardeza, a fast natural striker and the only Quinta member not born in Madrid.

These players brought to Real Madrid a refreshing versatility and an engaging style of play which reflected the emergence of a more open and flexible post-Francoist society. To the old values of passion, strength and athleticism – the basis of the 'Furia Española' – the Quinta was adding skill, speed, mutual awareness and, in keeping with 'La Movida', a sense of artistry recently absent from the Spanish game.

The Quinta also injected into their apparent nonchalant assurance a steely determination and aggression, applied constant pressure on opponents and were committed to attack. Supported by Argentinian World Cup winner Jorge Valdano, another intelligent and creative forward, who had arrived from Real Zaragoza in 1984, long-serving Real defenders Ricardo Gallego and José Antonio Camacho, and forwards Santillana and Juanito, the Quinta was, by the mid-1980s, about to reassert Real Madrid's supremacy in Spain.

Real Madrid had an inauspicious beginning to season 1984/85, losing 3–0 to Barcelona under Barça's new manager Terry Venables, and the Catalan club won its first Liga title for eleven years, Real having to settle for fifth place. However, coached by the club's ex-player Luis Molowny, Real Madrid won that season's UEFA Cup.

In the first of what would become known by madrileños as the 'grandes remontadas' ('great comebacks'), Real overturned a first-leg 3–0 defeat by Anderlecht in Belgium by winning 6–1 in the return match at the Bernabéu, Butragueño scoring a hat-trick. In the semi-final 'los blancos' replied to a 2–0 defeat in Milan by overcoming Inter 3–0 at home. They won the trophy with a 3–1 aggregate victory over Hungary's Videoton.

In the summer of 1985 the Quinta was reinforced by the arrival of prolific Mexican striker Hugo Sánchez, who had spent the previous four seasons with neighbours Atlético Madrid, centre-back Antonio Maceda from Sporting de Gijón and midfielder Rafael Gordillo from Real Betis. The last two were essentially defensive players, acquired to add a tough support to the young forwards. Their arrival prompted Sánchez, who was paraded in front of 50,000 admiring fans at the Bernabéu, to rename the team 'La Quinta de los Machos' ('the Virile Squad').

That season 1985/86, Real Madrid were domestically dominant, winning the club's first Liga title for six years and ending eleven points ahead of second-placed Barcelona. They also again won the UEFA Cup. In another 'grande remontada' Real faced Bayern Munich at the Bernabéu after a 5–1 hammering in Germany and eliminated the German side 4–0 on away goals, these coming from Valdano and Santillana. They then repeated the previous season's dismissal of Inter Milan when a 3–1 Italian lead was equalled at full time in the Bernabéu, followed by a 5–1 extra-time Real win, Santillana claiming both late goals. After all this, Real Madrid deserved its 5–3 defeat of Cologne in the final.

Season 1986/87, with Real now coached by Leo Beenhakker, concluded with the club again topping La Liga, but president Ramón Mendoza's primary aim was to reclaim the European Cup, a trophy the club had not won for twenty years. This season Real had dispensed with Juventus and Red Star Belgrade, and met Bayern Munich in the European Cup semi-final. Defeated 4–1 in Germany, Real managed only one goal in reply at the Bernabéu, with no sign of a 'grande remontada', and were eliminated from the tournament.

Within Spain, however, this Real Madrid side was unstoppable. In the Quinta's finest season of 1987/88, Real won La Liga in style, eleven points ahead of second-placed Real Sociedad and twenty-three points in front of sixth-placed Barcelona, with the exuberant Sánchez picking up his second successive Pichichi.

In his book *Fear and Loathing in La Liga*, Sid Lowe recounts that when Jesús Gil, president of Atlético Madrid, was told about Real's 7–0 destruction of Sporting de Gijón, he commented, 'Well, they won't do that again.' The following week the Quinta won 7–1 against Real Zaragoza. These were heady times for the 'local lads', particularly in the ferociously partisan Bernabéu and, although Pardeza left to join Real Zaragoza in 1988, they had still not finished their extraordinary run.

Over the following two seasons the Quinta made it five Liga titles in succession. For 1989/90, new manager John Toshack replaced Beenhakker, who had the temerity to drop Butragueño but who had also secured a Liga and Copa double before his departure. Toshack's side concluded the Welshman's first season as boss with a nine-point lead over second-placed Valencia and a Liga record tally of 107 goals, Sánchez netting thirty-eight of them and equalling Zarra's long-time Liga record.

However, the European Cup proved to be beyond the Quinta, with the 1988 tournament proving a particular disappointment. Real Madrid brushed aside a Maradona-led Napoli as well as two ex-winners of the trophy – Porto and Bayern Munich – as they progressed to the semi-final against PSV Eindhoven. Despite Real being favourites to reach the final, a 1–1 draw in Madrid was followed by a 0–0 result in Holland, a brilliant performance from PSV keeper Van Breukelen denying Real an appearance in the final.

In the following season, now fielding ex-Barcelona German midfielder Bernd Schuster, Real accounted for PSV with an extra-time second-leg winner from Vázquez at the Bernabéu. The semi-final first leg was in Madrid against Silvio Berlusconi's AC Milan – the Dutch trio of Gullit, Van Basten and Rijkaard at its core – and again ended in a 1–1 draw. In the return match at the San Siro, a sluggish Real was destroyed 5–1 by an outstanding Milan display.

In the 1990 European Cup, Real was again knocked out by Milan, this time in the second round, and the side also lost the Copa 2–0 to Barcelona. With the departure of Schuster and Vázquez, and results beginning to favour Cruyff's Barcelona, the Quinta was entering into decline, both domestically and in Europe.

At the end of the 1994/95 Liga season, during which Butragueño had played only a handful of matches, he left the club. This revered player, after ten years of fan adulation, had been replaced by Raúl, a seventeen-year-old striker, also born in Madrid, who was to become one of the most admired and effective footballers in Real Madrid's history.

Spanish club record appearances

The following five players have made the highest number of senior appearances for Spanish Liga clubs during their careers (with goals scored in brackets). It is little surprise that the two leaders are goalkeepers, as goalies do tend to last longer.

1) Francisco Buyo (Francisco Buyo Sánchez)
680 appearances
Goalkeeper

1975–76	Real Mallorca	16
1976–80	Deportivo de La Coruña	122
1980–86	Sevilla	199
1986–97	Real Madrid	343

2) Andoni Zubizarreta
622 appearances
Goalkeeper

1981–86	Athletic Bilbao	169
1986–94	Barcelona	301
1994–98	Valencia	152

---

3) Raúl (Raúl González Blanco)
550 appearances (228)
Striker
1994–2010 Real Madrid   550

4) Eusébio (Eusébio 'Paco' Sacristán)
543 appearances (36)
Central midfielder
1982–87   Valladolid   117
1987–88   Atlético Madrid   27
1988–95   Barcelona   203
1995–97   Celta de Vigo   67
1997–2002 Valladolid   129

5) Manuel Sanchís (Manuel Sanchís Hontiyuelo)
533 appearances (43)
Sweeper
1983–84   Castilla   10
1984–2001 Real Madrid   523

Venables in Catalonia

In the summer of 1984, Terry Venables' arrival from QPR as the new coach of **Barcelona** came as a surprise to Catalan supporters, mainly because very few fans had ever heard of him.

However, club president Josep Luis Nuñez was one of those few and, acting partly on his and his associates' knowledge and also on the recommendation of Bobby Robson, he hired 'El Tel', as the Londoner was swiftly dubbed by the British press, or 'Meester Ben-a-Bless' as he became known to the 'blaugranas' support.

Venables was the seventh coach whom Nuñez had hired and fired since he had assumed the presidency seven years previously. El Tel's recent predecessors included Herrera, Michels, Kubala and Menotti and were daunting acts to follow. The Englishman, although well rewarded, knew the price of failure.

One of Venables' first decisions was whether or not to agree with Nuñez that Maradona was more trouble than he was worth. The Argentine star had scored thirty-eight goals in fifty-eight appearances in his two injury-affected seasons with the club. However, his special talent had been accompanied by his self-indulgent behaviour off the pitch, his frequent disputes with Nuñez, his uncontrolled lashing-out in the Copa final against Athletic Bilbao, and his recent demands to be transferred. Unsurprisingly, Venables sided with the president, so off to Napoli went Diego for another world record fee, leaving Barcelona with a £2 million paper profit and more relief than grief.

Venables bought from Spurs the Scottish striker Steve Archibald to replace Maradona, although Hugo Sánchez had been the club's and many supporters' preferred choice. It took some time to acclimatise, but both men became enamoured with the region and the club and they, in turn, gradually gained the support of the fans.

Venables normally adopted a pressing 4–3–3 formation, in which he was ably assisted by full-backs Gerardo and Julio Alberto, centre-backs Alexanko and Migueli, West German international midfielder Bernd Schuster, and an attack featuring wingers 'Lobo' Carrasco and Marcos Alonso and which was spearheaded by centre-forward Archibald. In his first season, Venables made a promising start by beating Real Madrid at the Bernabéu, and his team then embarked on a twelve-game unbeaten run.

In this, his opening season, he won La Liga nine points ahead of second-placed Atlético Madrid. This was Barcelona's first Liga title since 1974, with Venables repaying the opportunity he had received from Nuñez. Archibald, the frequent recipient of Schuster's deliveries from midfield, scored fifteen league goals during the season.

Archibald, a confident personality with an instinct for self-preservation, gradually developed a productive relationship with Schuster. Although the Scottish striker disarmingly disparaged himself as 'only a skinny motor mechanic from Rutherglen', his swift reflexes and awareness in front of goal soon won over the fans, who named him 'Archigoles'.

In the summer of 1985/86 Venables continued to buy British, acquiring Gary Lineker from Everton and Mark Hughes from Manchester United. Lineker immediately fitted into the Spanish game and Venables' coaching strategy, scoring a hat-trick in an early away Liga 3–2 defeat of Real Madrid and ending the season with twenty-one goals. Hughes, however, was regarded as tough and strong but clumsy, lacking the necessary skill to make his mark in the Spanish game. He was known as 'El Toro' ('the bull') while Lineker was hailed as 'El Matador'.

Barcelona lost their Liga title to Real Madrid in 1986 and were beaten 1–0 by Real Zaragoza in the April 1986 Copa final, but the team had knocked out Porto, Juventus and IFK Gothenburg to reach the club's second European Cup final. Barcelona's status as favourites was strengthened by the perceived 'weaker' opposition, Steaua Bucharest, and by the venue, Seville, which was almost a home game for Barça.

The crowd in the Sánchez-Pizjuán Stadium that May evening in 1986 was 50,000, with Romanian fans in a small minority, and, despite predictions, the game was far from a Catalan walkover. It drifted into extra time and then penalties. Barcelona's Basque keeper Urruti let in two, Romanian goalie Duckadam saved all four penalties and, against all odds, Steaua had won the European Cup. Venables described it as 'the biggest disappointment I have had as a manager'.

Beaten again by Real Madrid in La Liga, defeated by Osasuna in the Copa, and eliminated from the UEFA Cup in the quarter-final by Dundee United, Barcelona have enjoyed more memorable seasons than 1986/87. Nuñez, a man with a limited reserve of patience, paid off Venables in September 1987, and Luis Aragonés took over as caretaker.

Bernd Schuster had been subbed during the 1986 European Cup final, stormed off the pitch, and that was his last game for Barcelona. During his subsequent transfer to Real Madrid the following season, the Spanish tax authorities discovered the 'double contracts' (one for playing and one for other subsidiary rights) which Nuñez had negotiated with his players.

Several players claimed they were owed money by Nuñez. At a meeting in April 1988 at Barcelona's Hesperia Hotel, the entire squad – minus Lineker (international duty), Lopez (injured) and Schuster (couldn't be bothered) – demanded that the club paid them the outstanding money and insisted on Nuñez's resignation. In what became known as 'the Hesperia mutiny', Captain José Alexanko claimed that Nuñez 'deceived us as professionals and humiliated us as people'. Fourteen players, as well as coach Aragonés, left the club as a result of this episode.

At the season's end, Barcelona were sixth in La Liga. They had won the Copa but the atmosphere at the club was unpleasant. It was in debt, the team was performing badly on the pitch and seemed directionless, attendances were tumbling and Nuñez's presidency was under attack from several players and club members.

Then the president pulled off a neat stunt. In May 1988 he announced the arrival of a new manager. Not only did Nuñez's decision save his presidency, but the appointment was also to restore the status of Barcelona as one of the world's top clubs and to kick-start a legendary era for Barcelona FC. Johan Cruyff had agreed to return to the Camp Nou.

Cruyff and the 'Dream Team'

'El Salvador' ('the Saviour'), as Cruyff had been nicknamed by Barcelona's support after his first season as a player with the club in 1974, had not been idle during his ten-year absence from Catalonia.

He'd spent two years in the USA's NASL and while at Los Angeles Aztecs he'd been named NASL Player of the Year. He had considered retirement but he had lost a significant sum of money in, of all things, a pig-farming business. So he had another two-year spell playing for his first club Ajax, winning two Dutch league titles. When Ajax refused him a new contract in 1983, he joined rivals Feyenoord, where he was awarded Dutch Footballer of the Year for the fifth time. Finally, at the age of thirty-six he retired as a player and in 1985 he took over as manager of Ajax, leading the club to victory in the 1987 European Cup Winners' Cup final. The following year the call came from Nuñez.

When he was a player at Barcelona, Cruyff had encouraged the club in its development of La Masia, the youth academy, and had sold Barça the idea of copying the Ajax Youth Academy. When he became manager, Cruyff knew that La Masia had by then produced young players schooled in the manner he required. He also had a list of established, like-minded players whom he could bring into his new Barcelona side. With fellow ex-player Carles ('Charly') Rexach as his assistant, Cruyff set about building his team.

The 'Total Football' system which Cruyff and his Ajax manager Rinus Michels had developed in the late 1960s, and which Ajax had so effectively put into action in the early 1970s, was essentially a fluid 4–3–3 formation. It was based on fast attacking movement, possession of the ball, and the passing game.

It involved pressing the opposition while maintaining a high offside line and, crucially, ensuring the players were aware of the need for constant interchanging of positions and roles. For instance, if the left-back ran with the ball into attack, the left-winger would drop back into the defender's position to cover for him, and such positional interchanges were frequent, as they kept the ball moving forward and confused the opposition's markers. The markers were led into further disarray by Ajax's forwards continually switching wings. The bewitching 'Cruyff turn', however, was never perfected by anyone other than Johan Cruyff.

Finally, and importantly, 'Total Football' required players with the intelligence, awareness and experience to read the game as it unfolded and to react accordingly. A 'formation' was a guide rather than a diktat, and the players all knew this.

Mind reading

When Cruyff was at Ajax, one incident well illustrates the players' empathy. Ajax were about to kick off in a European Cup tie, when Cruyff and left-winger Piet Keizer both noticed a soggy puddle on the edge of the opposition penalty box, looked at each other and nodded, but said nothing. A few minutes later, Keizer sent in a low ball, the defenders hesitated waiting for the ball to bounce while Cruyff ran forwards towards the puddle. The ball landed on the puddle which significantly slowed down its momentum, as Keizer had intended. Cruyff had an open goal. A few minutes later, the two Ajax players did the same thing, and it was 2–0 before the opposition realised the move had been unplanned but was deliberate. Such mutual awareness was often described as 'habit football', a result of growing up and playing the game together.

Archibald had now left for Hibs, Hughes was on loan to Bayern Munich but Lineker was still at the club although only for one more season. A natural centre-forward, he was played by Cruyff as a right-winger, a position in which he grudgingly remained for that first season. Increasingly of the opinion that he formed no part of Cruyff's plans, the disenchanted English striker left Barcelona at the end of the season, as did Carrasco. Surprisingly, Alexanko, who had been the public face and most vocal of Nuñez's critics, remained at the club, and he retained his captaincy under the new manager.

During his first season Cruyff brought in three attacking players: José Mari Bakero and Txiki Begiristain from Real Sociedad and Julio Salinas from Atlético Madrid. Up from the academy came Guillermo Amor, Luis Milla and Sergi. With Cruyff's team bedding in, Barcelona won the Cup Winners' Cup in 1989, defeating Sampdoria 2–0, although Real Madrid's Quinta secured the domestic double.

In the summer of 1989, Cruyff signed two established players who were to form the core of his new Barcelona team. First to enter Camp Nou was the Dutch attacking sweeper Ronald Koeman, fresh from his club PSV's European Cup final success against Benfica and from Holland's victory in the 1988 European Championship. He was followed from Juventus by Denmark's Michael Laudrup, a gifted attacking midfielder with the flair and subtlety of touch on which Cruyff's system depended.

Nuñez and Cruyff were determined, single-minded individuals, each with a self-belief bordering on arrogance. The manager knew that putting together his team would take longer than the impatient Nuñez would like. As season 1989/90 drew to a close with Barcelona third in La Liga behind Valencia and Real Madrid, Cruyff's position was under serious threat. However, the team's 2–0 win in the Copa del Rey final over Real Madrid at the Mestalla Stadium in April 1990 calmed down the president and bought time for the manager.

Luis Milla and Ernesto Valverde (at the time of writing in 2019, the manager of the club) were among the departures in 1990 and, from the reserves, Albert Ferrer moved to right-back, with young 'Pep' Guardiola, also promoted from the reserves at Cruyff's insistence, assuming the important central defensive midfield role. The latter made his debut against Cádiz in December 1990 and became a mainstay of the side.

Cruyff now had his central defensive lynchpin, his calmly authoritative sweeper, his elegantly creative playmaker, and several exciting young players coming through from the reserves and youth team, but he lacked an aggressive forward to complement this stylish sophistication. At the time there were few better players around to provide this edgier, more threatening dimension than the European Golden Boot winner, CSKA Sofia's Hristo Stoichkov. The Bulgarian joined Barcelona in the summer of 1990, and the 'Dream Team' was in place.

Temperamental, disruptive and tantrum-prone he may have been, but Stoichkov's dribbling and goalscoring talents – he became quickly known as 'El Pistolero' – were unquestioned. His volatile nature appealed to Cruyff as much as did the Bulgarian's ability on the pitch. He had plenty of 'nice' players: what he needed were a few unpleasant ones.

That season, Barcelona won La Liga, eight points ahead of Atlético Madrid, the club's first Liga title since the emergence of La Quinta in 1985. Domestic honours were welcomed by Nuñez but, like Mendoza at Real Madrid, what mattered above all for the club's prestige was the European Cup. In the thirty years of the competition, Real could lay claim to six victories. Barcelona had none.

It had to happen, and finally it did at the end of the following season. On 20 May 1992 at Wembley Stadium, Barcelona won its first European Cup. Over 25,000 Barcelona fans travelled to London for the game against Italian champions Sampdoria, and they were joined in the 70,000 crowd by many more from London's large Spanish community.

Cruyff's final pre-match words to his players were 'Salid y disfrutad' ('Go out and enjoy yourselves'). It was a tight physical contest with players from both sides, particularly Gianluca Vialli and Stoichkov, missing scoring chances and the match ended 0–0 after ninety minutes and went into extra time. With only nine minutes remaining, Koeman's shot from a free kick outside the area eluded keeper Pagliuca and thundered into the net. The final whistle blew, and the Catalan club had done it. 'That was the most important goal of my life,' said Koeman.

Almost three weeks later, Barcelona again won La Liga, and Cruyff's team was also to win the following two Liga titles, making it four Ligas on the bounce, from 1990/91 to 1993/94, for the first time in the club's 104-year history.

If a club wins four successive league titles, it is normally fair to assume that there was a significant points lead at the end of at least one, at the very minimum, of these seasons. Although this was certainly true of the first Liga win, the following three could hardly have been closer. Not only was the destination of each of the three titles decided on the final day, but also in each case Barcelona's victories depended on a result elsewhere.

In 1992 and 1993, Real Madrid played Tenerife on the last day of the season, and a win on either occasion would have given the Madrid club the title. Tenerife was temporarily savouring a few years in Primera rather than in the more familiar surroundings of the lower leagues. Coincidentally, the manager of the Canary Islands' club was Jorge Valdano, a former member of La Quinta del Buitre. In 1992, Real had a 2–0 lead at half-time and the club's players thought the title was in the bag. but they handed the Liga to Barcelona by losing 3–2. In 1993 the situation was identical except that Real lost 2–0. Valdano accepted a coaching job at Real shortly after the latter game.

As I mentioned in more detail in the previous chapter (page 209), in the third season, 1993/94, Deportivo de La Coruña needed only to beat Valencia in Galicia on La Liga's last day to secure the title. With the score level, Dépor missed a last-minute penalty and had to settle for a draw. Barcelona were again Liga champions, almost by default.

In this last Liga-winning season, new signing Romário, playing alongside Stoichkov, won the Pichichi award, and the two forwards ran riot and scored over fifty goals between them. The little Brazilian was named World Footballer of the Year at the season's end. However, Spanish law then permitted only three non-Spaniards in a team, and Cruyff was forced to rotate his four foreigners, with Laudrup, in particular, becoming increasingly unhappy.

The influential Danish midfielder was again left out of the side for the 1994 European Cup final, a game in which Barcelona were caught off-guard and swamped 4–0 by a rampant AC Milan. The highlight of the match was Milan's third goal – an audaciously brilliant forty-yard lob over Barcelona keeper Zubizarreta from close to the touchline – which was scored by Yugoslavian winger Dejan Savićević.

Laudrup's omission, and his continuing disagreements with Cruyff, led to him joining Real Madrid for the start of the 1994/95 season. Later in that season both Romário and Stoichkov also left the club. Towards the end of the 1995/96 season, with Barcelona in fourth place in La Liga in 1995 behind winners Real Madrid and with no other titles heading in Catalonia's direction, the inevitable happened. Nuñez sacked Cruyff, who had become by now Barcelona's longest-serving continuous manager.

Cruyff's eight-year tenure had brought Barcelona eleven trophies and international acclaim. His footballing philosophy laid the groundwork for today's all-conquering club. Pep Guardiola, one of the Dutchman's many disciples, commented, 'Cruyff built the cathedral, our job is to maintain and renovate it.'

Many non-native Catalonians might consider this statement a touch grandiose, and reply, 'Pep, calm down, it's only a game of football,' but Pep was Barcelona FC to his core. A devoted believer in the club's marketing slogan 'mès que un club' ('more than a club'), Guardiola was a local boy and fervent Catalan nationalist who, in a few years' time, was to leave his own significant managerial mark on the club.

Cruyff's successor was Bobby Robson. In 1996/97, the affable Englishman finished second behind Real Madrid in La Liga, with powerful striker Ronaldo, bought for a world record £19.5 million, netting a third of Barcelona's 102 goals and winning the Pichichi. The twenty-year-old Brazilian also scored the only goal in the Cup Winners' Cup final against PSG, and claimed another six during Barcelona's journey to the Copa final where they beat Real Betis 3–2. Ronaldo was off to Inter Milan, and to even greater heights, at the end of the season.

None of these achievements appeared to impress the Barcelona board, and Robson departed after only one season to make way for Louis Van Gaal, manager of Ajax, in an attempt to continue the footballing methods which Cruyff had introduced. He brought with him his assistant Ronald Koeman, the man whose goal had won Barcelona the European Cup.

In his first season, Van Gaal won both La Liga and Copa, the first such 'double' since Herrera forty years previously. His second season produced another Liga title and, in his third season of 1999/2000, Barcelona were Liga runners-up behind Deportivo de La Coruña and also reached the Champions League semi-final.

Despite this admirable record, he was considered by some of the board to be a curt disciplinarian who lacked the cultural assimilation skills and casually effective manner of Cruyff. He was also unpopular with several of his star players, particularly Rivaldo, another Brazilian forward and top scorer who had also joined the club in 1997. Nor did Van Gaal's recruitment of a number of Dutch internationals help his cause. Many supporters and local media pundits felt that he was eroding the club's Catalan spirit and unravelling the sense of regional identity with which Cruyff had reimbued the club.

Shortly after the club had failed to win its third consecutive Liga, Van Gaal gave a press conference at which he said 'Amigos de la prensa. Yo me voy. Felicidades' ('Friends of the press. I am leaving. Congratulations'), with an ironic emphasis on the final word, and off he went to prepare the Dutch national squad for the 2002 World Cup.

'Socio' club ownership

In 1990, the Spanish Cortes, a two-chamber parliament established by the 1978 post-Franco Constitution, passed 'Ley 10/1990 del Deportivo'. This new law made it mandatory, beginning in June 1992, for all professional soccer clubs to become privately-owned S.A.D. organisations ('Sociedad Anónima Deportiva') – limited liability corporations – for the purpose of operating competitive sports teams.

There were exceptions made for four clubs: Real Madrid Club de Fútbol, Fútbol Club Barcelona, Athletic Club Bilbao and Club Atlético Osasuna. These clubs were permitted to maintain their existing legal structures on the grounds that:

i) their accounts had been 'in the black' for the five years between seasons 1985/86 and 1991/92, and

---

ii) they had special cultural and nationalistic significance for the ethnic groups from whom they primarily drew their support.

These clubs could continue as member-owned, non-profit sports associations, or 'socios'.

Those who supported the four clubs' exemptions from this law argued that these measures would permit the clubs to perpetuate their fans' distinct cultural bonds and socioeconomic status with the clubs; that a democratically elected club presidency would be appropriate for the members; that being owned by and answerable to the members would ensure the clubs were fiscally prudent; and that all profits and dividends would remain within the clubs and not be siphoned off to disinterested third parties who may not share the particular ethos and needs of the club.

Many others disagreed with the new law in its entirety, stating that financial capital could not be raised by share flotation and that funding of operations, player purchases, etc. would be reliant on income raised by the club; the requirement for presidential elections only every four years could lead to authoritarian rule by a president; it would be impossible to ensure continuous financial viability; it could serve as a veil for personal ambition; it could result in inherent institutional instability; and the 'Seventh Additional Provision', requiring a bank guarantee of fifteen per cent of budgeted expenditure to enter La Liga, could prevent financial chicanery but could also benefit the wealthier elitist clubs at the expense of the less financially secure clubs.

The model for European leagues is agreed by most observers to be Germany's '50+1' ownership rule, instituted in 1998, where private investors cannot own more than a forty-nine per cent stake in a Bundesliga club. This protects clubs and fans against reckless owners and financial corporate gambling, keeps stadiums full and tickets affordable, and promotes democratic decision-making. Because of this rule, said FIFA ex-president Michel Platini, 'German football is in remarkable health.'

In 1992 Jesús Gil, the president of Atlético Madrid, closed down his club's youth academy. Gil's decision meant the loss to Atlético of a Madrid-born, fifteen-year-old member of the academy who had the potential to have become one of the finest players in the history of 'los rojiblancos'.

This kid, Raúl González Blanco, travelled across town to **Real Madrid** where, under coach Jorge Valdano and after a spell in the reserve team, at the age of seventeen he was playing as striker for the Real 1994/95 first team, which won that season's Liga.

During the season following Raúl's debut, in 1995 Lorenzo Sanz was elected president of Real Madrid after Ramón Mendoza had been blamed for the club's recent problems and had been forced to resign. Sanz began to spend heavily on new players. In came left wing-back Roberto Carlos (Inter Milan) to support remaining Quinta centre-backs Fernando Hierro and Manolo Sanchís; midfielders Clarence Seedorf (Sampdoria) and Fernando Redondo (Tenerife); and forwards Predrag Mijatović (Valencia) and Davor Šuker (Sevilla). This array of talent was Brazilian, Dutch, Argentinian, Serbian, Croatian and, of course, Spanish.

Under the guidance of Italian coach Fabio Capello and, with Raúl scoring twenty-one league goals to accompany Šuker's twenty-four, this multinational Real side won La Liga in 1996/97. Germany's Jupp Heynckes, appointed by Sanz as coach for 1997/98, had two new players available: forward Fernando Morientes (Real Zaragoza) and Christian Karembeu

(Sampdoria) in midfield. Heynckes found it a problem to motivate and exert his authority over this team of experienced international millionaires, and Real finished the season in fourth place in La Liga.

The team's performance in Europe that season contrasted dramatically with its domestic discontents. At the newly constructed Amsterdam Arena, Real Madrid faced Juventus in the European Cup final in May 1998. The Italian side fielded a seemingly matchless forward line of Zidane, Del Piero and Inzaghi, and there was a total of twenty-one international players on the pitch. It was a tense, even match, with the only goal coming from Mijatović midway through the second half. Real Madrid's 1–0 victory brought the club its seventh European Cup, thirty-two years after it had gained its sixth trophy.

Shortly after the Juventus game, Sanz got rid of the German coach. He hired Camacho, who lasted less than a month, and Guus Hiddink, who endured seven months, and the club finished La Liga behind Barcelona in 1998/99. John Toshack was the next man for the job. Real paid Arsenal £23.5 million for the sullen centre-forward Nicolas Anelka, thereby netting Arsène Wenger's club a profit of over £22 million, which paid for a new training ground for the London club. The solipsistic striker's departure was greeted with relief by several ex-teammates. Winger Steve McManaman also arrived, on a free transfer from Liverpool.

Toshack was next to leave and, halfway through the 1999/2000 season, Vicente del Bosque took over from the Welshman and steered the club from seventeenth to fifth place in La Liga. Despite this lowly finish, del Bosque remained in his role for the following four years, aided by his quietly effective, non-combative manner, his persuasive personality, and by Real Madrid's defeats of Manchester United and Bayern Munich to reach another Champions League final, the club's second in three seasons.

The opposition in the Stade de France on 24 May 2000 was Valencia, the first time that two teams from the same country had met to decide the destination of the European Cup. Despite the presence in the Valencia side of Kily González, Claudio López and playmaker Gaizka Mendieta, on this occasion they were overwhelmed by the speed and flamboyant trickery of Real Madrid.

A header from Morientes opened the scoring, and the impressive McManaman, the 'Man of the Match', volleyed in the second from the edge of the box, becoming the first British player to score for a non-British club in the competition's final. With fifteen minutes remaining of the game, Raúl waltzed from his own half to skip round his old teammate and now Valencia keeper Cañizares to score the third.

Real changed from their all-black strip to all-white to receive the trophy, the club's eighth European Cup and one which their performance had fully deserved. However, club president Lorenzo Sanz had less than one month to savour the reflected glory as, on 16 June, Florentino Pérez was elected Real Madrid president. Still, it's difficult to think of a better way to begin a new century than by winning the major trophy in your sport.

***

So how did **Valencia** arrive at a European Cup final? The club from the Mediterranean port city had won four Ligas, five Copas and two Fairs Cups in the forty years between the end of the Civil War and 1980.

Indeed, 1980 was the year in which Valencia won the Cup Winners' Cup, and this was when we last encountered the club in this book. Valencia has long been regarded as one of the top five clubs in Spain's tortuous footballing history, so what had been going on during the intervening twenty years?

Surprisingly, for a club which had so recently claimed a major European trophy, and which had in the process defeated Rangers, Barcelona, Nantes and Arsenal, in the early 1980s Valencia oscillated between mid-table and the relegation zone. The club was heavily in debt and had problems in paying staff and player wages. At the end of 1985/86, Valencia was relegated to Segunda after fifty-five years in the top league in Spanish football.

New club president Arturo Tuzón asked Di Stéfano to take over as coach, the Argentinian agreed, and the following season, 1986/87, Valencia returned to La Liga as Segunda champions. Di Stéfano stayed on for the next season as the club reconsolidated, and he departed when the club secured an acceptable fourteenth place at the season's end.

The club remained in mid-table until the summer of 1991 when Guus Hiddink took over and raised the club to fourth in La Liga, also reaching the quarter-final of the Copa. Then the arrival in 1994 of Carlos Alberto Parreira, who had that summer managed Brazil's national side to victory in the World Cup finals, appeared to promise the club a return to its former exalted status. Parreira acquired keeper Andoni Zubizarreta, whom Cruyff had deemed surplus to his requirements in the 'Dream Team', as well as Russian striker Oleg Salenko. Results, however, remained disappointing. Aragonés and Valdano were also drafted in as coaches, and forwards Romário and Ariel Ortega joined the club.

However, it was not until Claudio Ranieri arrived as coach in 1997 that Valencia again became serious Liga contenders. He was instrumental in developing younger players, including Gaizka Mendieta and centre-forward Claudio López, the latter becoming known as 'el pijo' ('the louse') for his ability to irritate opposing defenders.

Playing in a tight 4–4–2 formation, and making effective use of the speedy counter-attack, his team came fourth in La Liga in

1998/99, and the club won the Copa. A 3–0 defeat of Atlético Madrid in the final, with two goals from López and one from Mendieta, brought the club its sixth Copa and showed that Valencia were back in business.

Under new coach Héctor Cúper, Valencia achieved third place in La Liga the following season, underlining the club's return to its old form and, although the team was beaten 3–0 by Real Madrid in the 2000 European Cup final, Valencia had eliminated Lazio and Barcelona on its way to the club's first final. After the game, striker López moved to Lazio.

Valencia finished fifth in La Liga at the end of the following season but again reached the European Cup final, John Carew scoring against Arsenal in the quarter-final second leg for a Valencia away goals win, and Juan Sánchez netting two in the 3–0 semi-final defeat of Leeds United. In the final, Mendieta opened the scoring but Bayern Munich equalised and the game went to penalties. Bayern took the trophy.

For 2001/02 Rafael Benítez replaced Cúper, who had been seen by many fans as overly defensive and cautious in his tactics. After a poor start, the team hit a winning streak in the second half of the season and won La Liga for the first time in over thirty years. The side was based around a solid defence, although playmaker Pablo Aimar was one of the most skilful and exciting players in Spain. Valencia managed only fifty-one goals during the season, and Real Madrid had to settle for third place.

Real Madrid topped the following season's Liga, with an eighteen-point gap between them and fifth-placed Valencia, but in 2003/04 'los che' again won the league title. They then captured their first European trophy for twenty-four years when they outplayed Marseille in the final to win the UEFA Cup.

However, the Barcelona/Real Madrid domination of the domestic game is proving increasingly difficult to counter, and since then there have been no more trophies for Valencia.

The otherwise disappointing season of 2007/08 under Ronald Koeman resulted in the club winning the Copa. The arrival of Unai Emery as manager was instrumental in steering Valencia to third place in La Liga on three successive occasions from 2010 to 2012, despite his having to oversee the sale of three of his top players – David Villa to Barcelona, David Silva to Manchester City and captain Juan Mata to Chelsea – in order to deal with the club's mounting debts.

But two Liga titles within three seasons did emphatically demonstrate that Valencia are never far away from Spanish football's top table.

2010 World Cup final: 'Passenaccio' meets pragmatism

It is normally the case that the greater and more intense the speculation surrounding a forthcoming event, the reality of its occurrence will inevitably generate an affronted sense of disappointment. In other words, an eagerly awaited game of football – one of crucial importance to both teams – rarely lives up to its advance billing.

This phenomenon is best illustrated when examining the history of the final deciding matches of arguably the world's two most famous football competitions: the annual European Cup (Champions League) and the quadrennial World Cup. In the former, it is difficult to see much beyond the (herein frequently mentioned) 1960 Real Madrid v Eintracht Frankfurt and the 1994 AC Milan v Barcelona finals, while in the latter tournament the 1970 Brazil v Italy final remains the benchmark, with little else to savour over the following fifty years.

True, many of these finals have highlighted moments of unparalleled individual brilliance, magnificent goals, superb team interplay and all the rest of it. However, memories of other such conflicts are generally of cautious, 'safety first', tedious encounters (does anyone, for instance, recall the 1990 World Cup final?). This is unfortunate yet understandable as, with the passing years, these games have offered the winners ever-increasing prestige and financial rewards. Correspondingly, the pressures on the players and managers to win at any cost have relegated skill and artistry and promoted pragmatism and ruthless efficiency as the dominant tactical factors in these supposedly epic encounters.

Although this book concerns itself with Spanish club football, it seems sensible to assume that the success or otherwise (normally the latter) of the country's national side has an impact on the self-images and European perception of the members of La Liga. In Part One I refer to the importance to the development of the Spanish game of the silver medal gained in the 1920 Olympic Games. For the following ninety years this was the highest honour Spain's national team had achieved in the world game until 2010 in South Africa when they faced the Netherlands in the concluding and conclusive game of the tournament.

Spain, managed by Vicente del Bosque and captained by goalie Iker Casillas, took to the pitch in Johannesburg on 11 July, in an unfamiliar navy-blue strip, to meet Bert van Marwijk's Netherlands side in the first World Cup final which did not include Italy, Brazil, Germany or Argentina since the competition's inception in 1930. It is little surprise to discover that Spain's starting XI comprised nine players from Real Madrid and Barcelona, the two non-conquistadores being Valencia striker David Villa and Villarreal right-winger Pedro.

Known for their tough, uncompromising attitude, speedy attack and hard tackling, the Dutch were more than a physical match for their smaller, seemingly more fragile opponents. The teams' tactics were also different, with the Dutch preferring a direct approach in contrast to Spain's more patient, passing and possession-based football. On the latter point, del Bosque's side appeared content to progress on the slimmest of margins. Having squeezed through the group stage by one goal ahead of Chile, Spain reached the final by knocking out Portugal, Paraguay and then Germany all by the same score: 1–0.

After a bad-tempered, disappointing final, with only four minutes remaining of extra time and the imminent dire prospect of penalties, Andrés Iniesta – described in the *New York Times* as 'the outstanding player on the field and also probably the most fouled' – adroitly finished off a cleverly fashioned Spanish move by scoring the only goal of the game in the 1–0 Spanish victory.

However, the game and referee Howard Webb's decisions were heavily criticised, particularly by the Dutch players and media. Webb handed out nine yellow cards (including a sending-off) to the physically intimidating Dutch side, who were frustrated by their inability to prise the ball away from the opposition and thereby permitted Spain to dictate the game's tempo, while he was accused of ignoring fouls in the Netherlands' favour. Also, Spain's constant 'passenaccio' – effective but on occasion yawn-inducing – combined with the persistent Dutch fouling, led to BBC Sport's description of the game as 'hugely underwhelming', while Johan Cruyff described it as 'vulgar anti-football'.

'The Battle of Johannesburg' may not have been a particularly appealing advert for 'the beautiful game' but, with the highest rating (almost sixteen million) for a live broadcast ever recorded in Spanish TV history and with FIFA's claim for a worldwide live audience of over 900 million, would Spain – also European champions in 2008 – have worried about the concerns of a few football pundits and purists? I think not.

Although it has also come back into domestic and European contention in recent years, one of Spain's more venerable clubs had also been having its ups and downs. **Sevilla**, still proclaiming itself as 'Spain's oldest club devoted solely to football' (a highly debatable point, as its Andalucian neighbour Recreativo de Huelva remains 'El Decano') was, when last I discussed the club, recovering from a humiliating European Cup hammering in 1958 by Real Madrid.

At the beginning of the 1958/59 Liga season, Sevilla officially inaugurated its newly built stadium with a 4–2 defeat of neighbours Real Betis. Named in honour of the club president who had been chairman for Sevilla's three Copa del Rey wins and who had died in 1956, the Ramón Sánchez-Pizjuán Stadium was one of the largest in Spain.

Although for the remainder of the twentieth century Sevilla was mainly to be found in La Liga, the cost involved in the construction of the new stadium drained its financial resources, particularly in the 1960s and 1970s which, in turn, contributed to a longer-term decline in its team's performances. Sevilla suffered its first-ever relegation in 1968/69 and again dropped down to Segunda for three seasons in the early 1970s.

By this point, the club was finding it difficult to compete with any success in La Liga, ending up most seasons in the lower reaches. Sevilla again dropped down to Segunda in the mid-1990s. Since returning to La Liga, however, Sevilla has been ever-present in the top half of Primera. Relatively unknown coach Joaquín Caparrós was appointed in 2000, and he organised Sevilla's return to La Liga for 2001/02. The manager developed youth team players, including José Antonio Reyes and Sergio Ramos, and bought Brazilians Júlio Baptista and Dani Alves. The club qualified for the 2005/06 UEFA Cup, and they defeated Middlesbrough 4–0 in the final. Under new coach Juande Ramos, in 2007 Sevilla won the Copa del Rey, finished third in La Liga, and again entered the UEFA Cup.

Español had in 1987 achieved its best-ever Liga season, finishing in third place under the direction of the Basque no-nonsense manager Javier Clemente. The club also reached the final of the UEFA Cup in 1988, then played over two legs, and lost to Bayer Leverkusen on penalties after a 3–3 draw. In 2006, the club defeated Real Zaragoza 4–1 in the final of the Copa del Rey, the fourth Copa win in its history.

In 1995, the club had changed its name from Español to **Espanyol** – the Catalan spelling – in order to increase its membership or, rather, to reflect its Catalan roots. When the club was formed in 1900, it had chosen the spelling 'Español' to demonstrate its Castilian centrist loyalties, to distinguish itself from its city rival and proudly Catalonian club FC Barcelona, and to emphasise that it was an all-Spanish club. However, ninety-five years later it accepted the inevitable, and Espanyol it became. 'O tempora, o mores', as Cicero once observed.

Espanyol entered the 2006/07 UEFA Cup along with three other Spanish clubs – Sevilla, Celta de Vigo and Real Osasuna

– and, remarkably, three of these clubs reached the semi-finals, with Celta eliminated in the round of sixteen.

The final in Glasgow on May 2007 was, therefore, an all-Spanish affair, the finalists being Sevilla and Espanyol, and the game attracted a crowd of 55,000. Perhaps as a gesture to the club's tradition, Ernesto Valverde's Espanyol had a starting line-up containing ten Spaniards, while that of Sevilla was multinational. A tense game ended after extra time with a 2–2 scoreline, and Sevilla won narrowly on penalties. This was Sevilla's second successive UEFA Cup victory, the first such double since Real Madrid in 1985 and 1986.

However, the record was shortly to be broken again by Sevilla between 2014 and 2016, under manager Unai Emery.

Three in a row

It is unusual in modern Spanish football to come across a successful Liga club coach who has not himself enjoyed a playing career at the highest level.

For example, in recent years, Real Madrid have employed Zinedine Zidane, Carlo Ancelotti and Santiago Solari (who had played for Real Madrid, Atlético Madrid, Inter Milan, etc); Barcelona have hired Luis Enriqué, Frank Rijkaard, Pep Guardiola and today's boss is Ernesto Valverde (Espanyol, Barcelona, Athletic Bilbao, etc.); and Atlético Madrid have played under Quique Sánchez Flores, Luis Aragonés, Marcos Alonso and Diego Simeone (Atlético, Sevilla, Inter Milan, Lazio, etc.). There are, of course, exceptions: José Mourinho and Rafael Benítez come to mind. Generally, though, small-club ex-players do not figure in many clubs' managerial searches.

This makes Basque-born Unai Emery's achievements even more remarkable. His playing career of less than nine years was spent with Real Sociedad reserves, and second- and third-tier clubs Toledo, Racing Ferrol, Leganés and Lorca Deportivo.

Emery began his rapid ascent of the managerial ladder in 2004, at the age of thirty-two, with modest Lorca. By the end of his first season, he gained Lorca promotion to Segunda for the club's first time, and in season two the club ended only five points away from promotion to La Liga. At his next club Almería, in his opening season of 2006/07 he secured the Andalucian club its first promotion to La Liga, and in the following campaign he led them to eighth place in Primera.

After an unfortunate few months with Spartak Moscow he took over at Valencia where, as I mention above, he remained from 2008 until 2012, with his club achieving third place for three successive seasons. He was clearly a young manager with a great deal of talent and tactical knowledge beyond his years.

Sevilla had taken note of his achievements, and shortly after the club had sacked coach Michel, Emery became manager at the Pizjuán in January 2013. Over the following three years he helped the old club to reach two fifth and one seventh Liga positions. More importantly, under his leadership, Sevilla became the first club in the history of the UEFA Cup / Europa League to win the trophy three seasons in succession.

In 2013/14, Sevilla beat Benfica on penalties in the final. They followed this with a 3–2 victory, striker Carlos Bacca scoring twice, in a 3–2 defeat of Dnipro Dnipropetrovsk in the 2014/15 final. Sevilla made it three in a row in the 2015/16 final in Basel by winning 3–1 against Liverpool.

In 2016 Emery moved to PSG, where the French club secured

all four of the French domestic trophies, although he was also in charge when Barcelona staged a quite astonishing, Neymar-inspired comeback at Camp Nou in the Champions League, when Barça overturned a PSG first leg 4–0 lead by scoring three times within the last two minutes to eliminate Emery's side.

Emery is currently manager at Arsenal, whose ex-manager Arsène Wenger was also far from being a household name as a player, although it seems unlikely that Emery will repeat his memorably unique European treble at the Emirates.

As with Valencia, Sevilla appears to have overcome the problems it faced in the final decades of the last century, and both clubs today play with flair, determination and renewed confidence, qualities which they had all too often lacked in recent years.

The problem in today's Liga, however, is how to break the duopoly of Barcelona and Real Madrid. As I look at La Liga today (mid-April 2019) with eight games remaining, Barcelona is top, Real Madrid is thirteen points behind in third, Getafe lies in fourth and is twenty-three points adrift of Barcelona, while Sevilla and Valencia occupy fifth and six positions respectively. Alavés sits in seventh place, which is admirable for a club in only its third season in Primera after ten years in Segunda and Segunda B, and one hopes the Basque club can in time maintain a top-three challenge. However, this appears improbable.

The second-placed club, currently sitting two points above Real Madrid in La Liga is also the only club, other than 'Real Barcelona', to have won La Liga in the last fifteen seasons. I am, of course, referring to the unpredictable 'rojiblancos' of **Atlético Madrid**.

After Atlético's successes of the 1970s, the following decade in La Liga was dominated by the Basque Country and Real Madrid (again). Few trophies found their way into the boardroom cabinet at the Vicente Calderón.

The only significant silverware to arrive over these years was in 1985 when Atlético lifted the Copa del Rey, Real Madrid-bound Hugo Sánchez scoring both goals in the 2–1 defeat of Athletic Bilbao. The club again lost a European final when they were outplayed 3–0 in the Cup Winners' Cup by Dynamo Kyiv in 1986. Atlético had won a European final way back in 1962 but, since then, this was the third final the club had lost.

In 1987, a new club president was elected. Jesús Gil, a ruthless operator with a controversial history and a man of extreme right-wing political views, was the popular choice. Almost twenty years earlier, Gil had been jailed for building a property near Segovia without recourse to such legal requirements as planning permission, an architect and a surveyor and, with the cement still not quite dry, opening it to the public. The roof of the building collapsed, killing fifty-eight people. Gil served only twenty-seven months of a five-year prison sentence before he was granted a pardon by Franco.

He was also accused of embezzlement and forgery when he was leader of Marbella City Council; he was foul-mouthed and quickly enraged; he threatened to feed his players, whom he constantly terrorised, to his pet crocodile; and he once physically abused a judge. So he was just the man for the job, and 'los colchoneros' began a fifteen-year roller-coaster ride under his presidency.

As he had promised the Atlético members, Gil immediately bought winger Paulo Futre, who had played for Portugal as a seventeen-year-old and who had made his mark in the previous year's European Cup final, won by his club Porto. A large sum of money to Porto and a yellow Porsche for Futre secured the deal. Gil's spending on players made him popular with the fans but brought in little in the way of success until, having spent lavishly on such players as Bernd Schuster (Schuster gets around), Atlético won two consecutive Copas in 1991 and 1992 as well as claiming a second-placed finish in La Liga.

Gil had a revolving-door policy with club coaches and, during his presidency, he managed to get through forty-three of them (including a three-month power struggle with Ron Atkinson: 'I deserve a testimonial,' said a weary Ron), with six different coaches hired and fired in one season alone. Raddy Antić, however, was less argumentative and more durable, lasting three entire seasons as coach. The Yugoslav, who took over at the beginning of 1995/96, assembled a blend of imports and ex-youth team players, including Argentinian Diego Simeone and Koke, and won the 'double' in 1996.

The extra-time defeat of Cruyff's Barcelona in the Copa was followed by the club winning La Liga for the first time in twenty years. To put Antić's achievement into perspective, the previous season Atlético avoided relegation only by drawing its final Liga game. A loss would have meant Segunda. A relieved Gil continued to spend, buying Christian Vieri, Juan Esnáider and Juninho. Arrigo Sacchi replaced Antić in early 1999, and his six-month tenure was followed by Claudio Ranieri at the end of that season. But disaster was looming for Atlético Madrid.

In 1992, Atlético, in common most other Spanish clubs, restructured the club to convert itself from a members' organisation into a 'Sociedad Anónima Deportiva' (S.A.D.) by means of which individuals could buy and sell shares: in effect, a public limited sports company.

This legislation, although intended to make all Spanish football clubs more open and competitive, increased Gil's power base. One of his first and, in hindsight, most ill-conceived decisions was, in 1992, to close down the youth academy, allegedly in order to save money. As we have seen, this forced Raúl to join the Real Madrid youth scheme, and Raúl was almost certainly not the only promising young player who was forced to move from Atlético to other Liga clubs. A young Fernando Torres, soon to become feted as 'El Niño' ('The Kid'), remained at Atlético largely due to his and his family's affection for the club. His decision was possibly helped by the inducement of a first-team berth when he reached the age of seventeen.

Although he appears to have had Atlético's interests at heart, Gil was not a man to lose much sleep over a few moral scruples, and he could immediately detect a personal advantage from this change in Spanish corporate law. So it was that, in late 1999, Gil and his board were eventually suspended pending government investigations into the club's parlous financial situation. Gil was later convicted by a court of fraudulently acquiring Atlético Madrid.

A financial administrator was installed by the government to take over the running of the club, and Ranieri resigned in disgust in early 2000, with Atlético sitting one place above the relegation zone. Antić returned but it was too late to prevent the inevitable and, with a squad of demotivated players on basic wages, Atlético was relegated to Segunda at the end of 1999/2000. This being Atlético Madrid, the club also reached the final of the Copa in the same month it was relegated, but an Espanyol victory in the game prevented the occurrence of an unhappy irony.

'Vamos Atlétiiiiiiiii. . .'

It's a truism, but one worth repeating and one which applies to all genuine football supporters. It states that when your club is consistently winning, you feel proud of your team's achievements, honoured to associate yourself with the club and its players, and are disdainful of the meagre efforts of your competitors.

However, it's only when your club is trying hard but consistently failing that you fall in love with it. The 'noble loser' captures the heart, while the 'arrogant victor' gains the material kudos.

As a lifelong supporter of the Scottish national football team, I can confirm the validity of this perception, self-deluding though it may be. Atlético fans appear to share this sentiment, although perhaps to a lesser degree in recent years as Diego Simeone's defensively inclined but highly effective managerial talents have brought success and trophies to 'los colchoneros' and have re-established Atlético as one of the top three Spanish clubs.

The opening of Atlético's new, state-of-the-art, 68,000-capacity Wanda Metropolitano Stadium at the start of season 2017/18 has added to its recently enhanced elite status. And, although the club was founded in 1903 as an offshoot of Athletic Club de Bilbao, Atlético's record over the years – ten Liga and ten Copa del Rey titles as well as three UEFA Cup/Europa League trophies – demonstrates that the club is far from being a Basque afterthought. But it remains by some distance Madrid's 'second' club.

Real Madrid's achievements on the pitch dwarf those of 'los indios'. Real is one of the world's largest and most respected clubs, and its world-famous seventy-year-old, 82,000-capacity stadium is named in honour of a genuine innovator in the Spanish game and not after a Chinese international conglomerate based in Beijing.

Atlético fans have always felt a simmering resentment towards their more fashionable, better-connected neighbours and a corresponding deeply felt, passionate commitment to their club, which they perceive as something of a 'noble loser' with a reputation for, and a history of, encountering and overcoming adversity, and fighting against the odds, but also of occasionally indulging in self-inflicted misbehaviours and self-pity at the unfairness of footballing life.

However, when Atlético was relegated at the end of 1999/2000, season ticket sales increased from 27,000 to over 40,000 at the club's old Vicente Calderón Stadium, and the ground was packed for every home game during the two seasons the club remained in Segunda. A cynic might say that the reason for the upsurge in ticket sales was because, being in Segunda, they were cheaper but this does not explain the overall maintenance of the size of the support.

The fans' loyalty was tested in Atlético's first home game of the Segunda season when the team lost to Recreativo de Huelva, who had only narrowly escaped relegation to Segunda B. But the 'rojiblanco' fans cheered on their team throughout the match. What is this if not devotion to the cause? The view of the supporters and the peñas is best expressed in the phrase 'Atlético hasta la muerte' ('Atlético till I die'), and they are among the most committed supporters in Spain.

Much of the Real-o-phobia probably stems from the contrast between their old location, the Estadio Vicente Calderón, which sat in a fairly nondescript part of the city close to a major motorway, and attracted a lower-class, scruffier support than did the bourgeois, fashionably located Bernabéu. Nor has Real's bulging trophy cabinet and its reputation as 'Franco's ambassadors' helped in fostering an enduring sense of friendship between the two clubs. The relative ease with which Real secured seemingly inexhaustible financing was another factor in minimising mutual camaraderie.

This disparity in wealth between the clubs was once again revealed by a Deloittes analysis released in January 2019. The report showed that, with an income of over €750 million in 2017/18, Real Madrid is Europe's richest club. In second place is, of course, Barcelona. The only other Liga club in the top twenty is Atlético, in fourteenth place with around €300 million generated in that season. Presumably, this is one of the reasons why Real can spend €40 million on an eighteen-year-old Brazilian left-winger, Vinícius Jr., with less than twenty minutes of senior football under his belt, and why Atlético can't. So there is also an element of envy in the supporters' righteousness.

On the pitch, Bayern Munich's last-second, extra-time, speculative forty-yard goal in the 1974 European Cup final deprived Atlético of the European Cup they felt they deserved (and which they still lack), and led to then-president Calderón describing his club as 'El Pupas' ('The Jinxed Ones'). This feeling of being hard done by was pervasive. The general dislike of Real's 'elitist' middle-class support and its privileged directors has been shared by Atlético's board. Jesús Gil said, 'The directors' box at the Bernabéu is like Franco's hunting trips,' (and Gil should know, having been pardoned by his friend Franco for the Segovia episode). Although fans of 'los rojiblancos' have been accused by fellow madrileños of over-playing the role of misunderstood martyrs, I can understand why these diehard supporters feel the way they do.

At Real Madrid's anniversary celebrations, Plácido Domingo was hired to sing the club's solemn anthem. When Atlético Madrid reached the same age, a band played the Rolling Stones song 'You Can't Always Get What You Want'.

'Los rojiblancos' spent two seasons in Segunda, but the returning ex-manager Luis Aragonés hauled the club back into La Liga and he gave seventeen-year-old forward Fernando Torres his debut in the first team. By the age of nineteen Torres was the club's influential captain and a hero to the fans.

Gil died in 2004, and his son Gil Marin took over. During the first four seasons back in Primera, Atlético drifted around mid-table, until the arrival in 2006 of Mexican coach Javier Aguirre. Aguirre sold Torres to Liverpool for £27 million and replaced him with Sergio Agüero and Diego Forlán, handing £21 million to Villarreal for the Uruguayan striker, and he also took the unsettled winger José Antonio Reyes off Arsenal's hands in return for £12 million.

In the Mexican coach's second season, Atlético finished in fourth place in La Liga, the club's highest position since 1997, and in 2008/09 the club was again fourth. Aguirre, to many of the players' dismay, was sacked midway through the season. Forlán, possibly with one eye on the Atlético boardroom, said 'he was not the cause of our problems'.

However, that season Forlán won the Pichichi and, with the promising keeper David de Gea emerging from the youth team, and new signing Juanito from Real Betis playing alongside Agüero and Forlán, Atlético were now looking like genuine contenders, domestically and in Europe.

Appearances, however, can be deceptive. In 2009/10 Atlético could only finish ninth in La Liga, the club's first game being a 5–0 defeat by Málaga, and they were beaten by Sevilla in the Copa final. Earlier in the season, after a 4–0 thrashing by Chelsea in the Champions League, the board had sacked Aguirre's replacement, former 'rojiblanco' goalie Abel Resino, who described Atlético as 'a madhouse'.

With Quique Sánchez Flores now having replaced Resino at the asylum ('to and fro, the coaches go. . .'), Atlético didn't win a single game in the elite European competition, and dropped down to the UEFA Cup, newly rebranded and reformatted as the Europa League.

You will not be surprised to know that 'los colchoneros' then became the first club to win this new tournament. Having disposed of Valencia in the quarter-final and Liverpool in the semi-final, they did the same to Fulham in the final in Hamburg, with Forlán scoring both goals in the 2–1 win, which brought a major European trophy back to Atlético Madrid after a wait of almost fifty years. This club certainly knows how to make life difficult for itself.

Return of 'El Cholo'

In the middle of the 2011/12 season a familiar ex-Atlético player arrived at Vicente Calderón. Diego 'El Cholo' Simeone was back, but this time as the club's new manager. 'Cholo' was originally a pejorative racist word used to describe people of a native Latin American Indian background, but its meaning varies and it would have been unwise to insult Simeone in his presence.

Simeone had been one of Argentina's best players in a national squad which included Fernando Redondo and Gabriel Batistuta. He had played in three consecutive World Cup finals, earned 102 caps, eclipsing Maradona's international total, and he had successfully managed clubs in Latin America before resettling in Madrid.

A tenacious, versatile and single-minded midfielder, mainly a deep-lying central role but also as a flanker and occasional goalscorer, Simeone's philosophy was to 'play with the knife between the teeth'. He had been a prominent and popular player in the 1995/96 Atlético Madrid 'double' team and, after spells with Lazio and Inter Milan, he had returned to play for Atlético from seasons 2003 to 2005. He was welcomed back by the 'rojiblancos' faithful.

Seeing red

English football supporters probably best remember Diego Simeone from the England v Argentina game in the last-sixteen stage of the 1998 World Cup finals in France.

Two minutes into the second half, Simeone launched an intimidating foul challenge on David Beckham, then patted the boy wonder on the head as Beckham lay dazed on the pitch. The young Englishman retaliated by petulantly kicking the Argentinian from behind. Simeone over-reacted by falling over in an impressively theatrical manner, and Becks was sent off presumably for serious ungentlemanly conduct.

Simeone later admitted that he dived in an attempt to persuade the referee to dismiss the Englishman. Ever since the 1982 Falklands War there had existed hostility from Argentina towards England, and the South American side used every trick it knew to exact revenge for Margaret Thatcher's devious electioneering gambit. The game ended 2–2, Argentina progressed to the last eight on penalties, and England was out of the World Cup. The English support was incensed by Simeone's antics and he became a hate figure for the tabloid press and middle England.

The two men were reconciled at the 2002 World Cup finals when England beat Argentina 1–0, but a good many England fans still blame Simeone for England not lifting the World Cup trophy in 1998.

Within six months of Simeone's return, he had coached Atlético Madrid to its second Europa League final within three years. On 9 May 2012 in Bucharest his team lined up against Athletic Bilbao in the final. Four months before Simeone arrived at the

Vicente Calderón, Atlético had paid Porto £23 million for the services of Radamel Falcao, and the prolific Colombian striker scored two well-crafted individual goals in the first half. Diego Costa added a third in the second half, and Atlético claimed the trophy with a convincing 3–0 victory over Simeone's compatriot Marcelo Bielsa and his well-drilled attacking Athletic side.

Simeone's preference was for a defensive 4–4–2 formation but one which could adapt speedily to fluctuating fortunes on the pitch. When defending, his team adopted two compact lines, each of four players, forcing opponents out to the flanks or to inter-passing until they lost possession. When Atlético had regained the ball, they quickly launched counter-attacks, with the midfielders and centre-backs pressing closely behind the attack. He stressed the attacking virtues of set pieces and corners, and he frequently made tactical adjustments during games to disrupt and confuse the opposition. Simeone and his players seemed to thrive on adversity and the team performed as a coherent unit, with the manager having effectively instilled discipline and confidence into his men.

In 2012/13, Atlético reached third place in La Liga, the club's highest finish for thirteen years. The club also achieved its first victory over Real Madrid in fourteen years, dismissing its neighbours 2–1 after extra time in the Copa del Rey final at the Bernabéu. In June 2013 Falcao completed his transfer to Monaco. Although his departure was a disappointment to many fans, the £55 million which Atlético received from the French club must have come in handy.

The following season of 2013/14 was the most successful in the long history of 'los rojiblancos'. At the season's culmination, Atlético faced Barcelona in La Liga at Camp Nou, knowing that a draw would be sufficient to win the league title. If they lost, the title was Barcelona's. Diego Costa, scorer of twenty-five goals that campaign, was forced off early in the game with a hamstring injury and Alexis Sánchez put Barça ahead. A header from Uruguayan centre-back Diego Godin equalised, the game ended 1–1 and Atlético had won La Liga, becoming the first club in ten years other than Real Madrid and Barcelona to win the league. Never a man to keep a rigid check on his emotions, Simeone commented, 'This is enormous, there are no words to capture this feeling of happiness.'

One week later in Lisbon, however, although Atlético reached the European Cup final – its first such final for forty years – Diego may have felt less elated, as Atlético crumbled late in the match to lose 4–1 to Real Madrid. The indefatigable Godin opened the scoring, Sergio Ramos headed in for a Real equaliser in the third minute of injury time, and Bale, Marcelo and Ronaldo all scored in extra time. Once again, so near for Atlético . . .

Over the summer of 2014, there was much coming and going at the club. Diego Costa, goalie Thibaut Courtois and left-back Filipe Luís all joined Chelsea, while David Villa went to play in the MLS. Arrivals included strikers Antoine Griezmann and Mario Mandžukić, keeper Jan Oblak and central midfielder Saúl Ñíguez, returning from loan at Rayo Vallecano. The following season was, by Atlético's improving standards, fairly uneventful. The club was knocked out of the Copa and Champions League at the quarter-final stage, and ended La Liga season in third place, trailing winners Real Madrid by sixteen points.

To cheer everyone up, however, in January 2015 the golden boy had returned from his travels. Fernando Torres had left Madrid in 2007 for Liverpool and Chelsea and had scored over 120 goals whilst in England. Although technically on loan from Milan, 'El Niño' was now to end his senior career at Atlético, his home club.

In 2015/16, Atlético again finished in third place in La Liga and once more met Real Madrid in the European Cup final, in May 2016 at the San Siro. Ramos scored first and, with ten minutes left, Belgian winger Yannick Carrasco, who had joined 'los colchoneros' at the beginning of the season, made it 1–1. The game went to extra time, and then penalties. Both teams scored with their first three attempts. Juanfran missed Atlético's fourth, his shot hitting the post, while Cristiano Ronaldo converted Real's fifth and secured Real Madrid's eleventh European Cup.

Sales of Juanfran's replica shirt soared after the match, as the fans displayed their sympathy with the ex-Atlético youth academy right-back, and the club offered him a two-year extension to his contract. Simeone also was far from disheartened. He described his team's progress in the tournament as 'a triumph of the collective', citing the fact that, as well as Juanfran, four of his other important players – Koke, Gabi, Saúl and Torres – had graduated from the club's youth academy. This team had also defeated PSV, Barcelona and Bayern Munich on its way to the final, and it had been assembled at a small fraction of the money paid by other leading European clubs to acquire their top players.

Over the following two seasons, Atlético Madrid confirmed its status as one of Europe's most consistent clubs in recent years. The team ended 2016/17 in third place and 2017/18 in second position in La Liga although, in the latter, they were a full fourteen points behind a rampant Barcelona. In the 2017 Champions League semi-final a Cristiano Ronaldo first-leg hat-trick gave Real Madrid a 3–0 win. In the return match at a passionate and pulsating Calderón, early goals from Griezmann and Saúl raised the fans' hopes but were insufficient to defeat a defensive Real side.

The following season, Atlético were eliminated from the tournament at the group stage, dropped down to the Europa League and again reached the final. In the match in Lyon against Marseille, the excitable Simeone was banned from the touchline and confined to the stand after 'insulting a match official and improper conduct' during the semi-final defeat of Arsenal. Two goals from Griezmann, his twenty-eighth and twenty-ninth of the season, and a late third from Gabi gave Atlético a deserved third Europa League title within eight years. Griezmann had proved to be an inspired acquisition, and the Frenchman's performance on the pitch led to Atlético's adoption of a more attacking edge to their play to complement what had previously been unfairly perceived as defensive obduracy.

In February 2019 Diego Simeone contractually committed himself to a further three years with Atlético. One must greatly admire his and his team's commitment, and there is clearly a good deal more to come from Madrid's 'second club'.

The Bosman ruling

In December 1995 the European Court of Justice found in favour of Belgian footballer Jean-Marc Bosman who, in the light of his experience with his club RC Liège, had challenged the rules governing foreign EU players in other EU national leagues.

Prior to this, UEFA had decided on 'quotas' to control the number of professional foreign players at each club, but these quotas made little real difference to the clubs' control of their players. Also, EU clubs had frequently manipulated the transfer fee system in their own financial interests. The Bosman ruling declared such behaviour to be in restraint of trade and a breach of the 1992 Single Market requirements.

The ruling banned restrictions on foreign EU players and allowed players in the EU to move to another club at the end of their contract with no transfer fee. This legislation quickly led to the larger EU clubs spending increasingly more on foreign than on homegrown players, and it fundamentally changed the way in which business in football was conducted. As Bosman said after the judgement: 'the law of the jungle has been abolished'.

The 'Galacticos'

In 2000, Florentino Pérez, the newly elected president at the Santiago Bernabéu, was a wealthy and well-connected businessman, but his forerunner had overseen **Real Madrid** capturing two European Cups in the previous three seasons, so Pérez had to make his mark, and quickly.

His presidency began in the most controversial manner possible, when he prised from Barcelona's clutches the Portuguese winger and 'Ballon d'Or' winner Luis Figo, who had been a fan favourite and honorary Catalan at Camp Nou. The £55 million which Pérez paid Barcelona helped to ease Figo's departure from the Catalan club. Figo was the first player in what Pérez hubristically termed his 'galactico' project, which involved bringing some of the world's finest and most glamorous players to what the president believed was the world's finest and most glamorous club, with a new 'galactico' to be added every season and paraded in front of the adoring Bernabéu faithful and an envious football world.

Figo was followed by Zinedine Zidane in 2001/02 and, the following year, by Brazilian striker Ronaldo, with their arrivals costing Real Madrid, a club already in debt, a total of close on £200 million. In September 2002, Pérez announced the sale of the club's training ground, Ciudad Deportivo, which had been re-zoned from a legally protected green sporting ground to an area of commercial development (Pérez enjoyed a close friendship with the then-ruling PP) and which, in the then-overheated construction sector of the Spanish economy, realised around £450 million. This sum was sufficient to pay off the club debts, as well as buy and equip a new training ground at Valdebebas, near Madrid's airport.

At the conclusion of season 2000/01, Real won La Liga for the first time in four years, finishing a remarkable seventeen points ahead of fourth-placed Barcelona. During Zidane's first season, 2001/02, the club celebrated its centenary, a highlight of which was a World XI v Real Madrid, the latter team including not only Hierro, Iker Casillas and Raúl but also, among others, Ronaldo, Roberto Carlos, Zidane and Figo. A neutral observer may well have found it difficult to discern which side was the World XI.

Despite the stellar quality of the leading actors and their supporting cast, the curtain fell on the season with Real Madrid occupying third place in La Liga. A further embarrassment was that, at the Bernabéu and despite a stirring operatic performance by Plácido Domingo, they lost the Copa del Rey final to Deportivo de La Coruña, whose Galician fans, raucously waving blue-and-white flags and cheerfully chanting 'Happy birthday to you', may have adversely affected the arias of the Italian tenor as much as the Copa loss dispirited the club.

However, there remained the Champions League and a semi-final against Barcelona, the first time since 1960 that the two clubs had met in the European Cup. In the first leg, Real managed to ignore the normal crowd hostility at Camp Nou and escaped with a 2–0 lead, courtesy of Zidane and McManaman. A 1–1 result at home meant Real's appearance at Glasgow's Hampden Park in its third European Cup final in five years. The opposition was Germany's Bayer Leverkusen, a fast attacking side who laid emphasis on ball possession.

Within the first fifteen minutes the score was 1–1, from a Raúl strike which was equalised by Bayern's Lucio. On the stroke of half-time, Roberto Carlos sent in a looping cross from the left wing, Zidane pirouetted outside the penalty box, connected perfectly with the ball and smashed a glorious left-foot volley into the net. It was a thing of beauty, one of the best goals ever scored in the tournament's final, and fully justified Zidane's 'galactico' status. The game ended 2–1 to Real Madrid, the club's ninth European Cup trophy.

Real regained the Liga title in 2003 but, in the summer of that year, Pérez finally sacked coach Vicente del Bosque, a man for whom he had not only nursed a personal antipathy, but Del Bosque's avuncular, modest style also contrasted sharply with the president's desired new dynamic image for the club. This dismissal was despite the coach having won two Ligas and two European Cups in his four years at Real Madrid. Pérez also dismissed the team's popular captain Fernando Hierro.

Around a dozen players also left the club in this shake-up, including Morientes, McManaman and Claude Makélélé, the latter being the defensive pivot in the team but who felt himself undervalued. Real Madrid were to gain no further major trophies over the following four years, and they had no one to blame but themselves.

Several of the remaining players were by now becoming disenchanted with the 'galactico' policy, feeling that the club was increasingly becoming a fashion cakewalk for individual egos when it should instead have been embracing the virtues of a cohesive and collective team. Indeed, Zidane shared this sentiment and said: 'There's a lot of players leaving when the normal rule is: never change a winning team.' However, Pérez seemed as concerned with the club's balance sheet as he was with the league table, and the money rolled in from replica shirt sales, TV rights and sponsorship for his superstars.

Another 'galactico' turned up at the Bernabéu in the summer of 2003, and this particular celebrity footballer confirmed the growing cynicism about Pérez's policy as an exercise in marketing rather than in the necessary team-building. David 'Becks' Beckham arrived from Manchester United, having fallen out with boss Alex Ferguson, and, although Real's subsequent promotional jaunt around the Far East raised £10 million from the sale of white replica shirts, Beckham's contribution on the pitch was rather less quantifiable in its impact. He remained a dead-ball expert but he appeared to lack the on-pitch creativity and quick thinking required by his teammates. Indeed, for this reason *Marca* magazine dubbed him 'Forrest Gump'.

Over the following couple of seasons, and under the supervision of a variety of coaches, Real Madrid finished fourth and second in La Liga, and reached no further than the Champions League quarter-final. In 2005, in came two Brazilians: Julio 'The Beast' Baptista, an attacking midfielder from Sevilla, and Robinho, a forward from Santos who took over Figo's number 10 shirt. The ex-Barcelona Portuguese winger had left Real in mid-season to join Inter Milan whose supporters, unlike culés (see page 42), tend not to hurl a pig's head at an ex-player when he's taking a corner.

A third newcomer that summer was a highly rated nineteen-year-old Spanish centre-back, Sergio Ramos, acquired from Sevilla for a record fee for a Spanish defender. Fourteen years later, Ramos is captain of today's Real Madrid team and, crucial though he was and is to the team's current success, he emanates that blend of insouciance, determination and a hint of arrogance which for many observers epitomises 'los blancos'.

But still they scrabbled. A 3–0 defeat by Barcelona at the Bernabéu in November was followed by a 6–1 Copa semi-final thrashing at the hands of Real Zaragoza which was then followed by elimination by Arsenal from the Champions League. At the end of February 2006 Real were ten points behind Liga leaders and eventual winners Barcelona, and it was little surprise when Pérez resigned that month as club president.

Ramón Calderón assumed the presidency before 2006/07, brought in Dutch striker Ruud van Nistelrooy and appointed Fabio Capello as coach. Although Capello won La Liga title on the very last day by head-to-head goal difference over Barcelona – Real's thirtieth Liga and its first for four years – his defensively cautious methods had little time for the free-flowing, attacking play which the Bernabéu wanted to see. He fell out with Beckham who was off to join LA Galaxy at the season's end, alienated several other main men, and was dismissed in June 2007.

New coach Bernd Schuster ushered Real to the Liga title in 2007/08, a full eighteen points ahead of third-placed Barcelona. Also, it was a pleasure to see Villarreal occupy the runner-up spot. The 'yellow submarine' were effectively only in their eighth-ever Liga season but, with players like Diego López, Diego Godin, Santi Cazorla and Robert Pires, the club deserved to break surface and 'up periscope' in such previously uncharted waters.

By the end of the 2008/09 season, with Barcelona building up a head of steam, a new captain was required for 'los blancos', so back came Florentino Pérez as club president. Undaunted by the evidence revealing the shaky underpinning of his 'galactico' project, Pérez continued where he'd left off. However, his first season back in charge did not proceed according to plan.

***

After Van Gaal's departure and Nuñez's resignation in 2000, **Barcelona** had taken some while to settle into the new century. The team under-performed on the pitch, and four seasons and several coaches came and went before the club managed to get its act together.

Before the 2000/01 season began, Nuñez was replaced by Joan Gaspart and Van Gaal by Lorenzo Serra Ferrer, but neither man could prevent the slow slide towards relative mediocrity. Gaspart spent the money the club had received from the sale of Figo on decent if not outstanding players, including Marc Overmars, Gerard López, Giovanni, Coco, Emmanuel Petit and a few others, but they made little difference to the club's on-pitch fortunes.

Ferrer was fired during the season and replaced by the dependable Charlie Rexach, who edged Barça back to a final fourth place and qualification for the Champions League. The last game of the Liga season was against Valencia. Barcelona needed to win, while for 'los che' a draw would suffice for fourth spot. Rivaldo scored twice, but Valencia equalised. In the eighty-ninth minute Rivaldo, from outside the box, executed an astonishing overhead kick which sailed into the net for the winner. An awestruck *Guardian* described Rivaldo's contribution as 'the greatest hat-trick of all time . . . a midsummer night's dream of a performance'.

Barcelona reached the semi-final of the tournament in 2002, but Real Madrid, on the way to winning the European Cup, knocked them out 3–1, and Rivaldo's sublimely lyrical efforts were ultimately to no avail. 'Lord, what fools these mortals be', as Shakespeare had presciently commented in the *Guardian*'s favourite play.

In 2001/02 Rexach had again achieved fourth spot in La Liga but, for whatever reason, Gaspart invited Van Gaal back as coach for 2002/03, and by February 2003 Barcelona found themselves fifteenth in La Liga. Van Gaal resigned and Raddy Antić then did what he could, which was to end the season with Barça in sixth place, twenty-two points behind Real Madrid.

Gaspart had little other choice than to resign his presidency, and a younger man, Joan Laporta, was elected as the new president of Barcelona. Laporta decided to sign up a new coach. In time for the start of the 2003/04 season Frank Rijkaard, who had been a more than effective defensive midfielder for Holland, Ajax and Milan, took over as team boss.

Laporta had already bought Ronaldinho from PSG for over £25 million. Rijkaard agreed with Laporta about the potential value to his team of the multi-talented Brazilian forward, but believed that Barcelona was also in need of other fresh talent. In the early months of Rijkaard's first season, he was frequently harangued by sections of the Barça support as the team continued to struggle. The arrival of Rijkaard's mate, Edgar 'Pitbull' Davids, in January 2004 on loan from Juventus, renewed the side's impetus, and they ended the season in second place in La Liga behind Valencia, Barcelona's best position for four years.

By the start of the new season, the coach had in place Deco, Samuel Eto'o, Rafael Márquez and Ludovic Giuly, and he had promoted such youth team players as keeper Victor Valdés, inside-forward schemer Andrés Iniesta and defender Carles Puyol to play alongside another La Masia graduate, the by now first-choice and increasingly influential central midfielder Xavi.

In season 2004/05, it all came together, and Barcelona regained La Liga title which it had last won in 1998/99. The Cameroonian striker Eto'o contributed twenty-four league goals and Valdés picked up the Zamora Trophy, with Ronaldinho's and Deco's outstanding technique reminding the supporters of what they had been missing in recent years.

At a Camp Nou celebration of the title, the unpredictable Eto'o chanted to the crowd 'Madrid, cabrón, saluda al campeón' ('Madrid, bastards, salute the champions') and was fined by the Spanish football authorities for his comments. The African player's first professional club had been Real Madrid and, as he couldn't hold down a regular place at the Bernabéu, he had joined Real Mallorca and had delighted in scoring against 'los blancos'. He later apologised for his intemperate remarks.

During the following campaign, the high point for Rijkaard and his side was the 3–0 defeat of Real Madrid at the Bernabéu in November 2005, as well as the unprecedented standing ovation from many madrileños which Ronaldinho received for his two goals and his overall scintillating performance. The team walked La Liga again that season, twelve points ahead of second-placed

Real, and Eto'o's tally of twenty-six league goals won him the Pichichi.

And there was still the European Cup final to come. In Paris on 17 May 2006, Barcelona faced Arsenal. The Gunners suffered a serious setback when keeper Jens Lehmann was sent off after fifteen minutes, but they held on to a Sol Campbell goal until, with seventeen minutes remaining, Eto'o levelled the score and then late substitute Juliano Belletti scored another for a 2–1 Barcelona victory and the club's second European Cup win.

As ever, however, self-satisfaction leads to hubris, which tends to laxity and inevitably nemesis, and the Catalan club won nothing of any significance for the next two years. The final straw for Laporta came on 8 May 2008 when Liga champions Real Madrid crushed Barcelona 4–1. Rijkaard was losing control of his ill-disciplined stars, particularly Ronaldinho, and his attempts at maintaining discipline were becoming routinely ignored by the players. He had to go and, after Laporta had profusely thanked the coach for 'making history', he fired the Dutchman.

Laporta had a replacement in mind. A gamble, certainly, but worth a shot, or at least a sideways pass. Step forward, head held high, Pep Guardiola.

What's on telly?

Until La Liga season 2014/15, the Spanish professional league was the only such league in Europe which permitted its clubs to negotiate their own individual TV and broadcasting rights, under an arrangement known as 'rights of arena'. This allowed Real Madrid and Barcelona to reach lucrative deals amounting to over one-third of the total revenue generated, while smaller clubs struggled, each receiving a disproportionately lower share of the overall sum. For instance, in 2014/15 Barcelona pulled in around €140 million while Eibar and Almería had to get by on €12–15 million each.

In May 2015 the Spanish government passed legislation to correct the existing 'imbalance' and 'adapt to modern times' by initiating a 'collective rights deal', whereby the forty-two clubs in Primera and Segunda would all receive through La Liga a centrally decided percentage of the TV money. This took full effect from 2016/17, when the total revenue was €1.24 billion, and was agreed as follows:

• Ten per cent of total revenue was divided equally between the twenty-two Segunda clubs
• Ninety per cent was allocated to La Liga with i) fifty per cent divided equally between the twenty clubs and ii) the remaining fifty per cent split half based on such 'metrics' as the number of TV viewers per match, and the other half allocated on results/performances over the previous five seasons. An important clause – at least for Barcelona and Real Madrid – was that no club should receive less than it previously earned.

Although this was more equitable than the existing arrangements, Barcelona and Real Madrid each still earned €140 million but Atlético Madrid (€99 million), Athletic Bilbao (€71 million) and Valencia (€67 million) began to catch up. The ratio between highest and lowest Liga earners reduced from 8:1 to 4:1 over the two seasons.

However, the same ratio in the English Premier League is maintained at 1.54:1, and the EPL agreement is for money to be paid 'based on current performance' and not 'based on the previous five seasons', as the latter militates against newly promoted clubs. But when levelling the playing field, the grass roller has to start from somewhere.

Pep Talk

Pep Guardiola may not initially have been Laporta's first choice as Rijkaard's replacement but, in hindsight, the president could not have made a wiser decision. During his four seasons as Barcelona's coach, Guardiola (henceforth 'Pep', for reasons of brevity) became by some distance the most successful coach in the history of the club.

As Cruyff's one-time protégé and now disciple, Pep's manner, style of playing and attitude to the game often mirrored that of the 'total footballer'. However, in terms of the number of trophies and plaudits received, and the enduring legacy of his 'tiki-taka' methods to Barcelona and to the Spanish national side, he eclipsed the extravagant contributions of his Dutch master. An inexperienced, thirty-eight-year-old manager but a proud Catalan and a Barça fan since childhood, with the help of his assistant Tito Vilanova he elevated his club to a previously unattained dominant status in La Liga and the European game.

It all began in the summer of 2008. When he was offered the job, he accepted it, on the condition that 'I do it my way with my own people' and therein, as he soon demonstrated, lay the basis of his custodianship. As a believer in the importance of discipline – individual and collective – and the work ethic, he felt that Ronaldinho and Deco were no longer necessary and that their 'relaxed' lifestyles were negatively affecting the younger players such as 'wunderkind' Lionel Messi. He transferred them both, along with Zambrotta, Edmilson, dos Santos and several others.

Eto'o was also on his original departure list but the Cameroonian's improved training routine over the summer impressed Pep, so he remained, as did Yaya Toure and Thierry Henry. In came right-back Dani Alves and inside-forward Alexander Hleb, and La Masia graduate centre-back Gerard Piqué came home from Manchester United. Promoted 'cantaneros' included defensive midfielder Sergio Busquets and winger Pedro.

After a wobbly start to 2008/09, Barcelona went twenty games unbeaten, including a 6–2 defeat of Real Madrid, and won La Liga by nine points ahead of 'los blancos'. The club also won its twenty-fifth Copa del Rey, beating Athletic Bilbao 4–1. Pep concluded his triumphant season with a 2–0 Champions League final victory over Manchester United in Rome on 27 May, the goals coming from Eto'o and Messi. Barcelona became the first Spanish club to win the 'treble', Pep was the tournament's youngest winning manager and he had only begun his remarkable adventure.

Over the summer, in came towering Swedish striker Zlatan Ibrahimović and out went Eto'o. Barça's season 2009/10 lacked the omnipotence of the previous campaign, losing in the quarter-final of the Copa and being knocked out of the Champions League by Inter at the semi-final stage. They compensated for these misfortunes in April 2010 by defeating Real Madrid in 'El Clásico' for a club record four times in a row and in May they again won La Liga, this time amassing ninety-nine points.

Pep's brand of 'tiki-taka' football was nominally 3–4–3 and based on the pressing game. It involved maintaining possession (he adopted a 'six-second rule', which meant winning back the ball in this brief interval before the opposition had time to recover or regroup), short passing, moving ever forward and relying on such midfielders as Iniesta and Xavi to feed the forwards, in particular Messi playing in a 'false' number nine role (or, indeed, wherever he felt like playing). The speed and movement on and off the ball was often bewildering, as were the 'collective pressing' and rotational positioning manoeuvres. The play was zonal rather than man-marking, and was heavily influenced by what Pep had learnt while playing under Cruyff. At its best, Barcelona's football was irresistible.

Still it continued. In the summer of 2010, as Pep's third season began, striker David Villa and defender/midfielder Javier Mascherano joined the club, Henry left and Ibrahimović went on loan to Inter. In November they extended their 'Clásico' run to five on the trot, but they lost to a last-minute extra-time goal from Cristiano Ronaldo in the final of the Copa. Pep's team gained revenge over the madrileños in the Champions League semi-final, when they took a 1–1 first-leg Camp Nou result to the Bernabéu and secured a 2–1 victory to reach the final. Barcelona then won La Liga for the third year in succession. Finally, on 26 May at Wembley, Barça outplayed Manchester United in a 3–1 win to claim the European Cup, with goals from Pedro, Villa and Messi, the last-named being, unsurprisingly, Man of the Match.

Phew, yet on it went, although the momentum was beginning to slacken a trifle. Newcomers for 2011/12, Pep's fourth season, included forward Alexis Sánchez and playmaking, ex-youth team midfielder Cesc Fàbregas. Also a product of La Masia, Thiago had by now established himself in central midfield. In November, Pep Guardiola oversaw his 200th game in charge. He had won 144 of them, had drawn thirty-nine and had lost only seventeen. There would have been few dissenters to his right to the title when, two months later, he was named FIFA World Coach of the Year. Barcelona won the Copa del Rey but they were eliminated by Chelsea from the Champions League at the semi-final stage, and they conceded the Liga title to Real Madrid.

As an indication of the depressing disparity between the top two and the rest of La Liga, at the conclusion of that season, 2011/12, Real Madrid had notched up 100 points and Barcelona were nine points behind. Third-placed Valencia had accumulated only sixty-one. In fairness to other Liga clubs, though, over the following few seasons to the present day the Liga final points totals have become less polarised due, in part, to the ascendancy under Diego Simeone of Atlético Madrid.

In mid-April 2012, a weary but seemingly indomitable Pep Guardiola announced that he would be leaving at the end of the season. This is exactly what he did, and he flew off to New York for a year's sabbatical. Awaiting his return were Bayern Munich and then Manchester City, the latter, at the time of writing, being where he today plies his trade with a degree of success not too dissimilar to that which he achieved with his home club where, no doubt, his arrival will invariably be a welcome one.

'Alcorconazo'

When the mighty are humbled, the world relishes the spectacle.

Such was the case on the evening of 27 October 2009 after Real Madrid had travelled across the city to play AD Alcorcón, a small club then in Segunda B – the third tier of the Spanish league – in the first leg of the Copa del Rey round of thirty-two.

Watched by a full house of around 4,000 spectators crammed into the Estadio Santa Domingo, Alcorcón had three shots at goal within the first two minutes and ended the game with a 4–0 victory over the disbelieving 'galacticos'. The Real Madrid side contained players of the apparently invincible stature of Raúl,

Guti, Cristiano Ronaldo, Benzema, van Nistelrooy and Marcelo, and they had been comprehensively taken apart by a team of unknowns.

The next morning, this astonishing result was the lead story in the footballing pages of the Western European press, and had been labelled 'Alcorconazo'. Over the summer, Real had spent over £120 million on new players, Chilean coach Manuel Pellegrini had joined as the club's new manager, and the average annual salary of an Alcorcón player was less than one day's wages for Ronaldo.

This ranked as one of the most embarrassing episodes in the recent history of Real Madrid. The Bernabéu switchboards were jammed by calls for Pellegrini's instant dismissal. *Sport* newspaper described the game as a 'ridículo histórico', *Marca* called it 'a historic disgrace', and Sid Lowe in the *Guardian* invoked what is clearly that newspaper's footballing playwright authority, William Shakespeare, saying 'like Lady Macbeth, there's no way Madrid can properly rid itself of this stain'.

In the second leg at the Bernabéu, it took Real Madrid eighty-one minutes to score the only goal of the game, and they were knocked out of the Copa by their suburban minnow neighbours. Coincidentally or not, Alcorcón began a major stadium renovation the following month, and at the end of this season of their historic triumph, they were promoted to Segunda, where they remain today.

The most popular number in the Spanish national lottery that Christmas was 27, 109, or 27 October 2009. Well, if Alcorcón can do it, anything's possible . . .

In the aftermath of the 'Alcorconazo' debacle, **Real Madrid** failed to collect any trophies in 2009/10 and, inevitably, Pérez fired Pellegrini. His replacement coach – Real's eleventh in seven years – was also appointed sporting director and was described as another 'galactico'.

José Mourinho quit as manager of Inter Milan and joined Real Madrid in May 2010. After an indifferent career as a player in Portugal, Mourinho had served as an assistant to both Robson and Van Gaal at Barcelona. His alarmingly sensitive ego had been bruised by his being overlooked by Barça in favour of Pep Guardiola, and Mourinho had a point to prove.

The new coach hit the transfer market, acquiring midfielders Sami Khedira and Mesut Özil, defender Ricardo Carvalho and winger Ángel Di María. Mourinho's first season at the Bernabéu was obviously one of acclimatisation, as Real were eliminated from the Champions League in the first knockout stage by Lyon, were runners-up in La Liga, and they again lifted no trophies.

Things picked up a bit in 2010/11 as Real Madrid won its first Copa for eighteen years in a 1–0 defeat of Barcelona in the final. However, Real had earlier in the season suffered a 5–0 hammering by Barça at Camp Nou, a result described with some hyperbole by Pérez as the 'worst defeat in the history of the club', and they had been knocked out of the Champions League semi-final by, again, Barcelona. They then again reached the Champions League semi-final in 2011/12, only to lose the second leg on penalties to Bayern Munich. However, Real won La Liga for the first time in four long years, nine points clear of Barcelona.

With the aid of hindsight, Mourinho described season 2012/13 as 'the worst ever in my career', although he did have the good sense at the start of the season to buy from Spurs the Croatian playmaker Luka Modrić. Real Madrid were beaten, for the third successive year, at the Champions League semi-final stage, this time by Borussia Dortmund, while Atlético Madrid denied Mourinho's team victory in the Copa final.

The coach's erratic behaviour, and his deteriorating relationship with Ramos and Casillas, were causing problems, as was the club's final second place in La Liga, fifteen points behind Barcelona. At the season's end, Mourinho left the club 'by mutual agreement'.

***

While Pep Guardiola was window-shopping on Fifth Avenue and enjoying his sabbatical in New York City, 3,500 miles away across the Atlantic the new manager of **Barcelona**, Girona-born Tito Vilanova, was putting together his team for the 2012/13 season.

Vilanova had come through the Barcelona youth academy but, like a good number of other promising youthful players, he had not broken through the ranks and had a relatively undistinguished playing career elsewhere. After retiring as a player, however, he had been at Pep's side as his assistant for the previous four years and had shared in the club's triumphs.

Tito began 2012/13 by acquiring defender Jordi Alba from Valencia and midfielder Alex Song from Arsenal. In his season at the helm, Tito's team reached the semi-finals of the Copa, losing 4–2 to Real Madrid, and the same stage in the Champions League. In the latter, Barcelona were hammered 7–0 on aggregate by Bayern Munich, with Müller and Robben scoring five of them. However, helped by Messi's Liga tally of forty-six goals, Barcelona wrenched back La Liga trophy from Real Madrid, leaving the old enemy in second place and fifteen points behind. At the season's end, Tito resigned due to a recurrence of throat cancer, and he died from cancer complications in April the following year at the age of forty-five.

His managerial role had been assumed by Argentinian Gerardo 'Tata' Martino in July 2013. A couple of months earlier, Camp

Nou was buzzing with the news that the Brazilian Neymar was joining the club for the 2013/14 season. However, even with his team of superstars 'Tata' would win no trophies that season, and Barça narrowly lost La Liga title to Atlético Madrid. So, in May 2014, it was ta-ta to 'Tata'.

'Money doesn't talk . . .'

In May 2013 Barcelona signed one of the finest forwards ever to have emerged from the footballing hothouse that is Brazil.

Neymar da Silva Santos Júnior, otherwise known as Neymar, was a forward whose footballing skills were phenomenal. He joined the club from Santos on a five-year contract which was stated by Barcelona to be worth around €57 million. The signing ceremony was witnessed by club president Sandro Rosell, vice-president Josep Maria Bartomeu and sporting director Andoni Zubizarreta, before the Brazilian was paraded in front of 55,000 delighted culés at Camp Nou.

Although Neymar had also been approached by, among other European clubs, Real Madrid, the twenty-one-year-old striker/winger said that he had been persuaded to come to Barcelona by his international teammate and Barça player Dani Alves. 'My dream has come true,' said the young Brazilian genius. However, shortly before becoming an honorary Catalan, Neymar had commented, with a view to the forthcoming 2014 World Cup finals in Brazil: 'I'm saying once and for all that I'm not leaving Santos right now.' Obviously someone or something – possibly the financial inducements dangled in front of him – had changed his mind.

During Neymar's spell at Barça he scored over 100 goals for the club and, in conjunction with Lionel Messi and Luis Suárez (known collectively as 'MSN'), he terrorised Spanish and European defences and the three forwards broke goalscoring records with impunity. In 2017, amid acrimony concerning alleged breach of contract, he departed Barcelona to join Paris St Germain.

Shortly after Neymar had joined Barcelona, a club member had challenged the stated size of the transfer fee, alleging that the actual fee had been closer to €74 million, and he took out a legal action attempting to prove 'misappropriation of funds'. Also, Santos and other interested parties to the transfer had questioned the relatively small sums they received, while Neymar's parents had benefited to the sum of €40 million from the transaction.

In January 2014, a judge found in favour of the club member's allegation. The day before the judge announced his decision, Rosell resigned with immediate effect as club president. Furthermore, in February Barcelona and Bartomeu were found guilty of tax fraud in relation to this matter, although these charges were dropped later that year.

As the details concerning Neymar's transfer were complicated and were subject to counter-allegations from Barcelona, I will not elaborate on the whole business other than to say that, aside from Neymar, few of those involved emerged from the transaction with any great credit. (Also, my personal experience in the book publishing business of the wrath of m'learned friends is a salutary one.) However, one thing is clear today when observing a supremely gifted player, a category to which Neymar most certainly belongs. This is that, in today's game, a player of this outstanding calibre is not simply a footballer but also virtually a multinational company, with financial advisers, lawyers, agents and probably pension funds profiting abundantly from his talents.

When observing Neymar, Ronaldo or Messi effortlessly weaving their ways through bewildered defences, it's easy to forget this. Such players bring a special magic to the game. But they also enrich their non-footballing 'advisers' who 'protect their client's interests' often to the detriment of those who foot their astronomic wages and, more importantly, those spectators who pay to watch them parade their unique talents. Sadly, such is the reality of modern international football at the highest level.

With Uruguayan striker Luis Suárez arriving from Liverpool for a reported £65 million, and with Messi and Neymar already in place, in the summer of 2014 Barcelona could with justification boast the world's most prolific attacking trio. The new manager was ex-Real Madrid and ex-Barça attacking midfielder and captain Luis Enrique, who acquired Chilean keeper Claudio Bravo and Croatian midfielder Ivan Rakitić to lend support to this 'MSN' forward line.

Suárez, who could be described as a 'temperamental' player, had been banned from the game by FIFA for four months after having bitten (yes, bitten) Giorgio Chiellini during that summer's World Cup finals, and therefore he didn't play his first competitive game till late October. Barcelona had a poor start to season 2014/15 but quickly recovered. In May the club won La Liga – its seventh title in eleven seasons – and also the Copa, beating Athletic Bilbao 3–1 in the final. In June, Barcelona claimed its second European Cup in six years, beating Juventus 3–1 in the final. The club had gained its second 'treble', helped by an MSN goal total of 122 in all competitions, and once more Barcelona were rampant at home and in Europe.

It was a similar story in 2015/16. Well, almost. Luis Enrique's side, under Bartomeu's re-elected presidency, were domestically unassailable. They again won the Spanish 'double', pipping Real Madrid to La Liga title by one point and winning the Copa with an extra-time 2–0 defeat of Sevilla in the final. The team of the moment Atlético Madrid, however, were their nemesis in the Champions League, beating the 'blaugranas' 3–2 in the quarter-final. Yet the MSN trio surpassed themselves that season by scoring an extraordinary 131 goals in total.

Celebrations in Barcelona were muted in March 2016 when the death of Johan Cruyff was announced. The Dutchman – 'El Salvador' – had created an enduring legacy at Barcelona as player and manager. Jürgen Klinsmann, himself no mean exponent of the game, said: 'Barcelona was not born in the last couple of years. It was born in the early 90s through Johan Cruyff.' As Cruyff had commented: 'We showed the world you could enjoy being a player. I represent the era which proved that attractive football was enjoyable and successful, and good fun to play too.' There were many, myself included, who believed that he was the greatest player of all time and that, as a manager, he had few equals.

But football continues, and Enrique's final season as coach was relatively disappointing. Although Barça won the Copa, beating Alavés 3–1, they were second to Real Madrid in La Liga and were beaten 3–0 by Juventus in the Champions League quarter-final. At the season's end, Neymar left for PSG and Luis Enrique made way for Ernesto Valverde as coach. Yet despite these changes, the club claimed La Liga in 2018, fourteen points ahead of Atlético Madrid.

FC Barcelona, a remarkable footballing institution and one of the oldest and most successful clubs in Spain, shows little sign of ceding its mastery to anyone. Barcelona remains one of the most exciting and skilful clubs in Europe, a status which, at least in the near future, it is unlikely to relinquish.

***

After José Mourinho's dismissal from his position, Carlo Ancelotti, with his assistant Zinedine Zidane, took over as manager of **Real Madrid** for the start of season 2013/14. Ancelotti was followed to the Bernabéu by Spurs' speedy winger/striker Gareth Bale, a world record acquisition at €100 million.

Real was an impressive side: keeper Casillas was defended by Ramos and Varane in central defence; midfield was patrolled by Modrić, Khedira and Di María; and up front lurked strikers Benzema, Ronaldo and Bale. It was a classic Real combination of firm defence, midfield guile, speedy wingers and ruthless striking power. This team possessed more than sufficient skill, strength and determination to hold its own against virtually any other European side.

In the Copa final 2–1 win against Barcelona at the Mestalla, Bale demonstrated his lightning turn of speed for the eighty-fifth-minute winner when he sprinted from his own half to plant the ball firmly in the Barça net. Real stuttered in La Liga, finishing in third place behind Atlético Madrid and Barcelona. However, they compensated for their inability to beat Atlético in La Liga by winning 4–1 after extra time against their city neighbours in the Champions League final in Lisbon in April 2014. This was Real's first European Cup win for twelve years and the first time that two teams from the same city had met in the final. It was Real Madrid's tenth European Cup, so it was dubbed 'La Décima'.

The 2014 World Cup finals had taken place over the summer before the Liga 2014/15 season kicked off, and three of that tournament's star players – Costa Rican keeper Keylor Navas, German midfielder Toni Kroos and Colombian forward James Rodríguez – now found themselves playing for Real Madrid. The season began haltingly but Real then embarked on a twenty-two-game winning run. This laudable achievement, however, brought in no trophies. They were eliminated from the Champions League by Juventus in the semi-finals, they failed to retain the Copa and they occupied second spot in La Liga. So Real did as they always did, which was to blame and then fire the manager.

The supposedly steady hand of Rafael Benítez was brought in to replace Ancelotti for 2015/16, and he guided the club to an unbeaten run in their first eleven games. But Real were embarrassingly thrashed 4–0 by Barcelona, and they were disqualified from the Copa for fielding an ineligible player against Cádiz. As Benitez was failing on the pitch, and was making enemies within the club, he was dismissed as coach in January 2016 and replaced by assistant coach Zidane.

Zidane's methods turned the club around and secured an end-of-season second place in La Liga, just behind Barcelona. More importantly, Real reached their second Champions League final in three seasons. At the San Siro, Real again faced Atlético and, with the score 1–1 after extra time, they won on penalties. Naturally, this was 'La Unidécima'.

With Zidane now firmly in charge for 2016/17, by January Real had set a new Spanish record of forty undefeated matches. They won La Liga for the thirty-third time, their first league title for five years. Furthermore, a resounding 4–1 defeat of a strangely subdued Juventus at Cardiff's Millennium Stadium in June 2017 in the Champions League final resulted in 'La Duodécima'. At the Olympic Stadium in Kiev the following season, 2017/18, Real reached its third successive Champions League final. Two second-half goals from Bale – the first coming from an acrobatic bicycle kick only two minutes after he had come on as substitute – helped Real to a 3–1 win over Liverpool, whose keeper Karius is probably still suffering nightmares over his two basic errors which allowed Real to score.

After having achieved what had not been seen since Bayern Munich's three-on-the-trot European Cup wins in the mid-1970s, Zidane stunned the football world by announcing his resignation from Real Madrid with immediate effect. Still, that's Real Madrid for you.

Going down

Although the performances and achievements in recent years of Real Madrid and Barcelona have been wholly admirable, one does develop a slightly weary, almost jaundiced attitude towards the recounting of all the victories gained and the trophies acquired by the 'big two'.

As this book is titled *Life in La Liga* and not *Life in Madrid / Barcelona*, a useful corrective is to move briefly away from the constant emphasis on 'Real Barcelona' and to look at the other end of La Liga – relegation – over the last ten seasons.

Although such grand clubs as Athletic Bilbao, Espanyol, Valencia, Sevilla and Real Sociedad rarely venture down to the depths of La Liga, it is instructive to discover the number of supposedly established and highly regarded Spanish clubs who did get their fingers burnt. Over the ten-year period between seasons 2008/09 and 2017/18, there were thirty vacancies for promotion from Segunda to Primera and the same number in the opposite direction.

Most of these clubs fell victim only once over this period to

---

these status downgrades. These included such names as Málaga, Las Palmas, Granada, Rayo Vallecano, Racing Santander, Real Zaragoza and 'El Decano' Recreativo de Huelva. A few of these clubs suffered the further embarrassment of relegation at the end of the very same season in which they were promoted. These 'one-season wonders' consisted of: Tenerife, the Canary Islands club which had made its previous appearances in La Liga during the 1990s; Xerez, from Jerez in Andalucia, which enjoyed its Liga visit for the one and only time in its lifetime of over sixty years; Hércules, the Valencia Community club which savoured its second La Liga season for forty-five years; and other somewhat loftier sides – Córdoba, Osasuna, Numancia and Deportivo de La Coruña – also made nodding, in-and-out, one-off appearances in this humbling category.

Out of all the relegated clubs, Deportivo de La Coruña hold the record for these ten years, as they were relegated no fewer than three times. A number of other clubs – Real Betis, Almería, Sporting de Gijón, Las Palmas and Valladolid – suffered the ignominy of Segunda on two separate occasions.

However, the larger the club, the stronger is the likelihood that it will soon be returning to Primera. The bigger clubs can more easily withstand the financial constraints of Segunda – and the temporary dwindling of the fan base when the supporters learn that next week's game is against Valencia Reserves and not Real Madrid – as they are confident they will soon return to the luxurious lifestyle of La Liga. And most of them do scramble back, and fairly quickly.

As far as promotion from Segunda to La Liga is concerned, the financially less well-endowed clubs find it difficult to enter and remain in Primera, as I mentioned in Part One when discussing

Eibar. However, Eibar are now in their fifth consecutive season in the top division and, as I write, with over two-thirds of the 2018/19 season gone, they appear to be well above the danger zone. Eibar's confidence in their ability to remain in Primera was no doubt assisted by their putting three goals past Real Madrid without reply earlier in this 2018/19 season.

In this ten-year period, and as well as Eibar, two other clubs – Girona and Leganés – made their Liga debuts, and they also appear to be out of trouble. However, Huesca – a new entrant in 2018/19 – is currently propping up La Liga and appears doomed to return to Segunda, although the gap between the bottom eight clubs is currently only a few points and who knows what may yet happen? Although it's tough competing against the wealthy head boys, it's heartening to see the smaller sides giving it their best shot in La Liga.

La Liga: 2018/19

The eighty-eighth Liga season kicked off in August 2018 after its usual flurry of comings and goings.

The many newcomers this season included two highly praised young Brazilian forwards. Malcom joined Barcelona from Bordeaux and eighteen-year-old Vinícius Júnior arrived at Real Madrid from Flamengo. Both players, essentially wingers, enjoyed encouraging opening seasons in La Liga.

Towards the end of the season, two particularly unexpected events were the departure of Cristiano Ronaldo from Real to Juventus for a reported £105 million and the return of Zinedine Zidane in March 2019 as coach of Real Madrid, only nine months after he had unequivocally resigned from the same position.

Ronaldo's record with 'los blancos' is unparalleled. Between his arrival from Manchester United in 2009 and his move to Serie A, the thirty-three-year-old Portuguese winger-cum-striker had played a critical role in helping his club to capture two Liga and two Copa titles and four Champions League trophies; he is the club's all-time top goalscorer, including thirty-four Liga hat-tricks; he is the first player to win the Ballon d'Or five times; and his footballing genius is obvious to all who watch him.

Zidane's departure, and its timing at the conclusion of the previous season, had itself seemed odd, given that he had just managed 'los blancos' to the club's third successive Champions League victory, a feat unmatched since Bayern Munich's European Cup treble between 1974 and 1976. Also, the Frenchman had been a popular figure with the players, partly due to his own unimpeachable history as a player, and his Real Madrid team had lost only sixteen of the 149 games they played under his managership. His explanation for leaving when he did – 'I think the players need a change' – clearly had its origins in Real's third place that season in La Liga behind neighbours Atlético and winners Barcelona.

The tenure of his successor, Josep Lopetegui, began with an embarrassing confrontation between RFEF and Real Madrid and ended in October with a 5–1 defeat at Camp Nou by Barcelona. Zidane's ex-teammate Santiago Solari took over in early November and oversaw a 3–0 away defeat by lowly Eibar as well as humiliating home losses to Real Sociedad, Girona and Barcelona. Although they perked up a bit under Solari, the Barça game coincided with Real's expulsion by Ajax from the Champions League, so out went Solari. Although defender Daniel Carvajal stated after the second leg of the Ajax game that the real reason for Real's failings was that 'we have had a shit season', the manager was yet again blamed.

VAR

This season's campaign witnessed the arrival in Spanish Liga football of a new, highly questionable 'benefit': Video Assistant Referee (VAR). The technology had been used in the summer World Cup in Russia and, seduced by its apparent objectivity and its claim to minimise on-pitch errors, it was adopted by La Liga, despite the indisputable facts that the appeal of football has always been about mistakes, that VAR relegates the essential authority of the referee by faceless technocrats and thereby diminishes his ultimate authority in the eyes of the players, that it interferes – to no one's benefit – with the impetus of the game, that it has the potential to incite crowd violence, and a good deal more besides. However, no doubt time will reveal VAR's inherent failings, and it will be discarded to the dustbin of footballing history where it will join the 'golden goal', 'catenaccio' and other failed attempts to intrude on the enjoyment of such a simple game as football.

Another victim of the 'let's sack the manager' game was Pablo Machin who took over in May 2018 as manager of Sevilla after having led Girona, in 2016/17, to the Catalonian club's first Liga season in its eighty-five years' existence. He was fired only nine months later, the morning after Sevilla's defeat by Slavia Prague in the last sixteen of the Europa League. Sevilla were sixth in La Liga – a respectable position – when he joined, and sixth in La Liga when he was fired. What do these club presidents want?

Meanwhile, back at Real Madrid and after a brief, unproductive flirtation between the club and José Mourinho, 'Zizou' was lured back to oversee operations, with 'los blancos' sitting twelve points behind the leaders and now out of Europe. Season 2019/20 should be an interesting test for Zidane and Real.

Otherwise, life continued more or less as normal in La Liga. Barcelona won its second Liga on the bounce, and its eighth title within the previous eleven seasons, leading Atlético Madrid, under Simeone's astute stewardship, by eleven points and by a crushing nineteen points ahead of Real Madrid. Valencia (in their final match) and Getafe did particularly well, securing respectively fourth and fifth positions, while Sevilla and Espanyol completed the line-up for European competition in 2019/20. Alavés began well but faded away towards the end, while their unfancied neighbours Eibar maintained their unpredicted proud status in La Liga for a fifth successive year. Athletic Bilbao hovered close to the relegation zone, and the club's first demotion in its ninety-year Liga history, but recovered to mid-table as the season drew to a close.

Victims of relegation in 2018/19 were the trio of Rayo Vallecano (constantly up and down), Huesca (up and down in one season) and Girona (up and down in two seasons), and the two automatic promotions from Segunda were, to no one's surprise, Osasuna and Granada.

The third club to be promoted from Segunda emerged from a play-off between Málaga, Albacete, Real Mallorca and Deportivo de La Coruña. In the final home and away games of the play-offs, Real Mallorca narrowly defeated Dépor 3-2 on aggregate and, seven years after relegation, were back in Primera for 2019/20.

Copa del Rey

The 117th anniversary of this venerable Spanish football tournament was held during season 2018/19. By early October there were thirty-two clubs battling it out in the Copa: six from Tercera and Segunda B, six from Segunda, seven clubs who had qualified from European competitions, and the remaining thirteen from Primera. The lowest-ranked club left in the competition – Sant Andre, a Barcelona-based club from the Tercera División – was defeated 5–0 by Atlético Madrid in this round.

By the end of February in the Copa, the semi-finals had taken place, the finalists had been decided and the smaller clubs had all disappeared. Barcelona's 4–1 dismissive displays against Real Madrid, and a 3–2 Valencia defeat of Real Betis, saw Barcelona face Valencia in the Estadio Benito Villamarín on 25 May.

On a raucous evening in Seville, in a heatwave temperature exceeding 30 degrees and with 'cooling breaks' welcomed by the players, reigning Copa champions Barcelona – seeking a record fifth consecutive victory in the tournament – had all the early possession but fell victim to two counter-attacking Valencia goals within twelve first-half minutes. A goal from Messi midway through the second half was all that Barcelona could manage in response, and the Catalan club was beaten 2–1. Valencia had won its eighth such title and the club's first Copa for eleven years.

Meanwhile, in Europe . . .

Spanish football clubs have long dominated European tournaments, and seven Liga clubs – Sevilla, Real Betis, Villarreal, Valencia, Real Madrid, Atlético Madrid and Barcelona – entered the two main continental competitions in 2018/19. For only the third season in the previous fourteen years, however, none of them won a trophy, nor even reached either final.

In the Europa League, Betis and Sevilla were eliminated in the early knockout stages. To lessen further the opportunity of a Spanish club reaching the final, Valencia met Villarreal in the quarter-final and 'los che' won 5–1, although an energetic performance by Arsenal resulted in a 7–3 drubbing of Valencia in the semi-final.

Two English clubs – Arsenal and Chelsea – met in the Europa League final.

In the Champions League, Atlético Madrid won 2–0 at home but suffered a 3–0 defeat by Juventus in Turin, the apparently ageless Cristiano Ronaldo picking up yet another hat-trick for his new Italian employer. Barcelona took a 3–0 semi-final first-leg win to Anfield, decided to protect the lead, and were as a result defeated 4–0 in an epic comeback by a determined Liverpool performance on a thrilling evening of football.

To round off a bad season for 'los blancos', Real Madrid had been eliminated from the competition at the last sixteen stage. In the first leg in Amsterdam, a young Ajax team – six of whom had emerged through the Ajax youth system and had all fought their way through the early qualifying rounds – had the bad fortune to lose 2–1 to the mighty madrileños but the Dutch side's skill, passing, tackling, constant pressing and unceasing determination frequently bewildered the Real players. Ajax's performance brought to mind the Johan Cruyff-inspired side of the early 1970s and gladdened the hearts of all football enthusiast neutrals.

In the second leg at the Bernabéu, Ajax had the effrontery to demolish Real Madrid, the reigning champions. The Dusan Tadic-inspired Dutch team were two goals ahead within the first eighteen minutes, winning the tie 4–1 and 5–3 on aggregate. The post-match Spanish media comments were damning, ranging from *AS*'s 'a tragic week' to *Marca*'s 'failure of the century', and captain Sergio Ramos's last-minute decision in Amsterdam to provoke a booking and suspension, so as to be in top shape for the following round, revealed Real's condescending certainty that the second leg would be a formality.

Ajax, who fully deserved all the praise lavished on their

performances, were knocked out of the tournament in the semi-final by Tottenham Hotspur.

Two English clubs – Liverpool and Spurs – met in the Champions League final.

***

Given the presence of four English clubs competing in the two 2018/19 European competitions, it's legitimate to ask if this signals the arrival in European football of the Premiership's impending dominance over La Liga.

This is quite possible. In recent years, the English Premier League is now in fourth place (after the NFL, Major League Baseball and the NBA) in terms of revenue generated by the world's leading professional sports leagues. La Liga is now in seventh place, behind the Bundesliga. Although money is not the sole factor in determining excellence – as has been demonstrated by this season's performance from Ajax among others – it certainly helps in acquiring the world's most talented coaches and players.

Also, it is interesting to note that the managers of these four English finalists are all non-English by birth and footballing upbringing. The number of English managers in the Premier League has nearly halved over the last ten years or so. Along with this, every Premier League season sees the arrival of non-English quality players to the league. Both such groups bring with them different methods of playing and understanding the game, and the results are obvious.

It's still too early to answer the question, and La Liga has shown it can surprise all observers. But it is far from unlikely and, if so, La Liga is more than capable of overturning neutral predictions on the European stage. It has done so before, on frequent occasions.

What next?

In the fourth century BC in Greece there lived a philosopher known as Zeno of Elea. Described by Aristotle as 'the inventor of dialectic', Zeno outlined four arguments – Zeno's Paradoxes – which 'proved' the impossibility of motion.

One of these paradoxes is as follows. Achilles, the fastest man alive, runs a race with a tortoise who has a start of n metres. Assume that the tortoise runs one-tenth of the speed of Achilles. Therefore, by the time Achilles has reached the tortoise's starting position, the tortoise is n/10 metres ahead of Achilles. When Achilles arrives at this point, the tortoise is now n/100 metres in front of the speedy Greek. This continues ad infinitum and means that Achilles cannot catch up with the tortoise.

You may ask yourself, and quite rightly, why I am invoking, in a book on the history of Spanish club football, the philosophical musings of a Greek philosopher from 2,500 years ago. The reason is not simply due to my fascination for philosophy, but rather because Zeno's proposition reminds me of Real Madrid and Barcelona, and these two clubs' relationships with the other clubs in La Liga.

If one imagines the two conquistadores collectively as 'the tortoise' and all the other Spanish clubs as 'Achilles', and if there is any correlation between Zeno's speculations and football, then this is a useful (if somewhat strained) analogy for the current state of the club game in Spain. No matter how hard they try, no one is ever going to catch up definitively with Real Madrid and Barcelona. Occasionally, another club – for instance, today's Atlético Madrid – may confound Zeno's conjectures but, as a general rule, overtaking 'Real Barcelona' appears, in any meaningful sense, to be an impossibility. The dominant position of the two big boys in recent years, and the ease with which they maintain this, suggests that their masterful supremacy will continue ad infinitum.

However, one does not need recourse to ancient Greek wisdom to confirm the difficulty of unseating these two old clubs from their thrones in La Liga. Although since the beginning of La Liga, a number of clubs – Athletic Bilbao, Valencia, Atlético Madrid, Real Sociedad, Real Betis, Sevilla and Deportivo de La Coruña – have assumed temporary ascendancy in Primera, the story of Spanish club football has been and remains essentially the constant and continuing battle between Real Madrid and Barcelona.

In this respect, Spain is not too dissimilar to several other European leagues. For instance, in Scotland between 1904 and 1939 only one club (Motherwell) other than Celtic and Rangers won the top division. The hegemony of the two Glasgow clubs was again briefly interrupted by the 'New Firm' of Dundee United and Aberdeen in the late 1970s and early 1980s, but normal service was soon resumed.

Likewise, in the German Bundesliga it is rare indeed in recent years to see a league-winning club which is not Bayern Munich or Borussia Dortmund. In Holland, there have been only two seasons over the last thirty-five years when the league champion has not been Ajax, PSV Eindhoven or Feyenoord. In Italy's Serie A, over the last thirty seasons there have only been four occasions when the league winner was not Juventus, AC Milan or Inter.

From the beginning of the English Premier League in 1992/93, for all but two seasons the title has been won by either Manchester City, Manchester United, Chelsea or Arsenal, so it's slightly more competitive than in Spain. Also, although PSG in France appears today to be picking up the winning habit, several other clubs – including Lyon, Monaco, Nantes and Bordeaux – have been recent title winners. Generally, however, and particularly since football has become an international business as much as a sport, each European country's league has been dominated, more or less, by the same (wealthy) names. This being so, Spain's footballing duopoly is not as unusual as many observers may suppose.

As I have said in this book, the growth and increasing inclusivity of European football has allowed other leading Spanish clubs – principally Sevilla, Valencia, Atlético Madrid, Deportivo de La Coruña, Real Zaragoza, Villarreal, Espanyol, Valladolid and Celta de Vigo – to compete at a high level with other major European sides, and to be rewarded financially and with their profiles significantly enhanced. Clubs such as these will no doubt continue to benefit from these European tournaments, and also from the domestic opportunities offered by the Copa del Rey.

But it does seem unlikely in the foreseeable future that a third club will emerge to offer a serious and lasting challenge to 'los blaugranas' and 'los blancos'. Their financial strength and international reputation allow them to take their pick of the world's leading players, and their influence and infrastructures overshadow that of any other Spanish club side.

Real Madrid have won the European Cup – the continent's flagship tournament – a remarkable thirteen times, almost twice as many as the second-placed AC Milan, with Barcelona having claimed five trophies. The only other Spanish clubs to have reached the European Cup/Champions League final are Atlético Madrid (on three occasions) and Valencia (twice), but neither club has been victorious.

However, in the 'second tier' UEFA Cup/Europa League (a tournament which the 'big two' have largely tended to ignore, although Real Madrid did win the UEFA Cup twice), Sevilla head the winners' list with five trophies, followed by three for Atlético Madrid and one for Valencia, while Athletic Bilbao, Espanyol and Alavés have each reached the final.

But the disparity is also evident in domestic tournaments, with Madrid having claimed La Liga thirty-three times, with Barcelona on twenty-six and, third on the list, Atlético Madrid with ten. As is generally the case in national cup tournaments, the Copa del Rey has a wider range of winners. Fourteen clubs have held the Copa, headed by Barcelona although, in this case, Athletic Bilbao is in second place and Real Madrid is an ignominious third.

So the Spanish game is not all about 'Real Barcelona', as matches in La Liga and the Copa del Rey do result on several occasions in the defeat of both these two clubs, and the other Spanish clubs frequently compete successfully in European tournaments against some of the continent's top teams. Also, and despite the financial and logistical barriers to Primera entry, it has been heartening over the last few years to see such 'small' clubs as Alavés, Eibar, Girona, Leganés, Huesca and even Xerez make their first appearances in La Liga. In particular, the first-mentioned two clubs appear to have settled well into Primera and look likely to remain there, for a few more seasons anyway.

Club football in Spain, even although a relatively late starter and brutally interrupted during its formative years, is today regarded as representing the game at its finest, and not entirely because of Real Madrid and Barcelona. Despite the traumas and tragedies which it witnessed in the previous century, Spanish club football has generally dealt well with obstacles and setbacks, and has emerged intact and energised.

When played at its best, Spanish club football – from Real Betis to Celta de Vigo and from Real Sociedad to Getafe – is without parallel in Europe, and there is every reason to suppose that this will continue over the years to come. Let's hope so anyway. There's still plenty of life left in La Liga.

FURTHER READING

This is only a brief guide to a few other books you may wish to read. The brevity is mainly due to the fact that there is a multitude of published titles on Spanish history, culture and society – one which could conceivably fill an average-sized public library – and it would be invidious of me to suggest books which I haven't read. Also, as this is a book on football, the list narrows considerably and, as there are no doubt a good many Spanish football books which I haven't read (this book is an introduction not an encyclopedia), my recommended publications diminish in number still further.

On a general, comprehensive level, both the *Rough Guide to Spain* and *DK Witness Travel Guide to Spain* provide what one would expect, as do Raymond Carr's *Spain: A History* and Jan Morris's *Spain*. Other histories abound from a variety of publishers.

On the Spanish Civil War – a subject I deliberately don't cover in any detail in this book – you would benefit from reading Gerald Brenan's *The Spanish Labyrinth*, covering Brenan's insights from the late nineteenth century to the early consolidation of Francoism. Other titles which also demand serious attention are Anthony Beevor's *The Battle for Spain*, Paul Preston's *The Spanish Holocaust* and, for a vivid account of the US experience during the War, Adam Hochschild's *Spain in Our Hearts* is invaluable. George Orwell's personal experiences of the savage conflict are well captured in *Homage to Catalonia*. More recent books include Giles Tremlett's *The Ghosts of Spain*, which well describes the author's personal post-Francoist travels and discoveries in Spain, and *Spain: What Everyone Needs to Know* by William Chislett, an essential factual guide to the people and events which created modern Spain. There are many other insightful and revealing titles but those I mention here are a good start.

These is an abundance of books on the history and current state of European football (including the *Rough Guide to European Football* and my own *The European Cup: A History*), and obviously Spain is prominently represented in these. The story of Spanish football is equally well covered, although many of the available books, inevitably and understandably, tend towards a concentration on Real Madrid and Barcelona. For instance, I greatly enjoyed Jimmy Burns's *La Rioja: A Journey Through Spanish Football* and *Barca: A People's Passion*, and Sid Lowe's *Fear and Loathing in La Liga: Barcelona vs Real Madrid*. I also discovered much of value about some other clubs – for instance Eibar and Atletico Madrid – from Euan McTear's books *Eibar the Brave* and *Hijacking La Liga*, and Robbie Dunne's *Working Class Heroes* provided fascinating information on Rayo Vallecano. Also, Phil Ball's entertaining journey between the leading Spanish clubs is engagingly documented in *Morbo: The Story of Spanish Football*. And, again, you could profitably begin your researches into the Spanish game by reading these titles.

The internet was also invaluable (so long as one double-checks the accuracy), and I was continually surprised at the availability of so many English language websites on Spanish club football, including the leading Spanish football magazines and, indeed, magazines and newspapers worldwide.

With so many sources on which to base this book, and added to my own observations and other reading, I frequently faced the enviable dilemma of what to omit rather than include. I hope you feel I made the right choices.

INDEX

A

Aarhus FC 150
Abalo, José Maria 52
Aberdeen FC 202
AC Milan 158, 159, 161, 171, 212, 226, 236, 247, 256, 310
Acheson, Dean 142
Acuña, Juan 132
Adam, Charles 15
Adams, Tony 23
Adelardo 61, 185
AEK Athens 226
Agrupación Deportivo Plus Ultra 174
Aguirre, Javier 270
Agüero, Sergio 270
Aimar, Pablo 255
Ajax FC 41, 154, 184, 200, 242, 243, 302, 306, 307
Alavés FC 39, 40, 01, 106, 218, 219, 228, 296, 304, 310, 311
Alba, Jordi 292
Albacete Balompié 41, 84, 304
Alberto, Julio 239
Alcorcón AD 85, 86, 289, 290
Alcoyano FC 71
Aldridge, John 191
Alexanko, José 239, 241, 244
Alfonso XII, King 4
Alfonso XIII, King 16, 20, 33, 34, 69, 97-99
Alhambra Palace 22, 23, 78
Allardyce, Sam 82
Almería UD 18, 262, 285
Alonso, Marcos 239
Alves, Dani 260, 287, 293
Amadeo (forward) 124
Amaro, Amancio 132, 181, 182, 203, 208, 233
Amnesty Act (1977) 178
Amor, Guillermo 244
Amsterdam Arena 252
Ancelotti, Carlo 297, 298
Anderlecht FC 226, 234
Anelka, Nicolas 252
Años de Hambre, Los 119
Antić, Raddy 265, 282

Antwerp 9
Aragon 7, 56
Aragonés, Luis 183, 185, 218, 241, 254, 269
Arana, Sabino de 27
Aranzadi, Rafael Moreno – see Pichichi
Arbroath FC 41
Archibald, Steve 239, 240, 244
Arenas Club de Getxo 33, 49, 50, 101
Arsenal FC 58, 164, 188, 212, 215, 220-22, 224, 252, 255, 263, 275, 280, 284, 306
Asensi, Juan Manuel 124, 201
Athletic Club Bilbao 19, 26-28, 32, 42, 49, 124, 169, 183, 189, 195-99, 219, 232, 272, 287, 304
  Basque derbies 35
  'cantera' policy 124
  Copa success 27, 195, 199
  'golden years' 104, 105
  La Liga success 148, 183, 197, 198
  TV money 286
Atkinson, Ron 265
Atlético Aviación 121, 122, 132
Atlético Madrid 27, 42, 84, 89-91, 122, 148, 151-54, 263-76, 296, 304
  Champions League 275, 297, 306
  Copa del Rey success 152, 171, 183, 186, 264, 265, 273
  Europa League 271-73, 310
  European Cup 151, 269, 274, 310
  European Cupwinners' Cup 152, 153, 264
  La Liga success 122, 165, 186, 265, 273, 297
  merger with Air Force team 122
  'Pupas' 269
  Stadio Wanda Metropolitano 121, 267
  TV money 286
  Vicente Calderón Stadium 171, 264, 268
Ávila 76
Ayala, Rubén 184
Ayr United FC 41

B

Bacca, Carlos 262
Badajoz CD 82
Bakero, José Maria 191, 244
Bale, Gareth 274, 297, 298

Ball, Phil 60
Ballon d'Or 302
Baptista, Júlio 260, 280
Barcelona 61, 65
  University of 69
Barcelona FC 23, 27, 40, 52, 65-69, 134-38
  Barcelona derbies 70
  Camp de Les Corts 67, 68
  Camp Nou 138, 197, 201, 242, 244, 263,
273, 283, 291, 293, 302
  Champions League 310
  Copa del Rey victories 33, 40, 68, 136, 137,
200, 219, 248, 287, 288, 295, 296, 310
  dominating La Liga 213
  European Cup 161, 162, 200, 240, 241,
245, 246, 256, 284, 288, 295
  European Cup Winners' Cup 200, 201, 244
  Fairs Cup success 164, 200
  first La Liga champions 104
  first match v Real Madrid 27
  Latin Cup winners 135
  La Liga successes 68, 136, 137, 161, 201,
206, 240, 245-48, 283, 287, 288, 292-96,
304, 310
  relationship with Real Madrid 110, 111,
126-28
  tour of N America 115, 116
  TV money 285-87
Barnes, Billy 32
Bartomeu, Josep Maria 293, 294
Basel FC 66
Basque Country 7, 26, 27, 189, 198
Basten, Marco van 236
Bata (striker) 105
Batistuta, Gabriel 271
Bayer Leverkusen FC 260, 278
Bayern Munich FC 185, 186, 212, 235, 236,
255, 269, 275, 289, 292, 299, 302
Bebeto (striker) 209, 210
Beckham, David 223, 272, 279, 281
Beenhakker, Leo 235, 236
Begiristain, Txiki 191, 244
Belauste 10
Belletti, Juliano 284
Benfica FC 150, 162, 163, 179, 182, 215,
262
Benitez, Rafael 255, 261, 298
Benzema 297
Bergkamp, Dennis 224

Berlusconi, Silvio 236
Bernabéu, Santiago 129-31, 138, 146, 157,
203
Bernabéu Stadium, Madrid (originally Nuevo
Estadio Chamartin) 17, 137, 151, 152, 162,
174, 199, 234-36, 268, 279, 283, 290
  as Estadio Chamartin 130, 131
  character of 157
  Copa del Rey finals 211, 273, 278
  directors' box 269
  opening of 138
Betancourt, Rómulo 180
Betis – see Real Betis
Bielsa, Marcelo 273
Bilbao 26 (see also Athletic Club Bilbao)
  British miners in 26
  La Cantera policy 31
  San Mamés Stadium 27, 29, 42, 105
Blackburn Rovers FC 32, 90
Blackpool FC 32
Blanco, Admiral Luis Carrera 176
Blanco, Raúl Gonzalez – see Raúl
Boavista FC 226
Bonhof, Rainer 188
Bordeaux FC 228
Borussia Dortmund 210, 226
Borussia Mönchengladbach 188
Bosman, Jean-Marc 276
Bosque, Vicente del 252, 257, 258, 279
Bourbon dynasty 2, 4, 97, 99
Brady, Liam 188
Bravo, Claudio 295
Breitner, Paul 203
Brenan, Gerald 6
Breukelen, van 236
Brighton & Hove Albion FC 76
Bru, Paco 113
Bruges FC 186, 187
Burgos CF 76
Busquets, Sergio 287
Butragueño, Emilio 232-37
Buyo, Francisco 237

C

Cadiz CF 22, 37, 48, 173, 231, 232, 245,
298
Calderón, Ramón 280
Calderón, Vicente 269, 275

Camacho, José Antonio 234
Camp Nou stadium, Barcelona 138, 197,
201, 242, 244, 263, 273, 283, 291, 293, 302
  Champions League 278, 288
  financing of 200
Campbell, Sol 284
Campeonato Levants 112
Campionat de Catalunya 62, 113
Canário (winger) 145, 160, 168
Canary Islands 7, 79
Cañizares 253
Caparrós, Joaquin 260
Capello, Fabio 251, 280
Carew, Jon 255
Carlist Wars 4
Carlos, Roberto 211, 223, 251, 278
Carniglia, Luis 159
Carrasco, Yannick 'Lobo' 239, 244, 275
Cartagena CF 74
Carvajal, Daniel 302
Carvalho, Ricardo 291
Casillas, Iker 257, 278, 292, 297
Castile and León 8, 75
Castilla-La Mancha 8, 83
Castellon FC 71
Catalan Generalitat 61
Catalonia 7, 198
catenaccio system 181, 303
Cazorla, Santi 226, 281
Celta de Vigo 42, 43, 52, 53, 94, 136, 150,
172, 214, 215, 222, 260, 310
Celtic FC 37, 38, 154, 192
Cervantes, Miguel 78
Champions League, inauguration of 146, 147
  see also under individual clubs
Chiellini, Giorgio 295
Chelsea FC 164, 202, 256, 270, 274, 288,
306
Ciriaco (defender) 106
Ciudad de Caceres 82
Ciudad Deportivo, Madrid 277
Clemente, Javier 196, 199, 218, 260
Club Gimnàstic de Tarragona 62
Clyde FC 41
Coco 281
Cologne FC 235
Columbus, Christopher 78
Comisiones Obreras 176
Communist Party 176, 178

Compostela SD 51
Conceição, Flávio 210
Confederación Nacional de Trabajo (CNT) 98
Constitutions 4, 178, 249
Copa de la Coronación 27, 97
Copa de la España Libre 114
Copa del Generalisimo 33, 148, 150, 172
Copa del Presidente de la Républic 33
Copa del Rey 33, 97, 100, 120, 304, 305
  See also under individual clubs
copper mining 13-15
Corcuera, Julio 132
Cordoba CF 23, 43
  Los Califas 43
Coruña, La 52, 207
Costa, Diego 273, 274
Costa da Morte 207
Courtois, Thibaut 274
Cowdenbeath FC 41
Cruyff, Johann 41, 154, 200-02, 242-49,
258, 286, 288, 296
  total football 154, 243
Cruyff, Jordi 201, 219
CSKA Sofia 192
Cullis, Stan 161
Cultural y Deportriva Leonesa CF 77
Cundi (left back) 193
Cunningham, Laurie 203
Cúper, Héctor 255
Czibor, Zoltán 137, 148, 161, 163

D

Dani (striker) 196, 223, 224
Daučik, Ferdinand 148
Davids, Edgar 283
Deco 283, 286
Del Sol, Luis 145, 160, 181
Denilson 216-18
Deportivo Alavés 39, 40, 219
Deportivo de la Coruña 43, 52, 132, 137,
207-12, 247, 300
  Copa del Rey success 210-12, 278
  La Liga success 208, 211, 212
  Los Herculinos 43
  Los Turcos 43, 44
  Riazor Stadium 52
Desastre, El 5, 25
Diaz, 'Panadero' 184

Didi 160, 181
Dinamo Moscow 171
Djalminha 210
Dnipro Dnipropetrovsk 262
Domingo, Placido 269, 278
Donato 209
Dukíc, Miroslav 209
Dylan, Bob 206
Dynamo Kiev 264

E

Edmilson 287
Eibar SD 35-37, 285, 301, 302, 304, 311
  Ipurua Stadium 35-37
Eintracht Frankfurt FC 145, 156, 185, 209, 256
Elche FC 36, 72, 166, 186, 206
Emery, Unai 18, 256, 261-63
Enlightenment, The 3
Enrique, Luis 219, 295, 296
Epi (winger) 124
Escola, Josep 114
Eskozias (Eibar) 37
Esnáider, Juan 222, 265
Espanyol FC 44, 65, 69, 172, 186, 228, 260, 261, 304, 310
  Barcelona derbies 70
  Copa del Generalisimo success 172
  Copa del Rey success 260, 266
  Estadi de Sarrià 44
  UEFA Cup 260, 261
Esportiu Europa 64
Esquerra Republicana de Catalunya 109
Estadi de Sarrià (Espanyol) 44, 70
Estadio Benito Villamarin (Real Betis) 108, 171, 205
Estadio de Cerámica (Villarreal) 72
Estadio de Son Moix (Palm) 59, 60
Estadio de Vallejo (Levante) 45
ETA (Euskadi Ta Askatasuna) 27, 176, 189
Eto'o, Samuel 224, 283, 284
Europa League 262, 270, 305
  see also under individual clubs
European Cup 143-47
  see also under individual clubs
European Cup Winners' Cup 147, 152, 153, 216, 220-222
  see also under individual clubs

Eurosamop 17
Eusébio (Benfica, 1960s) 179
Eusébio (Sacristan, 4 clubs 1982-2002) 238
Euzkadi Selezkioa, tour in 1937 117, 118, 132
  in Russia 118
Evaristo (winger) 137, 162
Extremadura CF 82, 83
Extremadura UD 84

F

Fàbregas, Cesc 288
Falcao, Radamel 273
Falklands War 272
FALN, Venezuela 180
Fausté, Josep Maria 200
Federació Catalana de Futbol 109
Felipe, Pedro de 182
Ferdinand II, King of Aragon 22, 78
Ferguson, Sir Alex 279
Ferrer, Albert 245
Ferrer, Lorenzo Serra 218, 281, 282
Ferrero, Enzo 193
FIFA 203, 259
Figo, Luis 211, 277, 278
First Republic (1873) 4, 97
Flamengo FC 217
Flores, Quique Sánchez 270
Floro, Benito 41
food shortages 119
Football Associació de Catalunya 62
Ford, Richard 1
Forlán, Diego 220, 221, 270, 271
Fortuna Düsseldorf 201
Fowler, Robbie 219
Fran (winger) 209
Franco, General Francisco 100, 109, 118-20, 141, 142, 159, 177, 189, 264
Fulham FC 76, 164, 271
Furia Español 11
Future, Paolo 264, 265

G

Gaal, Louis van 248, 249, 281, 282, 291
Gabi 275
Gaínza, Agustin 124
Galicia 7, 51, 207

Gallego, Ricardo 234
Gamper, Joan (formerly Hans Kamper) 67
Gárate, José 183, 185, 186
Garbutt, William 105
Garcia, Oswaldo 132
Garriga, Josep Sunyol 109-111
Garrincha 216
Gaspart, Joan 281
Gea, David de 270
Gento, Paco 139, 145, 158, 159
Gerardo (full back) 239
Getafe CF 85-87, 263, 304
  Stadium Alfonso Pérez 86
Gil, Jesús 235, 251, 264-66, 269, 270
Gil, Marin 270
Gijón (see also Sporting de Gijón) 47, 54, 194
Gimnástica Segoviana CF 77
Giovanni 281
Girona FC 63, 301-04, 311
Girona Football Group 63
Giuly, Ludovic 283
Godin, Diego 274, 281
Goikoetxea, Andoni 196, 197
González, Felipe 21, 232
González, Fernando 'La Bandera' 44
González, Kily 253
Gonzalvo, Mariâ 137
Gordillo, Rafael 234
Gorostiza, Guillermo 105, 124
Granada CF 23, 44, 137, 172-74, 182, 227, 300, 304
Great White Cross 16
Greenwell, Jack 67
Griezmann, Antoine 274, 275
Grosso, Ramon 182
Guadalquivir River 20, 23
Guardiola, Pep 63, 245, 248, 284, 286-89, 291, 292
  World Coach of the Year 288
Guardiola, Pere 63
Guarrotxena, Endika 199
Guernica, bombing of 117
Gullit, Ruud 236
Guttman, Bela 162

Hanot, Gabriel 146
Hartson, John 222
Haynes, Johnny 164
Henry, Thierry 224, 287, 288
Hercules, Tower of 43
Hércules FC 72, 300
Heredia, Ramón 184
Herrera, Helenio 132, 150, 161, 172, 181, 248
Hewitt, John 202
Heynckes, Jupp 81, 251
Heysel Stadium, Brussels 149, 159, 182, 185
Hiddink, Guus 252, 254
Hierro, Fernando 251, 278, 279
Higuera, Francisco 222
Hleb, Alexander 287
Hoeness, Uli 186
Honved FC 148
Horton, Cliff 164
Huelva 13-17
Huesca SD 57, 301, 304, 311
Hughes, Mark 240, 244

H

Habsburg dynasty 2
Hampden Park Stadium 53, 143-45, 153, 278

I

Ibrahimović, Zlatan 287, 288
Iglesias, Arsenio 208
Ikurriña (Basque flag) 189, 190
Iniesta, Andrés 84, 258, 283, 288
Inter Milan 38, 154, 161, 181, 208, 218, 235, 248, 271, 280, 291
Inter-Cities Fairs Cup 147, 148, 163-65
Inter-Toto Cup 147, 225
Inzaghi 252Ipurua Stadium (Eibar) 35-37
Irureta, Javier 183, 210-12
Isabella, Queen 22
Isabella I, Queen of Castile 78
Isco (winger) 226

J

Jaén 24
Jairzinho 216
James I, King 47
Johnson, Arthur 92
Johnston, Edward Farquharson 19
Johnstone, Jimmy 'Jinky' 185
Juan Carlos, King 177

Juanfran 275
Juanito (striker) 203, 234, 270
Juninho 265
Jupiter CD 67
Juventus FC 81, 179, 181, 212, 215, 235, 244, 252, 296, 301, 306

K

Kaiserslautern FC 218
Kamper, Hans (later Joan Gamper) 66
Karembeu, Christian 251
Keizer, Piet 243
Kempes, Mario 188
Khedira, Sami 291, 297
Kilmarnock FC 182
Klinsmann, Jürgfen 296
Knights Templar 43
Kocsis, Sándor 137, 148, 163, 174
Koeman, Ronald 244, 246, 248, 256
Koke 265, 275
Kopa, Raymond 150, 158, 160
Kortabarria, Ignacio 189, 191
Kroos, Toni 298
Kubala, László 69, 75, 135-37

L

La Hoya Lorca CF 74
Lángara, Isidro 55
Lapetra, Carlos 168, 169
Laporta, Joan 282, 284
Las Palmas UD 44, 80, 166, 187, 206, 300
latifundio system 2
Lattek, Udo 198
Laudrup, Michael 244, 247
Lazio FC 224, 255
league system, structure of 18, 101-04
Leeds United FC 77, 225, 255
Leganés CD 44, 45, 85, 86, 301, 311
Lehmann, Jens 220, 284
Lendoiro, Augusto César 208, 210, 211
León 77
Les Corts Stadium, Barcelona 67, 68, 127, 128, 137
Lerida UD 64
Levante FC 45, 71-74, 220
  Estadio de Vallejo 45
  winning Copa Libre 114

Liège RC 276
Liga de Fútbol Profesional (LPF) 101
Liga, La
  formation of 39, 10
  restart in 1939 120
  wartime suspension 112, 113
  see also under individual clubs
Liga del Mediterráneo 113, 114
Lineker, Gary 240, 241, 244
Liverpool FC 215, 218, 262, 270, 295, 299, 306, 307
Lleida 64
Lleida Esportiu 64, 65
Logroñés SD 56
Logroñés UD 56
Lokomotiv Moscow 228
Lopera, Manuel Ruiz de 217
Lopetegui, Josep 302
López, Claudio 253-55
Lorca FC 262
Lorenzo, Juan Carlos 184
Los Angeles Aztecs 242
Los Angeles Galaxy 201
Lowe, Sid 21, 235, 290
Lucio 278
Lugo CD 52
Luís, Filipe 274
Lybster FC 15, 16

M

Maceda, Antonio 193, 234
Machin, Pablo 303
Madrid (*see also* Rayo Vallecano and Real Madrid) 8, 84, 85
Madrid FC 16, 27, 90-92, 105
Madrid derbies 90
Madrid, Pact of 142
Mackay, Jamesie 16
Mackay, Dr William Alexander 14-16
Makaay, Roy 210
Makélélé, Claude 279
Malaga 24, 225
Malaga CF 24, 45, 94, 161, 215, 225-27, 270, 300
  La Rosaleda stadium 225
Malcom 301
Mallorca (*see also* Real Mallorca) 59
Malo, General Emilio 99

Manchester City FC 63, 227, 256, 289
Manchester United FC 107, 149, 157, 212, 240, 252, 279, 287, 302
Mandzukić, Mario 274
Maradona, Diego 197-99, 239, 271
Marcelino (forward) 168
Marcelo 274
Marcial (midfielder) 186
María, Angel di 291, 297
Márquez, Rafael 283
Marquitos, Marcos 145, 158
Marseille FC 255, 275
Martino, Gerardo 'Tata' 292, 293
Marwijk, Bert van 257
Mascherano, Javier 288
Mata, Juan 256
McManaman, Steve 252, 253, 278, 279
Mendieta, Gaizka 253-55
Mendoza, Ramón 235, 251
Menotti, César Luis 198
Merchant Taylors' School 66
Mérida AD 45, 82
Merkel, Max 184
Messi, Lionel 30, 125, 126, 219, 287, 288, 292-95, 305
Mestalla Stadium (Valencia) 40, 73, 74, 108, 122, 123, 245, 297
Mezquita, Cordoba 23
Michel (winger) 233
Michels, Rinus 242
Middlesbrough FC 32, 260
Migueli (centre back) 239
Mijatović, Predrag 251, 252
Milla, Luis 244, 245
Millennium Stadium, Cardiff 298
Mills, Alfredo 31
Mirandés CD 77
Miró, Luis 128
Modrić, Luka 291, 297
Molinón Stadium, El (Gijon) 40, 54, 194, 195
Molowny, Luis 234
Monreal, Nacho 226
Moors 2, 22
Morientes 279
Mourinho, José 291, 292, 303
Movida Madrileña, La 232
Müller, Gerd 186, 292
Muller, Lucien 181

Mundo (centre forward) 124
Muñiz, Juan 227
Muñoz, Miguel 158-60, 181
Murcia 7, 74
Murrayfield Stadium, Edinburgh 38

N

Nantes FC 188
Napoli FC 236, 239
National Party 99
Navas, Keylor 298
Nayim 45m goal 222, 223
Netzer, Günter 203
Neymar (da Silva Santos Jr) 263, 293-96
Nice FC 69, 94
Níguez, Saúl 274
Nistelrooy, Ruud van 226, 280, 290
Numancia CD 46, 77
Núñez, Josep Luis 202, 238-42, 246

O

Oblak, Jan 274
O'Connell, Patrick 106-08, 114, 116, 170
Odense FC 179
Olympic Games 9-11
  Antwerp (1920) 9-11, 29, 52, 68, 113, 257
  football in 9-11, 29, 68
Omeyas Caliphate 43
Orleans, Maid of 48
Ormaetxea, Alberto 191
Ortega, Antonio 113
Ortega, Ariel 254
Orwell, George 58
Os Belenenses FC 131
Osasuna FC 49, 73, 121, 122, 160, 218, 224, 241, 249, 261, 300, 304
Overmars, Marc 281
Oviedo FC 32, 105
Özil, Mesut 291

P

Pachin, Enrique 145, 160
Pachón, Sergio 87
Pacto de Olvido 178
Padrós, Carlos and Juan 91
Pahiño, Manuel 133, 208

Palamós 62
Palamós FC 63, 69
  Palma 59, 60
    Estadio de Son Moix 59, 60
Pamplona FC 49
  El Sadar Stadium 49
Panizo, José Luis 124
Pardeza, Miguel 233
Paris St Germain (PSG) 262, 296
Parreira, Carlos Alberto 254
Partido Nacionalista Vasco (PNV) 27
Partido Socialista Obrero Español (PSOE) 179
Partizan Belgrade 182
Pasarin, Kuis 123
passenaccio system 258
Pedro (winger) 258, 287, 288
Peiró, Joaquin 153, 225, 226
Pellegrini, Manuel 221, 226, 227, 290
penalty shoot-outs 164, 171, 188
Pentland, Fred 32, 55, 91, 104
Pereira, Carlos 188
Pérez, Florentino 253, 277
Petit, Emmanuel 281
Pichichi (Rafael Moreno Aranzadi) 10, 28-30
Pichichi Award (Trofeo Pichichi) 28-30, 32, 55, 126, 168, 183, 194, 220, 235, 247, 284
Pico del Teide 81
Piero, del 252
Pina, Manuel 201
Piqué, Gerard 287
Pires, Robert 224, 281
Platáforma de Convergencia Democrática 177
Pontevedra 51
Popular Front 99
Porto FC 148, 157, 180, 236, 240, 254
Prat, Pitus 50
PSV Eindhoven 236, 244, 275
Puhades, Antonio 124
Puerto Rico, loss of 5
Puskás, Ferenc 75, 145, 149, 159, 160, 179, 181, 182
Puyol, Carlos 283

Q
Quincoces, Jacinto 106, 123
Quini 30, 126, 193-95

Quinta del Buitre, La 203

R
Racing de Ferrol 51, 150
Racing de Santander 55, 77, 139
Rakitić, Ivan 295
Ramallets, Antoni (El Gato) 94, 137, 168
Ramos, Juande 218, 260
Ramos, Sergio 260, 274, 280, 306
Rangers FC 169, 188
Ranieri, Claudio 254, 265, 266
Raúl (González Blanco) 237, 238, 251, 253, 265, 278, 289
Rayo Majadahonda CF 85
Rayo Vallecano de Madrid 37, 85, 87-89, 182, 228, 274, 300, 304
  anti-establishment status 88
  Bukaneros 37, 89
  charity work 88
Real Betis Balompié 20, 21, 122, 160, 169-71, 215-18
  Copa del Rey 206
  Estadio Benito Villamarín 171
  La Liga success 106, 170
  Seville derbies 21
Real Club Deportivo Español – see Español
Real Federación Española de Fútbol (RFEF) 16, 102, 114, 121, 182, 302
Real Jaén 24
Real Madrid 17, 46, 69, 92, 93, 126-34, 211
  as an ambassador for Spain 143
  beating Barcelona 11-1 127, 128
  Bernabéu Stadium 157, 174, 268
  Centenary season 278
  Champions League 275, 298, 299, 310
  Copa del Generalisimo success 165
  Copa del Rey success 131, 139, 244, 291, 310
  dominating La Liga 213
  Estadio Chamartin 92, 105, 127
  European Cup 144-46, 154-62, 179-86, 202, 235, 252, 253, 256, 275, 278, 282, 310
  European Cup Winners' Cup 202
  first match v Barcelona 27, 92
  La Liga success 139, 165, 180, 206, 235, 244, 251, 277, 279, 280, 298, 310
  Los Merengues 46
  Quinta dl Buitre, La 233-36, 244

relationship with Barcelona 110, 111, 126-28
  TV money 28486
  UEFA Cuo 234, 235
Real Mallorca 17, 33, 59, 60, 223-25, 237, 283, 304
  Copa del Rey success 60, 224
  European Cup Winners' Cup 223
Real Murcia CF 46, 75
Real Oviedo 54, 121, 166
Real Sociedad Alfonso XIII FC 60
Real Sociedad de Fútbol 32, 34, 60, 77, 101, 112, 173, 189-93, 196, 219, 235, 262, 302
  Basque derbies 35
  Cope del Rey success 192
  La Liga success 191
  record unbeaten run 191
Real Unión FC 29, 49, 50
Real Valladolid CF 48, 76, 78, 125, 172, 173, 238, 300
Real Zaragoza 57, 164, 166-69, 186, 222, 223, 260, 280
  Copa success 169, 222, 222, 260
  European Cup Winners' Cup 222
  Los Maños 168
  winning European Cupwinners' Cup 7, 168, 169
  winning Fairs Cup 164, 168, 169
Reconquista 2, 22, 47, 52
Recreativo de Huelva 13-19, 66, 206, 224, 259, 268, 300
  El Decano 13, 17
  Supporters' Trust 17
  Velodromo Stadium 16
Red Star Belgrade 195
Redondo, Fernando 251, 271
Reims FC 158, 160
Reina, Miguel 186
Republik Euzkadi (Basque team) 117
Resino, Abel 270
Reus CF 41, 62
Rexach, Charles 200, 201, 242, 282
Reyes, José Antonio 83, 260, 270
Rial, Hector 139, 158
Riazor Stadium (Dep. De la Coruña) 52, 132, 209, 272
Rijkaard, Frank 236, 282, 283
Rio, Paul del 180, 181
Rio Tinto 13

Rio Tinto Mining Company 14, 15
Rioja 7, 56
Riquelme, Juan Róman 221
Rivaldo 210, 249, 282
River Ebro 57, 167
River Nervión 29
Rivera, General Miguel Primo de 67, 98
Rix, Graham 188
Robben, Arno 292
Robinho 280
Robson, Bobby 238, 291
Rodríguez, James 298
Rodriguez, Manuel Ruiz 170
Romario 210, 247, 254
Ronaldinho 283, 284, 286
Ronaldo (Brazilian) 172, 173, 277, 278, 295, 297
Ronaldo, Cristiano 274, 275, 288, 290, 301, 302, 306
Roselada Stadium (Malaga) 225
Rosell, Sandro 293, 294
Russia, Basque team touring in 117, 118

S

Sabadell FC 64
Sacchi, Arrigo 265
Sacristán, Eusébio 'Paco' – see Eusébio
SAD regulations 249-51
Sadar, E, Stadium (Pamplon) 49
St James (Iago) 52
St Mammes 42
St Pauli FC (Germany) 88
Salenko, Oleg 254
Salinas, Julio 244
Samitier, Josep 10, 67, 68, 93, 135
Sampdoria FC 246
San Lorenzo FC, Argentina 132
San Mamés Stadium (Atlético Bilbao) 27, 29, 30, 42, 105, 149
San Sebastián 34, 190
San Siro Stadium 298
Sánchez, Alexis 274, 288
Sánchez, Hugo 30, 126, 234, 236, 264
Sanchez, José Martinez 182
Sánchez, Juan 255
Sánchez, Ramón 150
Sanchez-Pizjuán Stadium (Sevilla) 240, 259, 262

Sanchis, Manuel 233, 238, 251
Sant Andre FC 305
Santamaria, José 145, 156, 158, 182
Santander (*see also* Racing de Santander) 55
Santiago de Compostela 52
Santillana, Carlos 203, 232, 234, 235
Santos, Eleuterio 168
Sanz, Lorenzo 251-53
São Paulo FC 216, 217
Saporta, Raimundo 158
Satrústegui, Jesús María 191
Saúl 275
Savićević, Dejan 247
Schalke FC 81
Schuster, Bernd 227, 239, 241, 281
Schwarzenbeck, Hans-Georg 186
Scopelli, Alejandro 132
Second Republic (1931) 99
Secuéllamos UD 83
Seedorf, Clarence 251
Segarra, Joan 137
Segui, Vicente 124
Seminario, Juan 168
Sergi 244
Sergio (midfielder) 211
Sevilla Balompié 19
Sevilla FC 15, 20, 21, 49, 64, 79, 107, 122,
   132, 150, 151, 159, 259-61, 296, 303, 304
   Copa success 156, 172, 259, 270
   Europa League 218, 227, 262
   European Cup 150, 151
   La Liga success 150
   Sánchez-Pizjuán Stadium 240, 259
   UEFA Cup 261, 310
Shepherd, Mr (Bilbao manager) 32
Shilton, Peter 93
Silva, David 256
Silva, Mauro 209, 210
Simeone, Diego 'El Cholo' 267, 271, 272,
   274, 276
Sociedad Sky Football 91
Sola, Miguel 199
Solari, Santiago 302
Song, Alex 292
Songo'o, Jacques 211
Soria 46
Soriano, Manual Mas 115
Southampton FC 30
Spartak Moscow FC 262

Sporting de Gijón FC 30, 40, 47, 54, 77,
   136, 192-95, 206, 235, 300
   El Molinón Stadium 40, 54
Sporting Lisbon 192
Stade de France, Paris 253
Stadium Alfonso Perez (Getafe) 86
Stadio Wanda Metropolitano (Atlético
   Madrid) 121, 267
Standard Liège FC 179
Stéfano, Alfredo Di 30, 95, 126, 131-33,
   138, 139, 145, 150, 155, 158, 160, 166, 180,
   181, 231, 232, 254
Steaua Bucharest FC 240
Stewart, John 38
Stielike, Uli 203
Stoichkov, Hristo 245-47
Stuttgart FC 153
Suárez, Adolfo 178, 190
Suárez, Luis (Real Madrid/la Coruña, 1950s)
   23, 132, 162, 294, 295
Suker, Davor 251
Sunderland FC 30

T

Tablada Hippodrome, Sevilla 15
Tadic, Dusan 306
Tarragona, Gimnástia de 19
television, income from 284-86
Tenerife CD 80-82, 87, 246, 300
Teruel, Battle of 115
Thiago 288
Toledo CD 83
Torino FC 195
Torres, Fernando 266, 270, 275
Toshack, John 210, 236, 252
total football 154, 243
Tottenham Hotspur FC 153, 307
Toure, Yaya 287
Tribar, José Angel 189
Tristán, Diego 211

U

UEFA 147, 185, 227
UEFA Cup 227
   see also under individual clubs
Ufarte, Roberto Lopez 191
Ujpest Dozsa 167

Unamuno, Miguel de 28
Unión del Centro Democrático 178, 179
Unión Deportivo (Huesca) 57
Unión General de Trabajadores 98
Uranga, Josean 189
Urruti (goalkeeper) 240

V

Valdano, Jorge 234, 235, 247, 251
Valdés, Victor 283
Valencia 7, 47, 71
Valencia CF 47, 71, 73, 123, 124, 164, 166,
187, 188, 210, 247, 253-56, 262, 304
  Copa del Rey success 187, 188, 255, 256,
305
    European Cup 167, 253
    European Cup Winners' Cup 253
    Fairs Cup success 164, 167
    La Liga success 123, 167, 255
    Mestalla Stadium 73, 74, 122, 123
    TV money 285
    UEFA Cup success 255, 310
Valerón, Juan Carlos 211
Valladolid (see also Real Valladolid) 48
Valverde, Ernesto 245, 260, 296
Vasco da Gama FC 209
Vázquez, Rafael Martin 233, 236
Velázquez, Manuel 182 Velodromo Stadium
(Huelva) 16
Venables, Terry 234, 238
Vicente Calderón Stadium (Atlético Madrid)
171, 264, 268, 273, 275
Video Assistant Referee (VAR) 303
Videoton FC 234
Vieri, Christian 265
Vigo 53
Vikingur FC 192
Vialli, Gianluca 246
Vilanova, Tito 286, 292
Villa, David 223, 256, 258, 274
Villa, Juan 168, 169
Villalonga, José 'Papa' 153, 158
Villamarín, Beanito 170, 171
Villarreal FC 48, 72, 206, 220, 221, 226,
258, 270, 281, 305
  Champions League 221
  Estadio de Cerámica 72

Vinicius Junior 269, 301
Visigoths 2
Vizcaya FC 27

W

Wembley Stadium, London 245
Webb, Howard 258
Wenger, Arsène 252, 263
West Ham United FC 76
Whitty, Arthur and Ernest 66
Wild, Walter 66
Wolverhampton Wanderers FC 161
World Cup 256-59

X

Xavi 283, 288
Xerez FC 300, 311

Z

Zamora, Bobby 76
Zamora, Jesús 191, 192
Zamora, Ricardo 10, 67, 70, 93-95, 106, 122
Zamora CF 76
Zamora Trophy 9, 95, 283
Zaragoza (see also Real Zaragoza) 57
Zarraga, Juan 145, 158
Zarraonandia, Telmo (Zarra) 30, 124-26
Zenit St Petersburg FC 226
Zeno of Elea 308
Zidane, Zinedine 211, 252, 277-79, 298,
299, 301-04
Zoco, Ignacio 181
Zubieta, Angel 105, 132
Zubizarreta, Andoni 196, 237, 247, 254, 293
Zurich FC 66